The New Jew in Film

The New Jew in Film

Exploring Jewishness and Judaism in Contemporary Cinema

Nathan Abrams

Rutgers University Press
New Brunswick, New Jersey

First U.S. Printing 2021

Library of Congress Cataloging-in-Publication Data

Abrams, Nathan.
The new Jew in film : exploring Jewishness and Judaism in contemporary
cinema / Nathan Abrams.
   p. cm.
Includes bibliographical references and index.
Includes filmography.
ISBN 978-0-8135-5340-5 (hardcover : alk. paper) — ISBN 978-0-8135-5341-2
(pbk. : alk. paper) — ISBN 978-0-8135-5343-6 (e-book)
1. Jews in motion pictures. I. Title.
PN1995.9.J46A24 2012
791.43'652924—dc23

A British Cataloging-in-Publication record for this book is available from the
British Library.

First published in the United States 2012
by Rutgers University Press, New Brunswick, New Jersey

First published by I.B.Tauris & Co Ltd in the United Kingdom

www.rutgersuniversitypress.org

Manufactured in the United States of America

Contents

List of illustrations

Acknowledgements

Writing this book has been a pleasure. Rarely can one say that I have work to do, and that work involves watching a film a night. My gratitude for this must go to the School of English at what was then the University of Wales, Bangor which, in 2005, took a chance and hired me as a Lecturer in Film Studies, despite having had a background primarily in American History hitherto. It is not often that one gets the luxury of translating a hobby into a full-time job. My transfer (but alas with no attendant 'fee') to the National Institute for Excellence in the Creative Industries in January 2007, today known as the School of Creative Studies and Media, provided an extremely genial context in which to work, and I am particularly grateful to Professor Graeme Harper for his backing, support, and for providing the sort of working conditions in which I can thrive.

I would also like to thank my various friends and my partners for their respective patience and tolerance in not only watching these films with me but also for putting up with me when I stopped and rewound the DVD player ad nauseum, as well as my students and colleagues at Bangor University, the London School of Jewish Studies, the Spiro Ark and Limmud conferences for the useful discussions and comments, and also for sharing their DVDs with me.

Several individuals deserve singling out for their advice, insights and support. In alphabetical order they are: Michael Abrams, Becky Aizen, Caryn Aviv, Amy Chambers, Sarah Cramsey, Simon Dando, Howard Davis, Vinciane Duperthuy, Marc Michael Epstein, Santiago Fouz-Hernández, Martin Fradley, Norm Gutharz, Dyfrig Jones, Bruce Kaplan, Daniel Lichman, Dominique Moloney, Jacqueline Nicholls, Chris Pallant, Nick Poots, Steve Price, Goran Stanivukovic, Stephen Stern, Sonja Stojanovic, Kate Taylor, Renée Taylor, Lindsey Taylor-Gutharz, Naomi Wood and Raphael Zarum.

I am particularly grateful to Helena Miguélez Carballeira for many things and in many ways, but here for her typically close reading of my work and her very useful comments. 'Polish, medieval Chaucer' Sue Niebrzydowski, together with Cai, have been pillars of support, understanding, amusement and advice, and I thank them for putting up with me and my moaning. Sally Baker was always on hand with an amusing anecdote or useful bit of gossip. Marcus Brogden generously lent his voluminous and unparalleled DVD collection to me (sometimes he wasn't even aware of it). Anne-Marie Condron, Simon Dando, Ian Davies, Gerwyn Owen, Diana Pinto, Sofie Angharad Roberts, Rikke Schubart, Jenni Steele and Bryn Young-Roberts shared their as yet unpublished work with me, and allowed me to cite from it. Philippa Brewster saw the potential in this project, supported it from the outset, and has nurtured it to fruition. Her comments have been insightful and have improved the text immeasurably. Finally, I would like to thank the anonymous readers, whose comments were invaluable. Needless to say, any errors in fact or matters of interpretation remain my own.

Earlier versions of four chapters have been revised and expanded here. They are 'The Jew on the loo: the toilet in Jewish popular culture, memory, and imagination', in Olga Gershenson and Barbara Penner (eds), *Ladies and Gents: Public toilets and gender* (Philadelphia: Temple University Press, 2009), pp. 218–26; '"My religion is American": A *midrash* on Judaism in American films, 1990 to the present', in Jeanne Cortiel, Kornelia Freitag, Christine Gerhardt and Michael Wala (eds), *Religion in the United States* (Heidelberg: Winter Verlag, 2011), pp. 209–25; 'From Jeremy to Jesus: the Jewish male body on film, 1990 to the Present', in Santiago Fouz-Hernández (ed.), *Mysterious Skin: The male body in contemporary cinema* (London and New York: IB Tauris, 2009), pp. 15–29; '"I'll have whatever she's having": Jewish Food on Film', in Anne Bowers (ed.), *Reel Food: Essays on food and film* (New York and London: Routledge, 2004), pp. 87–100. I am grateful to the publishers for giving me permission to reproduce them in part here.

I dedicate this book to the memory of Duncan Tanner and Nina Fishman, as well as those who think that my work is 'too Jewy' but like it anyway.

Introduction

[T]he stereotype is a complex, ambivalent, contradictory mode of representation, as anxious as it is assertive, and demands not only that we extend our critical and political objectives but that we change the object of analysis itself.

Homi Bhabha (1994: 100)

Jews have big noses, eat bagels and love money.

The Hebrew Hammer (dir. Jonathan Kesselman, 2003)

This is a book in search of Jewish stereotypes and self-images in contemporary cinema, that is mainstream fiction film since 1990. It is not about how 'Jewish' a film is, if such a definition is even possible. But it does engage in discussions about the nature of the Jewishness and Judaism that such stereotypes and images exhibit. In this way, it seeks to map the metamorphosis of the modern and New Jew/ess in film.

A stereotype is a regularly repeated, simplistic, easily understood and inaccurate categorisation of a social group (Abrams et al. 2010: 365). Much has been written about the function of stereotypes in general, and Jewish ones in particular, especially how they perform cultural work in demonising minority groups from the outside, and perpetuating group solidarity and continuity from the inside. As Homi Bhabha suggests, the stereotype offers 'a *secure* point of identification' (1994: 99), that is reassurance. Daniel Boyarin calls this form of reassurance 'Jewissance' (1997: xxiii). Itself a play on the French term 'jouissance' (literally 'orgasm', but also meaning physical or intellectual pleasure, delight or ecstasy), Boyarin defines *Jewissance* as 'a pleasure' that 'brings to many men and women an extraordinary richness of experience and a powerful sense of

1

being rooted somewhere in the world, in a world of memory, intimacy, and connectedness' (1997: xxiii).

On a deeper level, stereotypes contain a 'surplus value', which provides 'enjoyment or jouissance [and] enables us to understand the logic of exclusion' (Zizek 1989: xi). Bhabha similarly suggests that the stereotype is characterised by a 'productive ambivalence' between 'pleasure and desire' and 'power and domination' (1994: 96). In other words, stereotypes are enjoyed because they allow us to see contested images at work and understand their ideological implications. They entertain us, as well as serve to ridicule the logic of exclusion, a menace that continues today (Neofotistos 2008: 16–17).

Stereotypes and self-images do not stay static. They 'change because the cultural patterns on which they are based are becoming anachronistic' (Antler 2008: 256). Likewise, cinematic stereotypes of Jews, existing almost as long as the medium itself, have evolved. During the early years of the nascent film industry, when Yiddish was still thriving, images of Jews were fairly common onscreen. However, the earliest representation of Jews which appeared in the first silent shorts of the twentieth century were crude and overtly antisemitic racialised portrayals. The image of 'the Jew', which erased all intra-group differences (religious, regional, national, linguistic, class, socioeconomic, political), was a subhuman, avaricious, unrefined, venal, grasping, greedy, shifty and menacing cheat and/or dangerous subversive. The Jew was an 'outsider' and 'invader' to be feared. Thus the Jew was paradoxically represented as a greedy capitalist and as a violent, anti-capitalist, radical reformer (Rocha 2010: 43–44).

Physically, the Jew was identified by his swarthiness, a hunched back, 'hook nose, bald head, oversize shoes, and round pouch' (Rivo 1998: 31). *A Gesture Fight in Hester Street* (dir. Anon, 1900), *Levi and Cohen: The Irish Comedians* (dir. G.W. Bitzer, 1903) and *Cohen's Advertising Scheme* (dir. Anon, 1904) marked the début of the screen Jew, an untrustworthy, money-grubbing, scheming Jewish merchant with gross features and vulgar habits. Subsequent films, such as *Cohen's Fire Sale* (dir. Edwin S. Porter, 1907) and *Levitsky's Insurance Policy, or When Thief Meets Thief* (dir. Anon, 1908), *The Robbers and the Jew* (dir. Jack Smith, 1908), *A Bad Day for Levinsky* (dir. T.J. Gobbett, 1909), *The Invaders* (dir. Percy Stow, 1909) and *The Antique Vase* (dir. H.O. Martinek, 1913) varied little in their characterisations on both sides of the Atlantic.

From the mid-1910s onwards, as Jewish moguls dominated Hollywood, more sympathetic portrayals resulted. These moguls included Adolf Zukor, Jesse Lasky and B.P. Schulberg at Paramount, Marcus Loew, Joseph Schenck, Samuel Goldwyn and Louis B. Mayer at MGM, Harry and Jack Cohn at Columbia, Jack and Harry Warner at Warner Brothers, Carl Laemmle and Irving Thalberg at Universal, and William Fox at Fox, among others. A shift in which Jewish representations changed from antisemitic racialised portrayals towards inside images created and/or perpetuated by Jews themselves occurred as a result. The first sympathetic Jewish character – a benevolent moneylender who saves a Gentile woman and her child – appeared in D.W. Griffith's *Old Isaacs, the Pawnbroker* (1908). This was followed by melodramas (*Threads of Destiny*, dir. Joseph W. Smiley, 1914), comedies (*Cohen's Luck*, dir. John H. Collins, 1915) and literary adaptations (*The Little Jewess*, dir. Anon, 1914). A tradition of Jewish cinematic stereotypes was established: the Stern Patriarch who clings to the old ways, the Prodigal/Rebellious Son, the Long-Suffering *Yiddische mama* (Yiddish: 'Jewish mother') and the Rose of the Ghetto, all of which were inside creations, stemming from the Jewish-American literature of Abraham Cahan, Mary Antin and Anzia Yezierska, some of whose works were adapted for film in the early 1920s by the moguls (Erens 1984). Sentimentalisation had replaced mean-spiritedness, and celluloid Jews became humorous and exotic foreigners, but they still perpetuated the link between Jews and particular trades, predominantly depicting them as pawnbrokers, moneylenders, tailors and peddlers.

Such representations peaked by the mid-to-late 1920s, the high watermark being *The Jazz Singer* (dir. Alan Crosland, 1927) in which Al Jolson, playing the son of an Orthodox Jewish cantor, sought to assimilate into the wider US culture by rejecting the ways of his cantor father and adopting the profession of singing jazz in blackface. Thereafter, cinematic Jews began to fade away, in what Henry Popkin called 'the great retreat', with the effect that by 1935 Jews had all but vanished from the screen (1952: 51). During this time Jews were hidden onscreen both literally and figuratively as the Jewish moguls, often prompted by pressure from Jewish organisations and the Hays Code, which exercised tight control over the portrayal of religion and ethnicity, promoted a strategy of assimilatory Americanisation. Jewish actors changed their names, as their Jewish bosses – for commercial reasons, as well as fear of inciting Depression- and Hitler-fuelled antisemitism even further – calculated that their predominantly white working-class audiences did not want to watch Jews onscreen (Popkin 1952, Gabler 1988). This period also encapsulated 'the desire for invisibility, the desire to become "white"' (Gilman 1991: 235) which, at that time, was essentially understood to refer to northern and western European. By this convention, Jews might look white; however, from their own perspective, as from the white Christians', they were still Jews, every bit as racially marked as black or Oriental (Boyarin 1998: 40).

Meanwhile, in other countries, such as the UK and France, Jews were present on film as early as the first two decades of the twentieth century. As in the United States, films of this period 'portrayed Jewish characters from the outside, as villains, scapegoats, or comic foils, and made no attempt to investigate either their situation or the prejudice directed against them and the social and political circumstances that allowed it to flourish' (Wright 1998: 339). During the 1920s and 1930s more sympathetic representations appeared, possibly as a response to antisemitism. Significant among these films was Lothar Mendes's philosemitic *Jew Süss* (1934), a clear 'condemnation of anti-semitism at a time when few films world-wide dared to broach political issues or speak the word "Jew"' (Epstein 2005: 366), and not to be confused with the antisemitic version *Jud Süss* (dir. Veit Harlan, 1940).

During the Second World War, Jews re-emerged. From 1942 onwards, they reappeared in US 'platoon' films, as one element in a spectrum of ethnic soldiers, including – anachronistically – African Americans. Such films were part of a war effort that sought to decrease racial, ethnic and religious differences and emphasise similarity and unity in fighting a common enemy. The post-war period was characterised as a 'golden age' in American Jewish history. Hitler had been defeated, overt and explicit antisemitism became unfashionable, to be replaced by a more hidden, subtle and genteel 'gentleman's agreement' type which itself was slowly being eroded as restrictive practices in hiring, university entrance and the professions were destroyed. Jews became more acculturated, assimilated and upwardly mobile. They entered the professions, moved out to the suburbs and became middle class. Yet, paradoxically, despite these socioeconomic changes, Jews were not necessarily any more visible onscreen, because melting-pot monoculturalism still dominated in the immediate post-war decades. Rather than being hidden entirely, however, Jews were idealised, 'de-Judaised' (that is turned into Gentiles) and 'de-Semitised' – 'the elimination of specifically Jewish characteristics from Jewish roles' – and played by non-Jews (Erens 1984: 136). Joel Rosenberg summed up this cinematic Jewishness as being defined by its absence: 'silence, disguise, implicit Jewishness, allegorisation, sentimentalisation, the soft focus of Gentile actors in Jewish roles' (2006: 27). This was not a 'simple invisibility' but an 'active vanishing, a selective approach to visibility that is consistent with the everyday behavior exhibited by the majority of American Jews during the 1940s and 1950s' (Bial 2005: 155).

The first film in this wave was *Body and Soul* (dir. Robert Rossen, 1947) in which John Garfield played a Jewish boxer. It was followed by Hollywood's first film about antisemitism, *Crossfire* (dir. Edward Dmytryk, 1947), in which the Jew is largely concealed onscreen by only appearing as a murder victim. His actual screen time was minimal, since the film devoted itself to exposing the roots of racism and bigotry rather than their consequences. Hollywood's other post-war film about antisemitism, the Oscar-winning *Gentleman's Agreement* (dir. Elia Kazan, 1947), ironically made by Twentieth Century Fox, the only Hollywood studio not headed by a Jew at that time, featured Gentile Gregory Peck as Gentile-cum-Jew Philip Schuyler Green.[1] As Popkin pointed out, 'Bent on showing that Jews are just like everyone else, these films so neutralised their Jewish characters as to deprive them of all reality' (1952: 46). Thereafter, Gentiles playing Jews became the norm: Millie Perkins as Anne Frank in *The Diary of Anne Frank* (dir. George Stevens, 1959); Charlton Heston as Moses and Ben-Hur in *The Ten Commandments* (dir. Cecil B. DeMille, 1956) and *Ben-Hur* (dir. William Wyler, 1959) respectively and Paul Newman as Ari Ben Canaan in *Exodus* (dir. Otto Preminger, 1960), to name just a few titles. It should be mentioned, however, that Newman, whose father, was, and name is, Jewish, was not by *Halacha* (Hebrew: 'Jewish law') Jewish, that is by Orthodox/ Conservative standards, but was so by Reform and Reconstructionist ones, and is listed as such in major websites.

By the late 1960s, however, 'we find a period marked by revolutionary changes in American film' (Rosenberg 1996: 24) which impacted on representations of Jews. The dissolution of the studio system allowed independent production companies to flourish. This was accompanied by major changes in the United States, and elsewhere, which made ethnicity itself respectable: the freedom marches in the South, the postcolonial independence of many nations around the globe, the growth of the New

Left and the US involvement in Vietnam. Crucial were the ethnic pride/ identity politics movements (Black Power, women's and gay liberation, the Chicano and American Indian movements), from which Jews benefited, and in which they participated. Furthermore, Israel's victory in the Six Day War in 1967 produced conflicting reactions. While many Jews were proud to identify with Israel's victory, some non-Jewish responses were clearly anti-Zionist and sometimes infused with antisemitism. Among Jews a greater consciousness about the Holocaust than ever before was promoted. The period of 'the great retreat', of invisibility and vanishing, was over.

After years of ignoring such issues, Jewish American filmmakers in the late 1960s and 1970s began making films that explored Jewish self-definition. The consequence was the ethnicisation of Jewishness, leading to a proliferation of such inside images of Jews (many of which were imported from Eastern Europe) as the Jewish American Princess, the Jewish Mother, the neurotic *schlemiel* (Yiddish: a sort of cosmic fool combined with cosmic victim). These 'unselfconscious representations of Jewishness' (Rosenberg 1996: 32) were also 'more aggressive, more pointed. There was a determined and concerted effort to stand up for Jewish identity and to throw Jewish practices back into the face of a film culture that had ignored them or shunted them aside', resulting in an 'explosion of Jewish references, associations, and even ambivalences' (Gertel 2003: 2). In this way, this period represented an extraordinary and unprecedented flowering of overt, complex, stereotype-confronting exercises in Jewish representation that marked a 'new acceptance of the textures of idiosyncracies of Jewishness' (Rosenberg 1996: 24) which, as I will argue, has become the hallmark of the post-1990s period. As Rosenberg put it,

> Along with a new frankness in language, sexuality, violence, and oral complexity came a similar openness in the representation of race and ethnicity. Interracial romance became more common in film stories, though still charged with meaning and mystique. Supposed ethnic traits that had once been considered impolite to discuss publicly were now embraced un-apologetically – for example, notions of the Jew as rude, pushy, ruthless, or subversive [1996: 25].

At this point, Henry Bial argues, there was 'a change in the way the sexual attractiveness of the Jewish body was perceived by both Jews and Gentiles. During this period, the Jewish body not only came to be recognised as sexually appealing, it also helped redefine sexual attractiveness in American culture more generally' (2005: 5). According to *Heeb* magazine (2009), as Benjamin Braddock in *The Graduate* (dir. Mike Nichols, 1967), Dustin Hoffman 'cracked open the door for the Jewiest of actors to be credible as romantic leads. (Let's put it this way: Without this film, there's no way Adam Sandler would be Jessica Biel's, Penelope Cruz's or Kate Beckinsale's leading man.) After Hoffman, conventional good looks never mattered the same way'. Prominent Jewish actresses also began to appear, most prominently Barbra Streisand, who, along with Woody Allen, Hoffman and others, helped to drive this change.

Yet the 1960s and 1970s betrayed a contradictory impulse. On the one hand, there was a retreat into affectionate, schmaltzy and sentimental nostalgia, as symbolised by *Fiddler on the Roof* (dir. Norman Jewison, 1971), while on the other we see neurotic, anxious stereotypes, as mastered by Allen, whose richest period was from 1971–89, or a combination of both, as depicted in the parodies and black comedies of Mel Brooks. Nonetheless, taken together, this period represented 'the first big "coming out"' of Jewishness in US cinema (Itzkovitz 2006: 232).

Elsewhere, Jews in many national cinemas were marked by their absence and invisibility onscreen, in spite of their heavy involvement in filmmaking. As late as 1994, Freda Freidberg could write that Australian film 'has to date excluded the Jew'. Where the Jew did appear, particularly in European cinema, it was often as the Other (either exotic or evil), most notoriously in the Nazi propaganda film *Jud Süss*. In the UK, for example, following the Second World War, Jews were portrayed both more frequently and realistically, normalising them by depicting them as equal citizens in a pluralist nation (Epstein 2005: 366, Abrams 2010). Moving into the 1960s, 1970s and 1980s, themes such as racial hatred and religious bigotry were tackled, most notably in *Sunday Bloody Sunday* (dir. John Schlesinger, 1971) and *Chariots of Fire* (dir. Hugh Hudson, 1981). Nonetheless, overall, despite these two conspicuous exceptions, the major British Jewish directors of these decades, namely Schlesinger, Mike Leigh and Michael Winner, preferred not to insert any direct or explicit Jewishness into their films, hence the observation that prior to 1990 'significant Jewish films are hard to find' in the UK (Tal 2007: 84).

Since 1990, films about Jews, together with representations of Jews across the world not only multiplied but also took on a new form, which, within the context of a century of cinema, marked a departure from the past. There had been a steady flow of such representations hitherto, particularly since the late 1960s, but from 1990 onwards it became a veritable flood. What has changed since 1990 are the sheer number of films, which were also less marked by the contradictions of the 1960s and 1970s. Furthermore, as we shall see, they 'essentially continued the 1970s trend of unselfconscious representations of Jewishness, while also occasionally making possible deeper and more nuanced treatments of specific themes' (Rosenberg 1996: 32). Given the predominance of Hollywood in general and in Jewish films in particular, this trend was particularly evident in the United States, where Vincent Brook observed a 'postmodern surge in American films featuring Jewish main characters and Jewish themes' (2003: 205) and Harry Medved (1998) proclaimed a 'new wave' in US Jewish film.

It was a visual manifestation of the comfort of US Jewry by the late twentieth century, that Jews had arrived, and were *at home* in the United States. The Jewish community had become one of the wealthiest and most highly educated in the United States, and many Jews had reached the highest professional levels. In 1988, George H.W. Bush spoke of a 'kinder and gentler America' even if this was not much in evidence in reality. The administration of Bill Clinton oversaw a softening of the United States' domestic and international image. The simultaneous growth of multiculturalism at home, where difference and cultural pluralism became much more acceptable and accepted, encouraged Jews not only to maintain but also to exhibit pride in their ethnic identities. Jews were appointed to high governmental (and other) positions, culminating in the nomination of the Orthodox Jew Senator Joseph Lieberman as the Democratic vice-presidential candidate in 2000. Many public figures, like Lieberman, spoke openly about their commitment to Judaism. This was combined with less identification with Israel as such and a concomitant growth of pride in American Jewishness as a distinct religious and ethnic branch of Judaism.

Indeed, some wondered if American Jews were not 'too much at home in America':

American Jews are products of an overwhelmingly middle-class background that is generally suburban and gathered in communities across the nation. With little direct experience of anti-Semitism in their formative years, little conflict over being a hyphenated American, and little pressure from within the community to hold onto religious beliefs (but little pressure from without to give them up), American Jewry is a comfortable, satisfied group [Desser and Friedman 2004: 319].

A new and younger generation of Jewish screenwriters, directors, actresses and actors, who were not immigrants, who were not required to acculturate or to fight for its rights, entered the US film industry, where they were able to express their Jewishness in a new fashion. This generation 'reached adulthood in a time of unprecedented Jewish accomplishment and acceptance in the United States' (Desser and Friedman 2004: 317), as well as elsewhere in the diaspora. They defined their Jewishness in different ways to those of their parents and grandparents, which Howard F. Stein and Robert F. Hill coined 'dime store ethnicity' – the ability to pick and choose from a variety of ethnic identities (1977). They had attained a high level of education, including post-secondary (university) levels. Their middle-class backgrounds, film-school training and access to national and international financial support assisted them. At the same time, they felt a sense of a recedingly distinctive Jewishness in postethnic America, which had to be reasserted, producing a dialectical tension *between* assimilation and multiculturalism (Brook 2003). The more Jews become accepted, therefore, the more their difference must be defined. Finally, there were a series of additional changes in television that paved the way: less opposition from Jewish advocacy groups, decent ratings for Jewish sitcoms, the Jewish stand-up legacy, industrial competition and programming changes (Brook 2003: 75–82).

In contrast to these earlier decades, this post-1990 cinematic shift was *global*. Beyond North America, there was a renaissance, or even birth in some cases, of Jewish filmmaking, clearly signalling similar trends to those in the United States. As Israel matured into a secure and economically viable state, diaspora communities no longer feeling the need to build up or be eclipsed by Israel began to prioritise their own development, and started to come into their own. Caryn Aviv and David Shneer thus even suggested 'the end of diaspora' because the majority of Jews outside Israel feel a sense of '*rootedness* in the places they live' and 'no longer see themselves "in diaspora" but instead see themselves at home, not pining for a Promised Land' (2005: xvi). They conclude that what they are witnessing is 'the emergence of what we have dubbed a new type of Jew – the New Jews' (2005: xvi). Jonathan Webber referred to it as 'a reconstruction of identity', especially by the young (1994: 22), and Lasse Dencik used the term 'ethno-cultural smorgasbord' (2003: 54). In this context, Judaism and Jewishness became 'fashionable' (Lustig and Leveson 2006: 3). The arrival (or greater highlighting of the presence) of other immigrant groups that took the spotlight off Jews, such as Muslims and Roma, assisted this revival of Jewishness and Jewish confidence. Such a significant non-white presence in Europe threw into relief the issue of minorities among whom there was not a wholesale desire for assimilation, made difficult by differences in skin colour (Alderman 1994: 189–90). Furthermore, in response to this new type of immigration, race-relations legislation and anti-discrimination policies were enacted, in particular by the European Union, from which Jews undoubtedly benefited. The media recognised, as a result, that it had to cater for an ethnically and religiously diverse population.

Greater Holocaust education also convinced many younger Jews that a low profile was useless given that antisemites were not so discerning in their discrimination. At the same time, hostility towards Jews was on the decrease, particularly towards the end of the twentieth century. A greater awareness of the receding distinctiveness of Jewish identity was partly overcompensated for by the proliferation of post-1990s Jewish images (Pearl and Pearl 1999, Brook 2003). In addition, what has been termed a 'Holocaust consciousness' (Novick 1999) was constructed in popular culture by landmark films such as *Shoah* (dir. Claude Lanzmann, 1985) and *Schindler's List* (dir. Steven Spielberg, 1993) and cemented by national educational curriculum changes, the growth of Holocaust modules and degree programmes at university level, the institution of annual remembrance days and the setting up of museums and memorials across the globe, including every major city in the United States and Europe. Together, these changes allowed 'younger Jews to become more assertive in declaring their Jewish identity', producing a tangible birth of Jewish confidence (Brook 1989: 417). In Britain during the 1980s, for example, Jewish screenwriter Frederic Raphael suggested 'assertiveness has now become a licensed form of behaviour, and Jews, having got the licence, have no intention of not using it' (quoted in Brook 1989: 420).

The fall of communism across Eastern and Central Europe and the former Soviet Union after 1989 led to a greater openness in filmmaking there, leading to a 'Jewish cinematic renaissance', heralding more films about Jewishness than had appeared beforehand. 'After decades during which Jewish topics in art had been silenced, bans were lifted, and films on Jewish issues started pouring onto the screens. This encompassed a wide range of subjects, genres, and authors' (Gershenson 2008: 179). The horizons of cinema 'broadened to encompass representational styles and subjects that had been avoided, if not altogether suppressed through censorship, during the post-World War II decades', resulting in an 'altered cinematic landscape' that foregrounded Jewish ethnic, religious and cultural identities (Portuges 2005: 121).

Finally, changes in the European film industry and funding helped to kick-start the careers of younger Jewish filmmakers. A growth of schemes and shorts competitions, along with the proliferation of film-production courses, created a climate of new-found energy, confidence and optimism in the 1990s. Jewish filmmakers obviously benefited from this context and from the financial support offered by a complex European network of funding bureaucracies, government film funds, television money and private investment.

Taken together, these changes led to the appearance of more Jews on European screens than ever before, as these new Jewish identities were increasingly mapped onto cinematic representations. Beginning with *Leon the Pig Farmer* (dirs Vadim Jean and Gary Sinyor, 1992), a group of British films were produced 'which sought to explore issues of national, cultural and ethnic identity in the form of narratives combining comic *and* dramatic plot developments, incidents and perspectives'. Among them was a new wave of films that 'meditated on what it meant to be Jewish [...] in contemporary Britain' (Mather 2005: 67). Almost as many films about or featuring Jews were released as in the previous eight decades combined (Abrams 2010). In France some of the most critically discussed films of the last two decades strongly featured Jewishness, most notably *La Haine* (dir. Mathieu Kassovitz, 1995). Germany witnessed a wave of post-1990 German heritage films dealing with Jews and Jewishness predicated on 'the resurgence of Jewish culture in postwall Germany' (Koepnick 2002: 57) such as *Viehjud Levi/ Jew-Boy Levi* (dir. Didi Danquart, 1999).

Other European nations saw similar films about Jews emerge. These included the Czech Republic (*Musíme si pomáhat/Divided We Fall*, dir. Jan Hrebejk, 2000), Holland (*Zwartboek/Black Book*, dir. Paul Verhoeven, 2006), Hungary (*Sunshine*, dir. István Szabó, 1999), Italy (*La vita è bella/ Life is Beautiful*, dir. Roberto Benigni, 1997), Poland (*Rewers/The Reverse*, dir. Borys Lankosz, 2009), Russia (*Lyubov/Love*, dir. Valery Todorovsky, 1991) and Spain (*Seres Queridos/Only Human*, dirs Dominic Harari and Teresa de Pelegrí, 2004). In Sweden, between 1990 and 1993 six films appeared – 'a significant number, given the relatively small annual output of the Swedish film industry' – that focused on the Jewish experience (Wright 1998: 323), such as *Kådisbellan/The Slingshot* (dir. Åke Sandgren, 1993).

Beyond the United States and Europe, new Jewish films appeared in Argentina (*Judíos en el espacio/Jews in Space*, dir. Gabriel Lichtmann, 2005), Australia (*Hey Hey It's Esther Blueburger*, dir. Cathy Randall, 2008), Brazil (*O Ano em Que Meus Pais Saíram de Férias/The Year My Parents Went on Vacation*, dir. Cao Hamburger, 2006), Canada (*The Trotsky*, dir. Jacob Tierney, 2009) and Mexico (*Novia que te vea/Like a Bride*, dir. Guita Schyfter, 1994). Bolder films emerged from Israel, too, tackling topics such as homosexuality in the military (*Yossi & Jagger*, dir. Eytan Fox, 2002), Palestinian–Jewish relationships (*The Bubble*, dir. Eytan Fox, 2006), suicide bombing (*Paradise Now*, dir. Hany Abu-Assad, 2005) and Israel's invasion of Lebanon in 1982 (*Beaufort*, dir. Joseph Cedar, 2007; *Waltz with Bashir*, dir. Ari Folman, 2008; *Lebanon*, dir. Samuel Maoz, 2009).

Clearly Jews began to feel accepted in the post-1990 period. As Ruth D. Johnston observed, 'the desire for assimilation waned in the 1970s and 1980s as the politics of multiculturalism gradually supplanted the politics of cultural pluralism, this time placing Jews in a peculiar post-assimilationist situation' (2006: 209). A generation of Jewish (and Gentile) producers, directors, actors, actresses and screenwriters emerged that is less anxious, less afraid of stoking an antisemitic backlash and thus more willing to put Jews onscreen regardless of plot imperative and without feeling the need to either explain or explain away their presence/absence. Daniel Itzkovitz remarks,

> Jewish characters abound in mainstream Hollywood cinema, for example, in numbers and varieties not seen since the first big 'coming out' of the 1960s, and Jewish artists and performers, dubbed 'new Jews' by some in the media, seem unabashed about their Jewishness – onscreen and off – as never before [...] There have, of course, always been large numbers of Jewish actors, writers, and directors in Hollywood, but never before have there been so many Jewish *characters*, particularly Jewish male characters, at the center of major Hollywood productions 2006: 232, 241.

Carolina Rocha called this 'a process of de-hiding or making minority groups visible to a larger audience' (2010: 39).

One of the results of this trend is an unselfconscious, normalised, 'casual' or 'matter of fact' Jewishness that has become ordinary or quotidien. Indeed, this is so much so that, at times, Jews frequently seem 'gratuitous' or 'superfluous'. It continues the 1970s trajectory of 'a tendency to make a character's (or actor's) Jewishness something other than the main point of his or her presence in the story' (Rosenberg 1996: 30). Often, in the past, in order to see onscreen Jews and Jewishness, films with a significant and overt Jewish content had to be viewed. Since 1990, however, there is a growing number of films in which the addition of the Jewishness to a character, or of a Jewish character, makes no major difference to the trajectory of the story, plot or narrative arc, except to insert a gag line or an 'in-joke' to be read by those who understand the cultural codes. Indeed, one can hardly see a mainstream US film these days without a Jewish character, reference or an in-joke appearing, often with no intrinsic value other than a nod and a wink to those members of the audience it is presumed will understand such insertions. Clearly a sense of *Jewissance* is a motivating factor here: the joy derived from placing and reading the Jew in the film text but providing the same pleasures that Boyarin and others outlined above. Furthermore, the increasing proliferation of in-jokes within films demonstrates that the New Jews neither know nor care if their Gentile audiences can share the laugh with them. This period can be described as post-melting pot and post-assimilatory, and it is not confined to any one country, although it is most prominent in the United States, the paradigmatic example of Jewish filmmaking.

This shift was illustrated by the advent of the very unapologetically Jewish *Seinfeld* (NBC, 1990–98) in 1990 that, according to the Nielsen ratings, was the most popular sitcom of the 1990s. *Seinfeld* was a sitcom that billed itself as 'a show about nothing'. It featured four nasty, selfish, self-serving, venal characters, setting the pattern for contemporary cinema. Since then, representations of Jews, Jewishness and Judaism recycle, reverse, mimic and mock the underlying stereotypes of the past, as well as what will be shown to be the polarities of the Jewish self-image that were limited to a strict set of binary oppositions hitherto. In doing so, a spectrum of representations has been introduced. Furthermore, these representations come from the inside: the *gaze* is that of Jewish directors, actors, actresses and screenwriters themselves.[2] If, as Rosenberg suggests, previous 'evasions of Jewish realities' were dictated or encouraged by the larger society, then in the contemporary period these characterisations were motivated from within the community itself (1996: 27).

This new use of Jewish stereotypes in contemporary cinema reveals a deeper strategy beyond *Jewissance* and pleasure. The reversal of insult, or 'victim humour', is a technique against antisemitism, to 'disguise the aggression and hostility by turning it on oneself' (Berger 2001: 9–18). This is comparable to what Michel Foucault labelled a 'reverse discourse', which seeks to 'demand that its legitimacy [...] be acknowledged, often in the same vocabulary, using the same categories by which it was [...] disqualified' (1990: 101). The recovering of such stigmatised epithets as 'Jew', 'Jewess' and 'Heeb' can be invoked here as examples. Initially offensive and negative, there has been a much more recent revival of these terms, paralleling recuperations such as 'queer'. Such scholars as Amy-Jill Levine, for example, issued a call 'to appropriate and transform the model of the Jewess' (1997: 153), and the blog of the Jewish Women's Archive in the United States opted to call itself 'Jewesses with Attitude' in order 'to reclaim this term for ourselves'. Similarly, one can point to the same trend with the very word Jew, once serving as a marker of difference, mystery and Otherness – a 'bloody grimace' in the words of Max Horkheimer and Theodor Adorno (1973: 186). Finally here, in 2001 a new, rebellious, alternative, self-consciously 'hip' Jewish magazine called *Heeb* was launched, underwritten by mainstream Jewish philanthropy.

Bhabha points out how, 'the same stereotype may be read in a contradictory way or, indeed, be misread' (1994: 100). This 'reverse stereotype', then, achieves the status of what Foucault calls 'a hindrance, a stumbling block, a point of resistance and a starting point for an opposing strategy' (1990: 100–1). Or what Sigmund Freud describes as 'a rebellion against authority, a liberation from its pressures' (1994: 149), glossed by Bhabha as 'a strategy of cultural resistance and agency committed to a community's survival' (1998: xvii). Reverse stereotypes may take the form of 'mimicry' (Bhabha 1994: 123), which 'is never a simple reproduction of those traits. Rather, the result is a "blurred copy" [...] that can be quite threatening. This is because mimicry is never very far from mockery, since it can appear to parody whatever it mimics' (Ashcroft et al. 2000: 139). Reverse stereotypes are a means for Jews to draw upon the traditional moderate and intellectual values of *Yiddishkeit* (Yiddish: lit. 'Jewishness', 'Jewish culture') to mimic, mock and critique the dominant ideas of *goyim naches* (Yiddish: lit. 'pleasure of/for the Gentiles'), which can be translated to mean the contemptuous Jewish term for Gentile/dominant values, that is 'preoccupation with the body, sensuality, rashness, and ruthless force' (Sammons 1988: 91), which are considered *goyish* (Yiddish: 'un-Jewish'). Reverse stereotypes are also a means to mimic, mock and critique the values and strategies of the older, more Zionist, assimilatory and placatory generation of establishment lay and rabbinic leaders, Jewish politicians and Hollywood studio executives of the past.

Apart from the odd article or chapter, however, this change has been largely overlooked by academic scholarship. Furthermore, in general terms, the field of Jewish film studies has tended to focus primarily either on the image of the Jew or the Holocaust on film (Friedman 1982, Erens 1984, Avisar 1988, Gabler 1988, Doneson 2002, Gertel 2003, Hoberman and Shandler 2003, Insdorf 2003, Hirsch 2004, Baron 2005, Bartov 2005, Taub 2005). In terms of the former – the image of the Jew – these studies were largely confined to the period before 1990. In being so, such scholarship showed the shifting formulation of cinematic Jewishness as a response to the ongoing crisis in the construction of Jewish-American identity during the twentieth century. Two such important and valuable studies stand out: Lester D. Friedman's *Hollywood's Image of the Jew* and Patricia Erens's *The Jew in American Cinema*. Both books cover a vast range of cinematic representations of Jews from the silent era to the early 1980s.

The New Jew in Film, then, attempts to build upon this pioneering work, as well as to update and expand it, by focusing on the 'contemporary' period, which I define as commencing in 1990, and continuing to the present. I also aim to take a wider and more ambitious remit than just 'Hollywood' or 'American Cinema' to redress the curious lack of writing on 'how Jews have been depicted through cinema as a whole' (Zimerman 2002: 934). While the US film industry certainly dominates film production and distribution, particularly in terms of Jewish representations, I include prominent examples of non-US films where appropriate. Furthermore, as I do not want to retread old ground, I include as many newer and perhaps less examined films as possible. Finally, unlike Friedman and Erens, there is no attempt at an overall periodisation here.

In this way, I hope to contribute to the existing scholarship by not only updating older monographs that covered the period up to the late 1980s, but also by tackling issues that, to date, have not achieved a great deal of attention, given the aforementioned foci of Jewish film studies. In its exploration of the new and changing depictions of Jews since 1990 until the present in mainstream cinema, this book does so through the organising lens of a series of themes, some familiar, as well as those that have traditionally fallen outside the scope of film studies, Jewish or otherwise. It is thus organised into overlapping thematic chapters: the Jew, the Jewess, sex, passivity, agency, religion, food and bathrooms. My final two chapters, in particular, are not only a departure into new Jewish territory – food and toilets – but are also a departure from the previous six. Unfortunately, an unavoidable consequence of this theme-based format, which necessitates a certain amount of overlap, is some repetition. Taken together, however, these chapters are 'reflections on images or stereotypes of Jews, particularly of Jewish bodies, for the most part bodies of Jewish men – with bodies being understood as physical bearers, literally embodiments, of community experiences, fantasies, and ideals' (Breines 1990: 4).

In addition to explicit representations of Jews and Jewishness, I will explore subsurface, sub-epidermic, 'implicit' (Rosenberg 1996: 18), symbolic or conceptual Jewishness, that is where Jews are 'literally *conceived*, more than *represented*' (Brook 2003: 124), thus hoping to challenge the widespread approach to the Jewish image on film as limited to overt 'content' analysis. Following Ella Shohat, I will suggest that in many films Jewishness is 'textually submerged' (1991: 215), producing 'Jewish moments' (Stratton 2000: 300) in which the viewer is given the *possibility* of what Bial calls '*reading Jewish*' (2005: 70), by 'employing a largely unconscious complex of codes that cross-check each other', of which the Jewish identities of actors/actresses is a key, but by no means the only, part. The 'real-life' status of the actor/actress behind the depiction can provide the viewer with an additional clue to reading Jewish in the conflation of cinematic role/persona with real life. As Rosenberg points out, 'In theory, the ethnicity, of an actor or actress should be irrelevant to the role – acting, after all, is just that: acting – but broader ideological factors influence casting decisions, and these in turn become relevant to the film depiction of ethnic experience' (1996: 26). However, an actor/actress's (or their character's) *actual* ethnic and religious status, whether s/he is Jewish only according to *Halacha*, that is born to a Jewish mother or converted by a recognised rabbinic authority, is not my overarching concern here.

Furthermore, reading Jewish relies on locating identifiably Jewish characteristics, behaviours, beliefs or other tics, either explicitly or by a range of other undeniable, if submerged, signifiers. Important clues include looks, intellect, behaviour, profession, name and physiognomy, all of which require a prerequisite knowledge of Jews, Jewishness and Judaism. As Rosalin Krieger explains:

> The Jewish-Yiddish symbols come in the form of historical and cultural references, names, foods, verbal and body language, phenotype, and religious rituals, all of which rely upon individual viewers to identify these clues that represent things Jews and elements that can be read as possibly Jewish [2003: 388].

Yet, at the same time, according to Bial, Jewishness is often 'double coded', that is 'a performance can communicate one message to Jewish audiences while simultaneously communicating another, often contradictory message to gentile audiences' (2005: 3). To quote Bial at length here,

> There is, I suggest, a Jewish audience that may glean Jewish specificity from performances that a general audience decodes as universal. The Jewish reader may decode Jewishness through aural, visual, or emotional/genre signs [...] speech patterns and accents, an actor's looks or hairstyle, a certain kind of anxiety or neurosis about the conflict between tradition and modernity – all of these things may be, and have been, read as Jewish by critics and audiences inclined to do so [...] Only Jews (or those who know the codes) will interpret these elements of performance as Jewish. While general audiences may recognize these performance practices as unusual, urban, or ethnic, they will not necessarily recognize them as indicators of Jewish cultural difference [2005: 152].

Such reading Jewish, the ability to tap into what may be perceived as a somewhat esoteric knowledge denied to those who do not know the codes, is arguably akin to Boyarin's notion of *Jewissance*. Where I depart from Bial, however, is in his notion that 'double coding functions to negotiate between the desire to assert the specificity of the Jewish experience and the apparently competing desire to speak to the universal human condition' (2005: 3–4). After 1990, in line with my argument above, there is no desire simultaneously to code specificity *and* universality; that latter category, I argue, belongs to an earlier era of assimilatory cinema, one that is rejected in the contemporary, postethnic period. Contemporary cinema operates in a mode summed up by David Mamet's response when it was put to him that the majority of his audiences would not recognise the Jewish symbolism within his work. Paraphrasing Maimonides, he replied,

'Those that do, do; those that do not, do not' (quoted in Kane 1999: 362 n. 40).

A note of caution, however: I will not deal extensively with Israeli cinema, because many Israeli films 'touch upon Jewish identity as it relates to Israeli nationality and Middle East politics' (Smith 2009: 393 n.12) rather than to Jewishness and Judaism per se. Indeed, 'Zionism has won, Jewishness has gone underground, and is in fact absent from the screen' (Tal 2007: 77). Nonetheless, where relevant to my argument, I will include references to Israeli films.

Finally, this book hopefully punctures the concluding comment in David Desser and Lester D. Friedman's *American Jewish Filmmakers*, 'perhaps, we have witnessed the final flowering of an American Jewish cinema' (2004: 320). Not only does American Jewish cinema continue to thrive and move in new directions, but also there is a blossoming of Jewish cinema across the globe.

CHAPTER 1

The Jew

A history in brief(s) of 'the Jew' in film

Given that the history of Jews in cinema is almost synonymous with the representation of the Jewish man, often conflated into the overarching term 'the Jew', it seems redundant here to rehash fully that history which I sketched out in my introduction. However, to summarise the period before 1990, representations and stereotypes of the Jew traditionally fell into one or more of the following categories: racialised and antisemitic; invisible or non-existent; idealised, de-Judainised and de-Semitised, often replaced by the Gentile mimicking the Jew; ethnicised, anxious and neurotic; or victimised and humiliated. Furthermore, since the 1960s, underlying these characterisations were certain recurring stereotypical tics, which stubbornly persisted, particularly in US cinema, including fast-talking intelligence, physical weakness, small stature and sexual preference for the blonde *shiksa* (Yiddish: a non-Jewish woman bearing derogatory connotations that objectify and sexualise her) (Desser 2001).

Self-images of the Jew traditionally fell into two opposing categories, both of which were 'openly resistant to and critical of the prevailing ideology of "manliness" dominant in Europe' (Boyarin 1997: 23), that is *goyim naches*. First, the 'tough' Jew, that is the idealised hyper-masculine, macho, militarised, muscled and bronzed, though not very intellectual, Jew of the Zionist project (Breines 1990, Yosef 2004) with its variations of

19

the 'Muscle-Jew' (Nordau 1898), and, later, the *sabra* (Hebrew: lit. 'prickly pear'; a native-born Israeli) (Almog 2000) – these will be explored in more detail in Chapter 5. Second, the 'queer' or 'sissy' diaspora Jew, which can be defined as the intellectual yet insufficiently, incompetently and inadequately masculine Ashkenazi (Central and Eastern European) male found in the diaspora – the subject of Chapter 4. This Jew is a 'nonmale' or an 'unmanly man'. He is feminised, effeminate, gentle, timid, studious and delicate. He never uses his hands for manual labour, exercises or pays attention to maintaining his body. The diaspora Jew of traditional Ashkenazi Jewish culture who devoted his life to the study of the Torah embodies him.

For centuries the diaspora Jew, especially his physiognomy and physiology, was tenaciously intertwined with notions of unmanly passivity, weakness, hysteria and pathology, all bred by the lack of outdoor and healthy activity. The Jew's legs and feet in particular were characterised as non-athletic, unsuited to nature, sport, war-making, brutality and violence. At the same time, *Yiddishkeit* valued timidity, meekness, physical frailty and gentleness, privileging the pale scholarly Jew who studied indoors, excluded from labour and warfare. This resulted in a number of self-images of the Jew: the *nebbish* (Yiddish: an unfortunate simpleton; an insignificant or ineffectual person; a nobody; a nonentity), the *yeshiva bocher* (Yiddish: a religious scholar), the *schlemiel*, the *mensch* (Yiddish: a decent, upstanding, ethical and responsible person with admirable characteristics) and the *haredi* (often conflated, but not synonymous, with 'Hasid').[3] All of these images were defined by their softness, gentleness, weakness and non-physical passivity, what shall be called 'queer' or 'sissy'.

This queer/sissy Jew was characterised as 'hysteric', the result of prominent nineteenth-century antisemitic prejudices. Psychoanalysts such as Freud and Jean-Martin Charcot worked towards understanding the Jew's hysteria. The Jew as an unmanly hysteric seeped into the Jew's own self-consciousness and identity. Boyarin noted how 'by focusing on hysteria, especially in light of his own self-diagnosed hysteria, Freud was fashioning a self-representation that collaborated with one of the most tenacious of anti-Semitic topoi – that Jews are a third sex: men who menstruate' (2000: 354). Franz Kafka, for his part, was morbidly preoccupied with his own insubstantial physicality, especially in relation to his physically imposing father (Gilman 1995, Pawel 1997). Otto Weininger concluded in his *Sex and Character* (1903) that 'Judaism was saturated with femininity' and that the

Jew was, 'found to approach so slightly and so rarely the ideal of manhood'. Like women, the Jew shared an 'exaggerated susceptibility to disease' (quoted in Friedman 2007: 15). Adding repressed homosexuality to his fragile self-consciousness, Weininger's self-hatred was so acute that he committed suicide shortly after the publication of his work. Boyarin noted the conflation between homosexual and Jew, that the same constructs were attached to both, namely, 'hypersexuality, melancholia, and passivity [...] the Jew was queer and hysterical – and therefore not a man' (2000: 355). Gilman summarised that 'the Jew is the hysteric; the Jew is the feminized Other; the Jew is seen as different, as diseased' (1991: 76). The Jew was both hysterical and homosexual; at once a man who menstruates, with menstruation a signifier of illness, incompletion and incapability, and not a man at all.

Since 1990, however, representations of the cinematic Jew have evolved. As we shall see, more and more explicitly identified Jewish actors moved from being leading indie men and secondary characters in mainstream film to the forefront of contemporary US cinema. In this new postethnic era in which masculinities were arguably gentled, replacing the hard white bodies of the 1980s (viz. Sylvester Stallone, Chuck Norris and Arnold Schwarzenegger), the queer/sissy Jew emerged as the vanguard of a new softer and kinder cinematic multiculturalism and cultural pluralism. This was facilitated by the creation of 1980s advertising images, the 'New Man', that is a 'de-masculinised' and feminised (Kirkham 1995: 107), emotionally sensitive, vulnerable, tender, loving but hunky male, a position for which the queer/sissy Jew was already almost ideally suited.

Furthermore, a cultural context emerged in which 'the multiple meanings of masculine identity, the existence of masculinities', was increasingly apparent (Tasker 1993: 1). Consequently, not only did the number of Jews on film multiply, but also they took on new and different forms, marking a departure from the past. Contemporary cinema introduced a spectrum of multiple Jewish masculinities that began to populate the ground between the poles of toughness and queerness. We are thus witnessing a shift towards more subtle, nuanced, playful and even outrageous representations of the Jew, in contrast to earlier representations. The variety of Jewish masculinities has proliferated to include Jews who are stoned, solitary, nasty, brutish, short, unprofessional, working-class and more. In doing so, the diaspora Jew's body is not just sissy/queer, that is a passive site often the locus for suffering, humiliation, victimisation, stereotyping, idealisation and sexual inadequacy, but has become a means of identification, pride and sexual prowess where the Jew, in all his variety, is openly and proudly identified.

In this chapter, in line with Steven Cohan and Ina Rae Hark's 1993 call for redefining the study of film masculinities to include a broader set of paradigms than before, and following the model provided by Santiago Fouz-Hernández and Alfred Martínez-Expósito (2007) among others, I will explore how this New Jew deconstructs conventional and hegemonic categories to include the non-normative and marginalised, in particular how Jewishness is deployed in a form of *Jewissance*. It is ironically a drive towards normalisation that motivates these more unusual representations. Furthermore, these new self-images are used as a means to mimic, mock and reverse the dominant tough values of the mainstream culture, whether Gentile or Jewish.

Solitary, nasty, brutish and short

Contemporary cinema is not afraid to shy away from the complexities of representing the Jew in the post-1990 period. As a consequence, the number of mean, nasty and venal Jews has proliferated onscreen. These Jews are often also represented as physically unattractive and non-erotic: short, ugly, fat, balding, frequently with brutish, self-serving and selfish characteristics to match. Such physical drawbacks are not necessarily ameliorated by wit, intelligence or sense of humour. This even affected an older generation of directors such as Woody Allen. From the early 1990s onwards, Allen changed his typical *shtick*, converted his leading men from the neurotic, yet lovable, *schlemiel* protagonist he personally excelled at playing to a series of darker monsters. With *Husbands and Wives* (1992), *Bullets over Broadway* (1994) and *Deconstructing Harry* (1997), Allen transformed 'the image of his lead actor from a caring, concerned individual into a rapacious, unresponsive one', an 'artist-monster figure, though hardly a heroic one' (Rubin-Dorsky 2003: 6, 19). 'Remote and unembraceable', his Gabe Roth in *Husband and Wives* is 'self-absorbed', 'unfulfilled', and in a relationship 'marked by unexamined resentment, full of deceit and dishonesty' (Rubin-Dorsky 2003: 6).

Allen's characters have always been flawed but none quite like Gabe, who is utterly uncharismatic. Without self-knowledge, indulging in avoidance and denial, or perhaps just attempting to hide his complaints and longings, he is unable or unwilling to say what he feels. Like one of the sperm in his novel, Gabe is minuscule and unformed, embryonic and voiceless [Rubin-Dorsky 2003: 7].

Harry Block (Allen) in *Deconstructing Harry* is 'morally reprehensible' (Rubin-Dorsky 2003: 20). He is 'a truly miserable antihero' (Girgus 2002: 152). Block is a 'black magician', an expert at 'spin[ning] literary gold out of human suffering'. Utterly lacking in compassion, principles and scruples, he 'doesn't care whom he hurts or kills off in his fiction, be it friend, sister, or parents. His world, in effect, is a moral vacuum' (Rubin-Dorsky 2003: 20). Block is a vulgar and violent misogynist given to cruel behaviour, choosing to cheat on his wives in particularly humiliating ways, sleeping with the sister of one and the patient of another. He is 'disturbed and unbalanced' (Rubin-Dorsky 2003: 20), a specialist in crude, combative and abrasive language, although taking it onto new levels of coarseness and misogyny: 'world class *meshugene* [Yiddish: crazy, mad female] cunt' and 'aggressive, tight-ass, busy-body cunt' being just two examples. He even teaches his son phrases such as 'banging beaver' and 'fuck God'. Block is, in his own words, 'spiritually bankrupt': 'I'm empty, I've got no soul'. Or, as his sister puts it, his whole life is 'cynicism, sarcasm, nihilism and orgasm'. As a clear marker of this, Block is a self-hater, with a penchant for ridiculing Judaism. 'No Woody Allen film has ever exhibited such a rough and inescapably unpleasant exterior', Rubin-Dorsky concludes (2003: 23).

Similarly, David Mamet's 1990s screenplays possess a set of unusual Jews, who utter relentless sexist and aggressive obscenity. They are also 'Jews of questionable morality' (Kane 1999: 306), set in a variety of atypical contexts, none domestic. Thus they are shorn of any redeeming characteristics, or associations which might engender sympathy; for example, they refer to, but we never see, a range of women who might ameliorate their worst excesses. Shelley Levene (Jack Lemmon), Dave Moss (Ed Harris) and George Aaranow (Alan Arkin) in Mamet's *Glengarry Glen Ross* (dir. James Foley, 1992) are three corrupt, unethical, petty and hard-up real-estate salesmen engaged in a cut-throat, Darwinian competition to sell worthless land to gullible investors. In their dark and degraded world (the words 'fuck', 'shit' and their derivatives are uttered over 180 times), Levene tries to bribe his superior for the best 'leads' while Moss and Aaronow conspire to rob their own office to steal those leads and sell them on to a competitor. Unlike their biblical namesakes (Aaron, Moses and the Levites), their only values are greed, ruthlessness and survival, and they are 'ready to resort to corruption, lying, and theft in order to conclude the sales that will prevent them from getting fired' (Piette 2004: 77). Soulless capitalism, *goyim naches*, has destroyed them, leaving them devoid of any humanity, warmth, compassion and *menschlikayt* (Yiddish: ethical responsibility, social justice and decency for others expressed in kindness).

In *American Buffalo* (dir. Michael Corrente, 1996), written by Mamet, Walt 'Teach' Cole (Dustin Hoffman) is 'a parody of the loud-mouthed pushy Jew obsessed with money' (Kane 1999: 51). Indeed, the first word out of his mouth in the film is 'fuckin'', and we are treated to various other obscenity-laden diatribes throughout the film, such as 'cocksucking fuckhead', 'cunt', and 'fuck the cocksucker'. And, in Mamet's *The Edge* (dir. Lee Tamahori, 1997), Robert Green (Alec Baldwin) is a duplicitous, jealous, envious and covetous Jew who attempts to lure his lover's husband to Alaska in order to murder him. Everything about Green defies cinematic convention. The casting of Baldwin as Green is intriguing, for, as played by Baldwin, one might never believe he was Jewish if not explicitly identified as such, so little does he conform to Jewish cinematic stereotypes.[4] Furthermore, Baldwin plays a role rarely assigned to the Jew: a fashion photographer, an atypical profession for a cinematic Jew, where he tends to be defined by his intellect. 'Mamet depicts Green as an individual seemingly devoid of ethical responsibility, personal integrity, and loyalty, his acts and artifice are driven, as is he, by profit' (Kane 1999: 306). He is a Jew of 'such apparent villainy. A predatory, aggressive artist-for-hire, Robert Green is a seducer, deceiver, and arch-exploiter.' He covets his lover's money more than his wife, inspiring 'boundless contempt and a paucity of compassion' (Kane 1999: 305). These are all characteristics that 'easily feed into a mythology of the Jew as excessive, dangerous, and suspect' (Garb 1995: 26). Green thus embodies many stereotypes: 'the marginal Jew-as-thief', 'the Jew-as-liar', 'a masterful manipulator' (Kane 1999: 305, 308).

The Coen brothers' post-1990 films manifest many of the trends that will be discussed in this book. Indeed, they are essential to understanding contemporary Jewish cinema. Walter Sobchak (John Goodman) in *The Big Lebowski* (dir. Joel Coen, 1998) is the epitome of the new trend towards normalisation. Walter is 'an oafish and occasionally psychotic gun-toting' as well as 'bombastically embittered' Vietnam veteran who is 'violently proactive, anal, socially crippled' (Tyree and Walters 2007: 10, 22, 23). Walter is not only a slightly deranged Vietnam veteran, he is – atypically – a convert to Judaism, having done so for love at the request of his wife – what, in the United States, would be called 'a Jew by choice'. And even though divorced, he still maintains his religious identity (which I discuss further in Chapter 6). Unusually for a cinematic Jew, Walter is not identified by any de-contextualised markers (indeed Walter is not ethnically Jewish), but by his beliefs, values and behaviour as he maintains a level of Orthodox Jewish practice. He quotes the founder of Zionism, Theodore Herzl, ('If you will it, it is no dream'), as well as talmudic lore, although rarely with much 'relevance to the original context' (Tyree and Walters 2007: 31). He even named his dog after the twelfth-century Jewish philosopher, scholar and physician Maimonides (anticipating the Fockers' dog Moses by some years). Walter is proud of his Jewishness, and does not mind shouting about it. He claims insistently, 'Three thousand years of beautiful tradition, from Moses to Sandy Koufax. YOU'RE GODDAMN RIGHT I'M LIVING IN THE FUCKING PAST!'

At the same time, Walter is a superficially unattractive figure both physically and mentally. He is overweight, close to unhinged, and prone to profuse profanity ('This is what happens when you fuck a stranger in the ass,' he frequently warns). Indeed, the work 'fuck' is used 260 times, a significant proportion of them uttered by Walter.

The extent of Walter's unusualness as a cinematic Jew is highlighted by John Goodman's previous appearance in the Coens' *Barton Fink* (dir. Joel Coen, 1991) as the serial killer CharlieMeadows/Karl Mundt, who shouts 'Heil Hitler' before killing two policemen, as well as his similarity with a later Coens creation, Mitch Brandt (Brent Braunschweig), an army- orientated, potentially antisemitic[5] character in their *A Serious Man* (2009). The most noticeable correspondence between Walter and Brandt is their physical resemblance. Both men are sturdily built, have identical 'crew cut' hairstyles, and wear similar casual shirts. Walter's appearance is the visual reminder of his past, his service in the Vietnam War. Although his clothing is not explicitly military, his shirts, combat jacket, waistcoats, haircut and aviator sunglasses evoke a style appropriate for an army man – practical, durable and comfortable. And where no reference is made to Brandt's occupation, his clothing mirrors Walter's, and his urgency to take his son hunting could imply his imminent departure for military service.

Walter's stint in Vietnam has instilled in him a desire for precise rules and regulations. His adopted Judaism becomes 'a logical replacement for the regimentation of his much-missed army life'. 'This need is most evident in Walter's dependency on institutionalised hierarchies, from his long-completed military service to his dissolved marriage, from league bowling to his highly dubious version of Judaism'. Walter's 'woeful notion of being Jewish' and 'put-on Jewish identity seems to be more about stiffly following a strictly regulated life than any deep and loving communion with God, his synagogue or other Jews' (Tyree and Walters 2007: 80).

The extent of Walter's obsession with systems and conventions is seen when he brings Cynthia's dog to the bowling alley. The dog's breed is unimportant; he confuses the scruffy terrier with a Pomeranian, but Walter is in no doubt that the dog is valuable, as he exclaims 'the fuckin' dog's got fuckin' papers!' The same approach to rules and regulations is seen in Brandt's attitude towards the Gopniks' lawn in *A Serious Man*. Larry believes Brandt is infringing upon the property line. Brandt tells him to measure. Larry protests that he does not need to measure, and that 'you can tell', to which Brandt forcefully replies that the property line extends to the poplar tree. Both Walter and Brandt use rules and regulations to their advantage, to quash and dismiss any contesting position. 'Walter's line-in-the-sand mentality of picking fights over the broaching of more or less arbitrary boundaries and working himself up into apoplexy simply to prove his intransigence' (Tyree and Walters 2007: 79).

Walter is single-minded, aggressive, belligerent, serious, rule-bound, and wound as tight as a coil ready to spring at any moment. He 'wears his trauma like a badge' (Körte 1999: 201). As befitting his hawkish, pro-Republican militaristic politics, he carries himself with military bearing. His body language and posture is diametrically opposed to that of his best friend the Dude (Jeff Bridges), who studiously avoids conflict, is relaxed, nonchalant, indifferent to social status, remarkably open, always slouching and putting his legs up and 'in a constant state of facial befuddlement' (Tyree and Walters 2007: 74–75).

Walter's character is revealed in its starkness when he believes that his bowling competitor Smokey (Jimmie Dale Gilmore) has committed a foul by stepping over the line of play. He insists, 'This is not 'Nam. This is bowling. There are rules.' When Smokey refuses to mark his score as a zero, as Walter insists, Walter produces a gun, warning, 'Smokey my friend, you're entering a world of pain.' He reiterates the last four words twice more for emphasis. Walter then primes the gun and points it at Smokey's head, and his tense, terse body is framed as he threatens Smokey. He shouts, 'HAS THE WHOLE WORLD GONE CRAZY? AM I THE ONLY ONE HERE WHO GIVES A SHIT ABOUT THE RULES? MARK IT ZERO!' 'Having pulled his gun', Tyree and Walters argue, Walter 'demonstrates his constitutional inability to back down from a confrontation, screaming as he breaks Lord knows how many federal laws'. Furthermore, they state, 'This exchange perfectly exemplifies the curious tension in Walter's personality between a demand for structure and a wrathful incontinence [...] Walter, in other words, is not quite housebroken' (Tyree and Walters 2007: 79). As Smokey puts it, he is a 'crazy fuck'.

Walter, therefore, is a complete reversal of the previous cinematic characterisations of the Jew – often no more than ciphers or stereotypes – if not an outright and deliberate satire and mockery of them. The embodiment of such characterisations can be found in *Fiddler on the Roof*'s cute, cuddly, kitsch, aphorism-spouting protagonist Tevye (Topol). So when Walter declares 'I'm as Jewish as fuckin' Tevye!', the irony here is that size and beard apart, he could not be farther from this product of a

Walter Sobchak in *The Big Lebowski*.

fantasised, Americanised image of *shtetl*-dwelling Jewry,[6] that embodies the assimilatory, nostalgic and placatory past.

The Coens, Allen and Mamet had all been writing and directing for some time prior to 1990, yet it was in that decade that their darker Jewish characters began to appear with more frequency. This marked shift in their collective output is further testament to the trend away from assimilatory to a postethnic normalising Jewishness in contemporary cinema. Taking Mamet as representative here, *Glengarry Glen Ross* takes the non-specific everyman Willy Loman of Arthur Miller's play *Death of a Salesman* (1949) and transforms and multiplies him into a set of unscrupulous and foul-mouthed Jews in a film otherwise known as 'Death of a Fuckin' Salesman'.[7] It clearly symbolises the generational shift from a playwright (Miller) who was concerned to downplay his Jewishness, and who reputedly hated *Glengarry Glen Ross*, to one (Mamet) who was happy to declare it, warts and all.

Unprofessional Jews

After the immigrant and ghetto period of film, and particularly following the Second World War, reflecting the suburbanisation, embourgeoisement and widespread entry of the Jews into the professions, the Jew in film was stereotypically professional, economically comfortable, middle class, well-to-do and whose parents and/or families lived in suburban affluence. While this trend continued in the post-1990 period, a socioeconomic spectrum has been introduced, and the range of films, especially those emanating from Europe, featuring Jews as lower-class deadbeats increased as a result. In the German film *Alles auf Zucker!/Go for Zucker!* (dir. Dani Levy, 2004), for example, Jakob 'Jaeckie Zucker' Zuckermann (Henry Hübchen) is a lowlife, debt-ridden, gambling pool hustler. As befitting a class-obsessed society, the British films *Solomon and Gaenor* (dir. Paul Morrison, 1999), *Wondrous Oblivion* (dir. Paul Morrison, 2003) and *Sixty Six* (dir. Paul Weiland, 2006) are rooted in either a lower-middle- or working-class environment (also a consequence of all three films being set in the past).

In this respect, French-Jewish director Mathieu Kassovitz repeatedly refuses to conform to cinematic conventions regarding the Jew. His 'fracture sociale' trilogy (*Métisse*, 1993; *La Haine*, 1995 and *Assassin(s)*, 1997), places the Jew in a present-day working-class milieu, far removed from the professional stereotypes outlined above by Desser. In this way, Kassovitz's films reverse 'preconceived stereotypical notions of race as they relate to socio-economic standing and marginalisation' (Higbee 2005: 125–26). In *Métisse*, Félix (Kassovitz) is the French descendant of Eastern European Jewish immigrants. He is a 'white', working-class Jew who delivers fast food for a living. He is somewhat stereotypically coded in his physical appearance – he has a skinny frame, oversized glasses,[8] and rides a bicycle (in one repeated joke, unable to free himself from the pedals of his bike, he crashes to the floor as he comes to a stop). This contrasts, however, with the athleticism of his brother Max (Vincent Cassel), who boxes and plays basketball and is known in the local community as a petty hood and drug dealer. Furthermore, Félix is involved in a *ménage à trois* with Lola (the *métisse* of the title) and Jamal, who is African. When Félix asks his father how his grandmother will react to this information, the response is 'your grandmother was in Buchenwald. She has seen much worse', providing an ironic reversal of Jewish philosopher Emil Fackenheim's 614th Commandment ('Thou shalt not give Hitler a posthumous victory'), the use of which coupled with the Holocaust is a means by which young Jews are warned of the dangers of intermarriage (1968).

Félix is defined both ethnically and religiously. His family celebrates the Shabbat meal. Félix works for a kosher restaurant. His grandfather has a thick Eastern European accent that occasionally lapses into Yiddish, and Max proudly sports a star of David tattoo. Thus, Kassovitz reminds his audience that Jewishness is an ethnicity and as such is not, an 'exclusively "non-white" issue' (Higbee 2005: 126). Yet, when Félix mixes in the clubs and streets of his local neighbourhood, these ethnic/religious markers disappear, as he mimics the urban street youth culture. He is 'noisy, boisterous, cocky, provocative, gesticulates all the time [...] invents and sings rap songs, lives in cramped quarters, wears jeans and sneakers, and speaks *verlan*' (a form of French urban slang that consists of inverting syllables), making him virtually indistinguishable from the black and *beur* (North African) youth with whom he mixes (Sherzer 1999: 155).

Likewise in *La Haine* Kassovitz refuses to resort to the simple stereotype. Vinz (Cassel) is a working-class Ashkenazi *banlieue* dweller; his best friends Hubert (Hubert Koundé) and Saïd (Saïd Taghmaoui) are black and *beur* respectively. Vinz is a blond, blue-eyed Jew, in contrast to a non-Jewish skinhead played by the dark-haired Jew, Kassovitz himself, thus inverting the real world. In this way, Kassovitz not only makes an oblique comment about the traditional representation of the Jew in European culture as 'the Other', but also questions the boundaries of such images. Furthermore, although Vinz postures as tough, he is essentially queer.

> Vinz's quest for violently authentic experience betrays deep anxiety about a possible masculine and ethnic deficit that stems from his ambivalent identity and social position as a French Jew [...] He is obsessed with performing hyper-masculinity, resulting in exaggerated behaviour possibly atypical for filmic Jews: punching, spitting and picking his nose [Rose 2007: 480].

The film juxtaposes contradictory images to convey Vinz's ambivalent status. In a dream sequence Vinz breakdances to Eastern European Ashkenazi *klezmer* music, coding the clash between his Jewish and street identities. But 'the moves that Vinz comically performs expose him to be a Jewish dork in hip-hop garb [...] not the ultra-tough authentic youth-from-the-street he tries to be in his waking hours' rather 'a schlemiel who might be quite out of place in the gritty world of the *banlieue*', as *klezmer* is clearly not cool on the street (Rose 2007: 481).

Vinz is ejected from the spaces that professional Jews typically occupy in film. This is clearest in a scene in an art gallery, precisely the sort of upper-middle-class arty space in which cinematic Jews are located. But Vinz's clothes and speech disclose that he does not belong. And, in a further irony,

Vinz in *La Haine*.

the owner of the art gallery is played by Kassovitz's father Peter, who – although nowhere explicitly identified as Jewish – for the culturally aware spectator able to recognise the codes further reinforces the Jewishness of the gallery from which Vinz is excluded. Yet, at the same time, unlike his *beur* and black friends, Vinz is able to pass as white, thus escaping the police brutality that is directed against non-white minorities in the film.

Some stereotypical elements, however, are hard to change. Vinz's diaspora Jewishness is inescapable. He is clearly a queer Jew, situated within 'a long tradition of insufficiently masculine Ashkenazi males' (Rose 2007: 482). He is 'feminised' by his socioeconomic status as a *banlieusard*, lacking work, money and sex. He and his friends are 'controlled', 'treated as passive', 'repeatedly rejected, ejected, and detained by nearly all those with whom they come into contact' (Higbee 2005: 129). Furthermore, Vinz carries a gun with him at all times, keeping it tucked into his trousers. Despite the risks associated with doing so, he shows it off to his friends. He talks about avenging Abdel's death, but his threats are empty, all of them able to 'be read as a desperate attempt to reassert his masculinity through the threat and symbols of violence' (Higbee 2005: 129). Vinz identifies Hubert as the masculine and racial stereotype he wishes to mimic as a means to compensate for his queer sissy Jewishness.

In the third film of his 'fracture sociale' trilogy, *Assassin(s)*, Kassovitz himself plays Max Pujol, an aimless unqualified twenty-five-year-old who works as a temporary employee in a welding shop. His prospects, like much working-class French youth in the 1990s, are bleak. He is

> an aimless delinquent who lives with his unsympathetic mother in a nondescript working-class house in the Parisian *banlieue*. With limited aspirations, and few future prospects beyond the short-term vocational training course on which he is enrolled, Max engages in acts of petty delinquency along with Mehdi (a Maghrebi French youth from the neighbouring cité) [Higbee 2005: 131].

Max is discussed further in Chapter 6. In all three films, therefore, Kassovitz produces Jews who are members of the 'disenfranchized youth underclass', belonging to marginalised, dysfunctional or absent families, in an anomic society dominated by violence' (Higbee 2005: 131). His choice to place his Jews squarely in a working-class *milieu* stands in sharp contrast to the middle-class professional space that the Jew in cinema traditionally occupied.

Within this non-professional, working-class milieu, contemporary American cinema has also introduced a range of non-professional Jews, seemingly devoting their lives to taking drugs, playing video games and *schtupping* (Yiddish: coitus), albeit without much success, rather than pursuing successful bourgeois goals such as careers and families. They are typically located in homosocial genres, variously called 'bromances', 'brom-coms', 'homme-coms' and even 'dick flicks'. Many of these films were directed or produced by the absolutely crucial post-1990s *auteur* Judd Apatow, whose role, similar to the Coens, is key to understanding and illustrating the trends under discussion in contemporary cinema. Apatow has been labelled the heir to Woody Allen's status as 'the king of awkwardness' (Kotsko 2010: 48). Indeed, like Allen, 'Apatow' now refers to a genre in its own right. Apatow's ensemble troupe, the 'Jew Tang Clan' (Seth Rogen, Jason Segel, Jonah Hill, Michael Cera, Paul Rudd and Jason Schwartzman), excels at playing these not particularly attractive overgrown adolescent or boy/man characters full of smart verbal wisecracks, sexual jokes and gross-out humour. Such slacker characters typically assume the role of the *badken* (Yiddish: a professional fun-maker, jester, entertainer, verbose Jewish jokester and showman). They are, as Kane put it, 'those arrogant, outspoken, pushy Jews always ready with a smart line' (1999: 300).

In *The 40-Year-Old Virgin* (dir. Judd Apatow, 2005), for example, Cal (Seth Rogen) is a not particularly bright blue-collar worker in an electronics store. He breaks the paradigm of Jews onscreen both intellectually and physically in that he is not in one of Desser's prescribed professions, nor does he fit into the paradigms of either tough or queer Jew. His body size is average, large, somewhat overweight, neither weedy and thin nor muscle-bound and hyper-masculine. He has no outwardly obvious ethnic characteristics (job, looks or name). On the contrary, he is fairly tall, hairy, and his arms are covered with tattoos (a very atypical characteristic). At the end of the film, he is shown dancing topless, a celebration of his physical ordinariness. His closest bodily analogue is Walter in *The Big Lebowski* or, at a stretch, Tevye. Such a depiction shows how the Jew is being normalised physically on film, neither being a skinny sissy/queer nor a muscled tough Jew.

In *Knocked Up* (dir. Judd Apatow, 2007) Rogen plays another *schlubby* (Yiddish: clumsy, stupid or unattractive) Jewish stoner, Ben Stone. He is 'cute in a chunky Jewish guy sort of way'. Unemployed, his Jewish and homosocial daily life is characterised by routine drinking and smoking weed, while attempting to construct a website that charts nudity in mainstream films. Apatow is unapologetic about Stone's stoner qualities, lovingly detailed in the opening sequence. Indeed, the film celebrates Stone, as he, somewhat surprisingly but entirely in keeping with cinematic tradition, sleeps with an attractive blonde, professional *shiksa* (Katherine Heigl).

In the film *When Do We Eat?* (dir. Salvador Litvak, 2005), a comedy about a Passover Seder, Zeke (Ben Feldman) is another Jewish stoner who secretly slips a tab of ecstasy into his father's drink just before the Seder meal, which he conducts while tripping (without knowing it). A similar occurrence happens to the brothers Jaeckie and Samuel Zuckermann (Udo Samel) in *Alles auf Zucker!/Go for Zucker!* when they mistakenly take Jaeckie's daughter's ecstasy, which they think is aspirin. Danny Gopnick (Aaron Wolff) and his Jewish friends in *A Serious Man* also smoke weed; in fact, Danny recites his bar mitzvah Torah portion while high, and clearly is not the only stoned person in synagogue either. Bernie Focker (Dustin Hoffman) in *Meet the Fockers* (dir. Jay Roach, 2004) may be a professional lawyer but he likes to smoke the occasional joint.

Sex-obsessed stoners Rosenberg (Eddie Kaye Thomas) and Goldstein (David Krumholtz) feature as superfluous and/or gratuitous secondary characters in *Harold & Kumar Go to White Castle/Harold & Kumar Get the Munchies* (dir. Danny Leiner, 2004) and *Harold & Kumar Escape from Guantanamo Bay* (dirs Jon Hurwitz and Hayden Schlossberg, 2008). Playing on the brand name of the sugary US American kosher sacramental wine (Manischewitz), they are referred to as 'Manny' and 'Shevitz'. It is not only a clear reference to their Jewishness, but also suggests that they behave like two sweet eighty-year-old Jewish men from New Jersey. It soon becomes clear, however, that they are contemporary, updated, hence stoned, versions of Jack Lemmon's and Walter Matthau's 'odd couple' characters. Their physical gesticulations and speech patterns reinforce this impression. In one snippet of dialogue, Rosenberg tells Goldstein, 'I think Kumar's a *faygele*.' His clear use of the Yiddish term for gay – literally meaning 'little bird' or 'fairy' – is not typically used by cinematic Jews of the younger generation.

Furthermore, these archetypal stoners are represented as proudly Jewish. Rosenberg and Goldstein have put up a highly atypical *mezuzah*,[9] in that it is decorated with an effigy of a topless woman below the usual Hebrew letter *shin*. Among the drug paraphernalia and other related debris in their apartment is clearly visible Judaica. Their coffee table has on it, among other things, a box of pastries inscribed with Hebrew writing, a jar of beef jerky, a broken menorah (Hebrew: the nine-branched candelabrum lit on Chanukah, the festival of lights) with one branch missing, and an empty KFC carton. This mixture of the sacred and the profane, kosher and *treyf* (Hebrew: lit. 'torn', explicitly non-kosher) clearly signifies that while Rosenberg and Goldstein identify as Jewish, they are not fully observant. They have even fashioned a bong out of a *shofar* (a ram's horn used as a musical instrument on the Jewish New Year and Day of Atonement) from which they proceed to smoke pot, proffered with the words 'Hey, you wanna suck on this?'

Taken together, these characters begin to reverse the cinematic stereotype of the professional, bourgeois Jew to introduce a range of unmotivated protagonists. They are embodied by Roger Greenberg (Ben Stiller) in *Greenberg* (dir. Noah Baumbach, 2010), the single, forty-something, part-time carpenter who is deliberately doing nothing with his life, except drinking, taking drugs and chasing women.

Jews in outer space

At the end of his *History of the World, Part 1* (1981), Mel Brooks offered up a humorous sequence depicting a promised sequel to his preview of 'Hitler on Ice' entitled 'Jews in Space', a sci-fi spectacular featuring star of David-shaped spaceships, flown by *haredim*, singing of the glories of 'defending the Hebrew race'. In his parodic *Spaceballs* (1987), Brooks delivered. This idea is developed elsewhere: in *Deconstructing Harry*, Allen provides a bar mitzvah party with a *Star Wars* (dir. George Lucas, 1977) theme, including the legend, 'May the force be with you, Donald'. But where Allen and Brooks offered up such visions for humour, contemporary cinema has reversed this paradigm to place Jews in outer space in a serious fashion. The Argentinean film *Judíos en el espacio/Jews in Space* set the Passover story to the backdrop of *Star Wars*.

In *Serenity* (dir. Joss Whedon, 2005), Mr Universe (David Krumholtz) is a recluse who lives alone on a moon with his blonde *shiksa* wife, Lenore (Nectar Rose), an automaton known as a 'love-bot'. A techno-geek, he adores data, and is skilled at intercepting electronic transmissions and recordings anywhere in the universe. He is also religiously identified as Jewish, shown wearing a *yarmulke* (Yiddish: skullcap) and crushing a cloth-wrapped glass on his wedding to Lenore. And after his death, stones are placed on his grave in the Jewish tradition. Similarly, *Independence Day* (dir. Roland Emmerich, 1996) features a 'neurasthenic hysteric' Jew in David Levinson (Rogin 1998: 48). David (Jeff Goldblum) is an MIT-educated eccentric intellectual scientist, a 'Jewish computer whizz', who is good at chess and a gangly 'geek' (Rogin 1998: 49, Itzkovitz 2006: 233). He is a 'loser brainiac' (White-Stanley and Flinn 2008: 161), a talker, or 'Jew is mouth as nervous brain' (Rogin 1998: 49), who *twice* marries his non-Jewish wife. David displays no *goyische* (Yiddish: non-Jewish) traits, and even mocks the stereotypical Jewish concept of cowardice with his fear of flying.

David and Mr Universe are both queer Jews, whose sissiness is reinforced by the presence of further unmanly Jews or 'not quite men' (White-Stanley and Flinn 2008: 161). David's father, Julius (Judd Hirsch), is a Yiddish-speaking male hysteric smothering Jewish mother stand-in who constantly berates him for being a failure and goads him about his relationship status. Marty Gilbert (Harvey Fierstein) is David's panicked, hysterical, effeminate and explicitly gay, mother-obsessed, cowardly *nebbish* sidekick, who calls his mother and psychoanalyst from beneath his desk and on his car phone. Indeed, the queer intellectual values of *Yiddishkeit* rather than bodily *goyim naches* are valorised in both films, as it is *Yiddische kopf* (Yiddish: lit. Jewish head) that brings salvation (Gertel 2003: 132). This is most notable in

David and Julius Levinson in *Independence Day*.

Independence Day, for it is Jewish hypochondria – a signifier of Jewish cinematic queerness – that becomes the key plot device when Julius asks David if he is getting a cold, and the idea of using a computer virus as a weapon occurs to him.

David's queerness stands in clear contrast to his companion Captain Steven Hiller (Will Smith). Hiller is a fast-talking, wise-cracking black fighter pilot who we first meet sprawled out, topless in bed with his beautiful girlfriend. His young son runs into the room and wakes them both up. Hiller's body is toned and taut; he is a father, patriotic soldier and the depiction of a *seemingly* adorable nuclear family, complete with dog, appears ideal (although he is in fact not married and his girlfriend is a stripper). Hiller's representation builds upon a cinematic racial economy that defines blacks by their bodies and the notion of athletic and physical superiority. In contrast, we first meet David playing a quiet game of chess with Julius in a park. Julius pesters him because he persists in wearing his wedding ring even though his marriage dissolved three years earlier. Whereas Hiller's figure and family girlfriend define and solidify his masculinity, David is decidedly queer and feminised, pining for his ex-wife and playing chess with an overbearing father. Thus, both *Independence Day* and *Serenity* feature smart nerdy, weak, Jewish bodies, defined by their intellectual rather than physical capacities – neither is shown nude, and they are both scientists in a genre in which such a profession is often coded as feminine and unmanly.

Ultimately, however, a shift has taken place in outer space. Previously, as mentioned above, the notion of Jews in outer space was one only mined for humour, and Jews could only *mimic* astronauts, but were out of place in outer space. It was also submerged in analogy. The series of *Star Trek* films (1979–2009) featured Leonard Nimoy as Vulcan scientist Dr Spock. The cerebral, pacifist, intellectual Vulcans were conceived along Jewish lines, and the Spock greeting sign is based on the raising of the hands during the priestly blessing. Yet, this was nowhere made explicit in the films, and Spock, the only non-human member of the *USS Enterprise* crew, thus functioned as a symbolic or conceptual Jew (Shandler 1994). He had to be read as Jewish employing that largely unconscious complex of codes and moments that cross-check each other. Indeed, 'viewers of *Star Trek* variously understood Spock's archetypal "otherness" as analogous to that of African-Americans, Asians, and other cultural groups' (Shandler 1999: 149). Mr Universe and David, in contrast, are contemporary incarnations of Spock who, unlike him, have come out of the ethnic-religious closet to assert unashamedly and explicitly their Jewishness and their queer Jewish values. Where Nimoy only indirectly and obliquely referred to his ethnicity, Goldblum and Krumholtz are open and explicit about theirs. The New Jew can now belong in outer space.

The *shmok*: foreskin envy

Discussion of the Jew would not be complete without reference to his penis, known in Yiddish as '*shmok*' or by its diminutive '*shmekl*' ('little penis'). Ever since Abraham, a key signifier of the Jew is his circumcision. It establishes his difference, as Judaism is literally and inescapably inscribed on his body. It is a physical marker of his status as 'almost the same, *but not quite*' (Bhabha 1994: 123). Contemporary cinema, in constructing the Jew, thus cannot help but allude to his genital organ, even when *there is no specific or explicit sexual content.*

An American Werewolf in London (dir. John Landis, 1981), points to the pattern. While backpacking across Europe, David Kessler (David Naughton) is wounded and taken to a hospital in London, where Nurse Alex Price (Jenny Agutter) is looking in on him when fellow nurse Susan Gallagher (Anne-Marie Davies) enters. 'Susan: Oh, I think he's a Jew/Alex: What makes you say that?/Susan: I've had a look.' Earlier, in *Annie Hall* (dir. Woody Allen, 1977), Alvy Singer (Allen) bemoans the fact that 'the failure of the country to get behind New York City is anti-Semitism... I'm not discussing politics or economics. This is foreskin.' Eric Kline Silverman glosses this remark thus: 'One rarely looks to Woody Allen for moral counsel these days, but Alvie Singer had a point: the Jew is often defined by his foreskinlessness' (2006: 242). As Salomon 'Solly' Perel (Marco Hofschneider) asks in *Hitlerjunge Salomon/Europa Europa* (dir. Agnieszka Holland, 1990), 'What set us apart, a simple foreskin?' A conversation between George Simmons (Adam Sandler) and Ira Wright (Seth Rogen) in *Funny People* (dir. Judd Apatow, 2009) mocks this notion: 'George: So, Ira Wright? That's not your real name. You're hiding some Judaism/Ira: I don't think I can hide that. My face is circumcised.' Similarly, in other films, the Jew is explicitly and verbally identified by reference to his circumcision: in *The Hebrew Hammer* (who is, as the theme tune tell us, a 'certified circumcised dick'), *Hostel* (dir. Eli Roth, 2005), *The History Boys* (dir. Nicholas Hytner, 2006) and *You Don't Mess with the Zohan* (dir. Dennis Dugan, 2008). Conversely, uncircumcised Jewish schoolchild Roland (Jesper Salén) in Swedish film *Kådisbellan/The Slingshot* uses this fact to argue he is not an outsider, asking his teacher, 'Do you want to see my wienie?' Circumcision in cinema, therefore, is 'the bedrock of [Jewish] identity. And yet that bedrock is precisely what mainstream cinema cannot show' (Coates 2005: 170).

Omer Bartov argues that the circumcised penis is 'a focus of identity, danger, and fascination' (2005: 341 n.33). Here, antisemitism conjoins with the Jewish self-image inherited from a traditional 'attitude of suspicion and alienation, or even distaste, toward the lower body', in particular the penis (Aran 2006: 86). Typically in cinema, representations of the Jew's nudity, with particular reference to the Holocaust, 'exposed' the Jewish penis in all its 'passivity', namely 'femininity' (Lehman and Hunt 2008). Often, his penis is the focus of this representation, as the nub of suffering, as seen in such films as *Schindler's List* and *Sunshine*. This occurs in other genres, in particular comedy. In *There's Something About Mary* (dir Bobby and Peter Farrelly, 1998), for example, Ted Stroehman (Ben Stiller) catches his genitals in his trouser zip (discussed further in Chapter 8) and, later in the film, a dog, and a little one at that, attacks his crotch.

Circumcision is also stereotypically linked to feminisation of the Jew, the bleeding male crotch suggesting menstruation. In *Transamerica* (dir. Duncan Tucker, 2005), the Jewish penis is complicated as the lead character Stanley/ Bree (Felicity Huffman) is a 'half-Jewish' pre-operative transsexual about to complete gender reassignment. Stanley/Bree is having his penis removed so he can become a woman. Articulating a Christian metaphor to her/his son Toby (Kevin Zegers), he says, 'Jesus made me this way for a reason so I could suffer and be reborn the way he was.' Mistakenly believing Bree, who is mimicking a Christian, is religious, Toby replies, 'You're cutting your dick off for Jesus?' Bree, as a pre-operative transsexual, points to an unusual double cutting of the Jewish penis. Danny (Ryan Gosling), a Jewish neo-Nazi based on an actual historical figure, in *The Believer* (dir. Henry Bean, 2001) explicitly articulates this connection between Jewishness and feminisation: 'a Jew's essentially female. Female. Yeah. Real men, white, Christian men, we fuck a woman. We make her come with our cocks! But a Jew doesn't like to penetrate and thrust. He can't assert himself in that way, so he resorts to these perversions. Oral sex is technically a perversion, you know that, right?' Josh (Derek Richardson) in *Hostel* is coded as feminised and passive because, when he has sex, he is underneath his female sexual partner, who rides him.

However, this circumcision imagery is mocked in a number of contradictory ways as other films seek to reverse the stereotypical paradigm of Jewish suffering. Even as it depicts the Jew in death, *Munich* (2005), Steven Spielberg's reconstruction of the Israeli government's response to the murder of 11 Israeli athletes at the 1972 Olympic Games, also symbolises almost the exact opposite: the reversal of the Holocaust paradigm from Jews who are killed to Jews who kill. Although the death of a Mossad (Israel's intelligence organisation) agent is depicted as humiliating – he is shown lying naked – particularly given that he was seduced and killed by a female mercenary, the image stands against the narrative trajectory of the film, which is a projection of the Jew's power and hence potency, discussed in more detail in Chapter 5. In the farcical comedy *One-Eyed Monster* (dir. Adam Fields, 2008), Jewish porn star Ron Jeremy, playing himself, is infested by an alien parasite that kills his body but leaves his penis alive to kill. His detached penis then embarks on a murderous rampage: as one character exclaims, while looking at a dead girl with a hole right through her head, 'Are you trying to tell me a disembodied DICK did this?' Thus, while Jeremy becomes the stereotypical victim, his penis outlives him and becomes the agent of humiliation, vulnerability, suffering, victimhood and death, rather than its object. Indeed, the film upholds the idea floated that the pornstar penis has 'the power to intimidate' (Aizen 2009: 4). Thus Jeremy's Jewish penis clearly explodes Hunt and Lehman's assertion that the Jewish penis is never potent, and always impotent.

The *schlemiel* – in which the Jew's body is represented as a site of fun, laughter and most usually ridicule – is also nothing new onscreen, but the penis as the locus of this laughter signals a shift. This plays on the other meaning of *shmok,* which is defined as 'jerk, fool, idiot, contemptible person; naive person, person easy to deceive'. Jim (Jason Biggs), the distinctively Jewish protagonist of the *American Pie* trilogy (dirs Paul Weitz, 1999; James B. Rogers, 2001, Jesse Dylan, 2003), is also the only character to feature in several sequences that focus (literally) on his (albeit unseen) penis as the source of his humiliation. In the first film, he is caught red-handed by his father (Eugene Levy) while penetrating a warm apple pie, thus giving the film its title. In the first sequel, Jim manages to glue his hand to his member when he mistakes a tube of superglue for lubricant. In the third instalment when Jim proposes to Michelle (Alyson Hannigan), there is more penis-centred humour. At the restaurant where Jim takes his girlfriend, she fellates him under the table. Meanwhile, Jim's dad walks into the restaurant, surprising both of them. Jim rises, his trousers around his ankles, much to the simultaneous disgust and amusement of his fellow diners, and when he proposes to Michelle, his zip is undone, showing, in close-up, his arousal. Jim is later caught in a position suggesting he is engaged in a sex act with a dog. Finally, Jim shaves his pubic area, before throwing the clippings out of the window; however, a fan blows them back inside the kitchen, covering his wedding cake and forcing its occupants to evacuate, choking on his hair.

Although these scenes contain superficial suffering, and Jim is indeed visibly humiliated, unlike the films identified by Bartov, Hunt and Lehman, we do not see close-ups of the *naked* Jewish penis. The genre is comedy and, in the final analysis, he always comes out on top, emerging as the hero. As David Buchbinder puts it, 'Yet, despite these assaults on [his] very manhood – first his penis, then his semen – he still manages to get the girl and the lifestyle he desires at the end of the film' (2008: 241). Furthermore, one only need compare Jim to Stifler (Seann William Scott) in the *American Pie* trilogy to demonstrate this point. Despite the suggestion implicit in his name that he is a symbol of hyper-masculine potency, Stifler suffers a series of humiliating reverses when he unwittingly drinks semen, eats dog faeces and must live with the knowledge that his mother was willingly seduced by his arch-enemy. Lehman wrote of 'the tradition of the representation of the penis in the 1990s' that he calls 'the melodramatic penis' whereby, 'At one pole, we have the powerful, awesome spectacle of phallic masculinity and at the other its vulnerable, pitiable and frequently comic collapse' (2004: 202). Jeremy and Jim both code these opposite ends of the spectrum. Overall, however, contemporary cinema manifests 'a sense of pride and solidarity in body and religion – the brotherhood of the circumcised' (Aran 2006: 85).

Menschlikayt

Drawing upon films of the past, the New Jew exhibits *menschlikayt*, and it is this characteristic that allows him to mock the dominant values of *goyim naches*. The code of *menschlikayt* was developed in response to antisemitism, as a means of articulating Jewish superiority through a refusal to share the aggressive values of the Jews' oppressors. Cal in *The 40-Year-Old Virgin* attempts to snap his best friend David (Paul Rudd) out of his two-year depression by hiring a completely unsuitable but attractive young woman to work in the stockroom with him. Saul Silver (James Franco) in *Pineapple Express* (dir. David Gordon Green, 2008) is a drug dealer with a heart. He only sells weed so that he can save up enough money to put his '*bubbie*' (Yiddish: 'grandmother') in a retirement home. Chuck Levine (Adam Sandler) in *I Now Pronounce You Chuck and Larry* (dir. Dennis Dugan, 2007) marries his best friend so that the friend can claim Chuck's insurance benefits.

Bernie Focker certainly 'revel[s] in anti-conformity, broadly liberal worldviews, and bodily pleasures' (Itzkovitz 2006: 236). He is a stay-at-home dad who has prioritised parenting over his own legal career. In a celebration of his son's mediocrity, he displays his ninth- and tenth-place trophies and ribbons. He is also very proud that his son lost his virginity to their Latina maid. Bernie thus provides a strict contrast to the dysfunctional 'politically conservative, suburban lockdown of anal-retentive anti-pleasure' of the *goyische* father of the family his son is planning to marry into (Itzkovitz 2006: 236). Very relaxed and tactile, as emphasised by his day-glo pink shirt unbuttoned to the waist, Bernie clearly contrasts with the uptight WASP Jack Byrnes (Robert De Niro), whom Bernie calls 'el Stiffo', especially when Bernie goes to hug and kiss him, much to Brynes's obvious discomfort. Bernie denigrates WASP pursuits like hunting as 'macho-wacho crap'. As his wife Roz (Barbra Streisand) says, 'Our people don't shoot ducks'. They only play American football in an attempt to appear more 'macho-wacho' for their son's benefit, but they even subvert the game's competitive spirit, playing it for fun. Bernie thus represents an alternative set of values, which he has attempted to implant in his son Gaylord/Greg (Ben Stiller). Bernie has 'Fockerised' Greg, rejecting the 'competitive drive' ethos of *goyim naches*, as advocated by Byrnes. 'We've always tried to instil a sense of self in Gaylord without being too goal-oriented. It's not about winning or losing, it's about passion. We just want him to love what he's doing,' clearly rejecting the predominant paradigm of *goyim naches* in favour of *Yiddishkeit* and *menschlikayt*.

Even those Jews who adopt and mimic toughness are usually masking a queer *mensch* persona. Vinz in *La Haine* cannot bring himself to shoot a neo-Nazi skinhead, and his rage is, in part, motivated by the fact that his friend is in the hospital with a coma, having been put there by violent riot police. Walter in *The Big Lebowski* is redeemed by his loyalty. Throughout the entire film, Walter abuses his other bowling partner Donny (Steve Buscemi), with the words 'Shut the fuck up, Donny', being a typical barb. Yet, in the final sequence, he 'reveals a deeper level of feeling for his friend at the moment that it matters most': reassuring Donny during a moment of potential confrontation, Walter rises to protect him and thus 'beneath his belligerent, unbalanced exterior' he is revealed to be 'a muddled, oafish softie' and 'an outrageous and impossible buffoon' who is yet 'bizarrely endearing' (Tyree and Walters 2007: 91, 102, 91). His *hesped* (Hebrew: 'eulogy') to Donny is a moving tribute to his friend that shows he cares deeply for him, as he does for the Dude, a fact acknowledged in the warm embrace they share after Walter accidentally empties Donny's ashes (irreverently contained in a Folger's coffee tin) into the Dude's face. Elsewhere in the film, showing a sense of justice and fair play, he invokes political correctness in correcting the Dude: 'Chinaman is not the preferred nomenclature. Asian-American, please.'

Conclusion

The New Jew in film embodies what Rowena Chapman called 'a hybrid masculinity' (1996: 235). Contemporary cinema reverses past imagery, and more subtle, nuanced, playful, sometimes ordinary, even outrageous, representations of Jewish masculinities populate a spectrum between the poles of tough and queer, collapsing the distinction between these categories, and working to normalise the Jew. In contrast to earlier representations, the Jew's body is not just a site of suffering, humiliation, victimisation, stereotyping and idealisation, but also one of positive identification, where Jewish masculinities, in all their variety, are openly and proudly proclaimed. It is a sign of the increasing normalisation of the Jew that we have witnessed the 'ascendance of the liminal Jewish man to normative American everyman' (Itzkovitz 2006: 245).

CHAPTER 2

The Jewess

Absent presences

Strangely, given the growth of women's and gender studies, little has been written about Jewish female representation in *contemporary cinema*, especially when compared with television. Perhaps this is explained by the fact that the Jewess on film suffered from consistent under-representation, being relegated to a limited number of secondary roles. If this book tends to concentrate on the Jew it is because he drowns out by sheer force of numbers the Jewess who, for the most part, is defined by her absence, as the majority of films focus on Jewish men. When she does appear prior to 1990, she rarely exists in her own right (although there are notable exceptions): she is defined largely by the viewpoint of and her relationship to the Jew. As late as 2006, one critic could entitle her article about Jewish women in film 'Invisible in Hollywood' (Dines 2006).

Lacking the obvious signifier of circumcision (which, though rarely shown, is frequently alluded to), the Jewess is harder to identify onscreen. Consequently, she was relegated to a limiting number of secondary roles, rarely straying from a prescribed range of characteristics that confine her to a set of unflattering and negative stereotypes. As Joyce Antler points out, 'erasure and exaggeration remain the dominant characteristics of the treatment of Jewish women in film' (1998: 243). These options are limited to the selfless, self-abnegating, overbearing, neurotic Jewish Mother or the materialistic Jewish American Princess (JAP). Furthermore, even the negative stereotypes of the Jew are 'much more positive' than those of the Jewess (Stratton 2008: 232). This is in part because the Jewess's body became a screen for the projections of the anxieties of acculturation, passing from 'blackness' to 'whiteness', shifts in women's workforce participation and male employment patterns and modernisation, all of which 'surfaced explosively in stereotypes about Jewish womanhood' (Brodkin 1998: 160, Prell 1999: 177–208). Paula Hyman explained how Jewish men produced these negative images of Jewish women in order to distance themselves from 'the Jew', and in this case, the typical Jew was a woman:

> Struggling to gain respect and power for themselves as men in a far from open larger society, male Jews defined an identity that not only distinguished them from women but also displaced their own anxieties upon women. Just as Jews remained the primal Other in secular cultures still marked by Christian prejudices, so did women in Jewish culture. Jewish men, first in the countries of western and central Europe and later in America, constructed a modern Jewish identity that devalued women, the Other within the Jewish community [...] Faced with the need to establish their own identities in societies in which they were both fully acculturated and yet perceived as partially Other because they were Jews, Jewish men were eager to distinguish themselves from the women of their community, whom they saw as the guardians of Jewishness. The negative representations of women they produced reflected their own ambivalence about assimilation and its limits [1995: 134–35, 169].

Because of the paucity of the range of representations, much of the academic literature on the Jewess in film, unfortunately, also tended to be restricted to these categories, thus is guilty of, to borrow a phrase from elsewhere, 'perpetuating asymmetries' (Miguélez Carballeira 2007). It is also confined to examining a limited range of women, in particular Barbra Streisand. Perhaps this can be explained by the fact that studies of the cinematic Jewess have generally been submerged within studies of 'the Jew in cinema' – 'the appellation "Jew" assuming a study of the Jewish man as representative of the Jewish community' as a whole (Lewin 2008b: 239) – such as Friedman (1982), Erens (1984) and Bartov (2005).

The study of the cinematic Jewess is further hindered by the theoretical trends within the wider field of Jewish studies of which it is a part. The Jew in many studies is 'implicitly masculine, and perceptions of Jews are frequently seen as projections of anxieties about masculinity. Cultural theorists, from Sartre to Fanon to Lyotard to Sander Gilman similarly assumed the masculinity of the Jewish subject' (Valman 2007: 3). Judith Lewin adds: 'Even in groundbreaking work on the representation and construction of the Jew as symbol such as that of Sander Gilman there remains the same frustrating tendency: in his words, "(The category of the female Jew all but vanishes)"' (2008b: 239). Explorations of the feminisation of the Jew (such as the work of Boyarin) further render invisible the Jewess and prevent the examination of her representation. As Ann Pelligrini stated, '*All Jews are womanly but no women are Jews*' (1997:109, emphasis in original). As a result, scholars have overlooked the shift in contemporary cinema, in which the representation of the Jewess has increased the range of available options and begun to introduce a spectrum that destabilises the above binaries to produce a variety of more nuanced, playful and subtle images than hitherto, and which begin to normalise her. It is these new self-images and stereotypes that this chapter explores.

From rose to frozen: a short history of the cinematic Jewess

The Jewess on film morphed reflecting changing circumstances and anxieties. Although the *OED* defines 'Jewess' as simply, 'A female Jew; a Jewish woman', the term is not without its problems. Amy-Jill Levine points out how *Merriam-Webster's Collegiate Dictionary* defines the term 'Jewess' as 'offensive' and, in rejecting the option of 'a Jewish woman', 'perpetuates the almost abandoned practice of gendering people according to ethnic, religious and racial categories' in a way that is not typically applied to other groups (1997: 149). Jordan Hiller (2009) refers to the 'graceful and beautiful' Jewess, 'the young, raven-haired, meek, mild, oddly pretty, blameless due to merely an unfortunate parentage, agreeable to fleeing her past and home Jewess'. Lauren Grodstein (2006) observes how the term 'Jewess' is certainly better than a hundred other derogatory names you could call a Jew. But still it rankles. The word Jewess brings to my mind heavy locks of thick black hair, long skirts, clinking bracelets, a musky odour. A Jewess sounds juicy and slightly dirty, like a lot of other words that end in the feminine suffix '-ess': mistress, seductress, stewardess. For Jean-Paul Sartre the phrase 'la belle juive' ('the beautiful Jewess') carried 'a very special sexual signification,' one of 'rape and massacre'. She was 'dragged by her hair through the streets of her burning village' by the Tsarist Cossacks. 'Frequently violated or beaten', he adds, 'she sometimes succeeds in escaping dishonor by means of death, but that is a form of justice; and those who keep their virtue are docile servants or humiliated women in love with indifferent Christians who marry Aryan women' (1965: 49). The general Jewish lack of athleticism, discussed by Gilman and Boyarin, among others, and described by Freud as the Jewish 'dike against brutality and the inclination to violence' (1967: 147), is thus reinforced here by the specific passivity, victimhood, and sexualisation of the Jewess who was an outcast(e). The literary construction of *la belle juive* predated cinema but undoubtedly influenced it.

But Jewesses have existed onscreen almost as long as cinema itself. The first recognisable film Jewess was Cohen's fiancée in *Cohen's Fire Sale*. As this was a crude and racialised antisemitic portrayal, she was as unattractive as the Jew, emphasised by her exaggerated and enlarged nose (Rivo 1998: 31). Thereafter representations become more sympathetic. Since the earliest silent films often dealt with the hardships of Jewish life in New York, particularly melodramas depicting young Jewish girls struggling to make ends meet as they toiled away in sweatshops, the so-called 'rose of the ghetto' or 'Ghetto Girl' (Prell 2009) was a familiar sight. 'In these early narrative films about the immigrant experience, Jewish women are consistently presented as victims of the immigrant experience, as objects of charity and symbols of the struggle for survival' (Rivo 1998: 32). The cultural milieu of the Jewish ghettos in New York, with its themes of sacrifice, despair and salvation, lent itself well to the burgeoning cinema industry and was romanticised in several popular films, notably D.W. Griffith's early shorts for Biograph: *Romance of a Jewess* (1908), *A Child of the Ghetto* (1910) and *Judith of Bethulia* (1914). In these films, the Jewess emerges as tragic, mysterious, domesticated, attainable, sexually conquerable, marriageable and even convertible. By the First World War, then, the polarities of representing the Jewess were established, overshadowing portrayals to the present day: '*belle juive*' and 'domineering hag' (Erdman 1997: 58–59).

Following the First World War, 'the image of Jewish women as vulnerable immigrants was transformed to that of capable, strong and independent mothers and daughters' (Rivo 1998: 34). The domination of the Jewish moguls in Hollywood from the mid-1910s onwards led to the replacement of racialised representations from the outside by inside imports from

Eastern Europe, as the number of films featuring the stock figure of the helpful and loving but 'long-suffering' *Yiddische mama* grew. 'Self-assured and energetic, she feels free to participate in every aspect of her husband's personal and business life. Unfortunately, these virtues coupled with intelligence and resourcefulness, often led the Jewish mother to dominate the lives of her husband and children' (Erens 1984: 90). Caught in the middle of the conflict between the stern, patriarchal, religious and therefore parochial father and his rebelling son, the *Yiddische mama* was generally represented as a kindly nurturing, sympathetic figure, 'generous with food, medicine and good advice, not only to her own children but to others' (Erens 1984: 257, 259). In films such as *His People* (dir. Edward Sloman, 1925) and *The Jazz Singer* she encouraged her son to pursue careers (boxing[10] and singing respectively) in the new American leisure culture that rejected the Old World.

As Ben Furnish put it, the *Yiddische mama* 'cooks, feeds, worries, and suffers' (2005: 135). She is known as the '*baleboosteh*' (Yiddish: lit. 'mistress of the house', but meaning a praiseworthy mother), which coincidentally sounds like a homonym for 'ball buster' (Aizen 2005), or 'the hysterical mother who stuffs her infant with forced feedings (thereby laying in, all unwittingly, the foundation for ulcers, diabetes, and intestinal cancer with each spoonful she crams down the hatch) [who] is motivated by a desire to give security to her child' (Rosenfeld 1949: 386). A-list actresses, whether Gentile or Jewish, rarely played such Jewesses in early cinema. Instead, they were the domain of character actresses, such as Vera Gordon, who came to represent the archetypal *Yiddische mama* in a series of onscreen roles. Hyman explains that this stereotype reflected 'Jewish men's profound ambivalence' about the transference of the responsibility within Jewish families for the transmission of *Yiddishkeit* to the children, with the effect that the mother now became the guardian of Jewishness, 'maintaining the integrity of the Jewish family as the locus of the formation of Jewish identity', while simultaneously pointing to the incomplete Americanisation of the Jewish family (1995: 154, 159).

These representations, however, peaked during the 1920s and early 1930s, when other pressures took over. This was a period of high antisemitism, when the desire for invisibility, for whiteness, led to the overt erasure, from the inside, of Jewishness from actresses like Paulette Goddard, Lauren Bacall and Judy Holliday. While a variety of constructions of the Jewess were represented – the *femmes fatales*, the innocent roses, the spoilt heiresses and the wisecracking equals – all were packaged and sold as ethnically 'neutral'. Such ethnic neutrality of Jewish figures in film was directly related to production codes and organised efforts by Jews and African Americans to censor racial stereotypes. This trend continued during the Second World War, but Jewish women were mainly defined by their absence. Although the post-war period saw the emergence of the biblical epic, as mentioned in the introduction, Jews tended to be de-Semitised, idealised and replaced by non-Jews. Furthermore, the Hebrew characters were overshadowed by non-Hebrew women such as Delilah and Sheba as portrayed by such glamorous actresses as Hedy Lamarr and Gina Lollobrigida in *Samson and Delilah* (dir. Cecil B. DeMille, 1949) and *Solomon and Sheba* (dir. King Vidor, 1959) respectively. In contrast, lesser-known character actresses played the Hebrew women, for example, Olive Deering as Miriam in *The Ten Commandments*. In turn, this had the effect of reinforcing orientalised and exoticised representations of the Jewess.

In the 1960s, however, a shift in the representation of the Jewess occurred. She became associated with the Jew's impotency, neurosis, guilt and castration. The Jewish Mother, in contradistinction to the pre-Second World War *Yiddische mama*, was particularly guilty of this. Where the portrayal of the *Yiddische mama* was affectionate, the post-war American Jewish creation of the Jewish Mother was not. With her meddlesome, domineering control that exceeded the boundaries between proper parental concern and overprotection, as well as pleading and excessive anxiety, the Jewish Mother was blamed for the Jew's own sense of vulnerability and emasculation, his lack of independence and self-confidence. He became a 'mama's boy', characterised by signs of immaturity, maternal over-dependence, adolescent sexual responses, hypochondria, undue fearfulness and other assorted phobias (Ravits 2000: 10, Erens 1984: 262). A series of films of the 1960s and 1970s, most notably *Portnoy's Complaint* (dir. Ernest Lehman, 1972), projected the view that, if the diaspora Jew was unmanly, that is not adhering to the normative values of Gentile masculinity, then it was his mother's fault and not because of any qualities that inhered in him.

And if the Jewish Mother became a monster, then the Jewish girlfriend provided no escape from her either. That she might turn out to be as controlling as his mother, coupled with her virginal nature, made her doubly unsatisfactory in the eyes of the Jew. These qualities were embodied in the negative, inside-created, stereotype of the JAP:

> Spoiled, whiny, materialistic and shallow, the Jewish American Princess dominates her father and then her husband, taking advantage of their money in exchange for the honour of being associated with her. If the Jewish Mother represented everything from the old world that the Jewish male sought to escape, then the JAP represented everything he hated about American culture. The JAP was the catastrophic blend of what is Jewish and American. She possessed none of the charm of her mother. She had her strength and assertiveness but none of her warmth or devotion [Weinfeld 2008: 190].

Beautiful and pampered, the JAP was inactive, non-reproductive and did not work at all. She was, according to Prell, 'demanding', 'withholding', and does 'not sweat' (1996: 76). Her body

> is at once exceptionally passive and highly adorned. She simultaneously lacks sexual desire and lavishes attention on beautifying herself. She attends to the needs of no one else, expending great energy on herself instead. This popularly constructed Jewish woman performs no domestic labor and gives no sexual pleasure. Rather, her body is a surface to decorate, its adornment financed by the sweat of others (Prell 1996: 75).

When she does perspire she produces *unproductive* sweat, expending energy on the tennis court, not in the kitchen or in the workforce.

The JAP, then, is, in general, repellent to the Jew because she is made in her mother's image. But, having been born into a more affluent and stable environment, she is shallow, materialistic and frivolous. The JAP, played by the non-Jewish actress Natalie Wood, made her film début in *Marjorie Morningstar* (dir. Irving Rapper, 1958). *Goodbye Columbus* (dir. Larry Peerce, 1969), based on the Philip Roth short story, cemented her position as an American Jewish stereotype.

The only possible mode of escape available to the Jew, in order not to be trapped by the undesirable Jewess, was to seek sexual gratification from the *shiksa* that bears no resemblance to his mother (or sister/s). Therefore, the *shiksa*, of which Meg Ryan (especially in *When Harry Met Sally*, dir. Rob Reiner, 1989) represents a particularly apt example, stands as the polar opposite of the Jewess, particularly in US film. Where she is attractive, lithe and blonde, the Jewess is a *zaftig* (plump), awkward and neurotic brunette, the female counterpart to the *schlemiel*. The key film that highlighted this *shiksa*/Jewess romantic dichotomy was Elaine May's *The Heartbreak Kid* (1972).

At work here was a process of whitening and displacement. In the transition from *la belle juive* and the racialised Jewess (both of whom were 'orientalised') to the JAP, as the Jewess's Otherness became less obvious, it simultaneously functioned as more of a threat to others; not only to Jewish men but also to all men, as she remained the creator of Jews, whether with Jewish men or not, and the guardian of the transmission of Jewish identity and culture. In part this explains the horror these stereotypes of the Jewess produce, as they are 'made into symbols of grotesque caricature, reminders of the unbridgeable distance between Jewish girlhood and dominant white cultures' (Byers 2009: 35). At the same time, these demeaning negative caricatures of the Jewess were the manifestation of the displacement of Jewish self-hatred in the years after the Second World War. Rather than internalising self-hatred, Jewish men 'directed their critique at Jewish women' (Hyman 1995: 157). For the Jew in the post-war decades, the JAP functioned as a means of transferring his fears about his own transgressions – and creating a space through which to legitimise his desire for *shiksas* who would help him shed his own sense of outsiderness – onto the Jewess.

As a result of the liberation and feminist movements of the 1960s, Jewish women began to move towards the forefront of US cinema. A greater range of multidimensional representations of the Jewess began to appear as a result, 'from being awkward, gauche, ugly and slovenly to being oversexed and undereducated' (Stuart Samuels 1978: 33). Alongside the Jewish Princesses appeared the 'Ugly Ducklings' (Erens 1984: 322), such as Lila (Jeannie Berlin) in *The Heartbreak Kid*, 'Nice Jewish Girls', for example Bernice Meyer (Anjanette Comer) in *Lepke* (dir. Menahem Golan, 1975) and '(Not-So-Nice) Jewish Radicals', represented by Katie Morosky (Barbra Streisand) in *The Way We Were* (dir. Sydney Pollack, 1973) (Aizen 2005). Perhaps the key change was the emergence of Streisand, who, in particular, contributed a great deal, both as an actress and as a director, to the more complete cinematic representation of the Jewess. Bernice Schrank observes: 'Many of Streisand's most memorable roles are as strong and often attractive Jewish women' (2007: 36). Bial, for example, argues that thanks to Streisand the Jewess came 'to be perceived (at least in part) as sexually appealing' (2005: 87). Beginning with *Funny Girl* (dir. William Wyler, 1968) and continuing through to *Yentl* (dir. Barbra Streisand, 1983),

Streisand brought to the screen a 'newly visible type of feisty, aggressive Jewish woman' in a succession of 'tough, unabashdedly ethnic' characters that could be described both as 'Jewesses with Attitude' (which I explore in more detail below), and even as foreshadowing them (Rosenberg 1996: 26). The mid-1970s saw the cementing of this variety with Joan Micklin Silver's 1975 *Hester Street* (to be later followed by her *Crossing Delancey* in 1988) and *Private Benjamin* (dir. Howard Zieff, 1980) produced by and starring Goldie Hawn as the eponymous, strong and feminist JAP who becomes a model US soldier, another forerunner of the Jewess with Attitude.

Yet, despite the strides made in this regard, such films conflicted with two other trends. First was the ongoing development of the Holocaust genre, reaching its height with *Schindler's List*, in which Jewish female passivity is embedded as a key device (to which I shall return later). The second was Woody Allen's considerable oeuvre, in which the Jewess did not fare at all well, often relegated to largely one-dimensional stereotypical representations. From *Annie Hall* onwards, his films featured the Jewess as fondly remembered, if loquacious and overbearing, relatives, uptight Jewish Mothers or simply undesirable. Sadie Millstein (Mae Questel) in Allen's segment of *New York Stories* (1989), 'Oedipus Wrecks', is possibly his most explicit and exaggerated representation of Jewish Motherhood. An Oedipal nightmare, she literally looms, larger-than-life, above New York City, booming orders at him, relentlessly *kvetching* (complaining) and perpetually pestering him about his love life. Rarely, if ever, is the Jewess an object of desire; indeed, a series of Jews leave their Jewish spouses for *shiksas*. His character Boris Grushenko in *Love and Death* (1975) encapsulates Allen's attitudes towards the Jewess: 'I hear Jewish women don't believe in sex after marriage.' The Jewess may have undergone a series of incarnations on film, therefore, but in mainstream American cinema, the predominant cinema in diaspora Jewish terms at least, up until 1990, 'Jewish femaleness is pictured as a kind of pathology' (Fishman 1998: 10).

The period since 1990, however, has witnessed the increased visibility of Jewish women in the film industry, at all levels, including as writers, actresses, filmmakers and other industry personnel in the less well-known areas behind the scenes. It was mainly in production, however, that they made the largest strides (Kronish 2009, Plotkin 2009, Erens 2009). Consequently, an 'unprecedented flurry' of films written and directed by, as well as starring, Jewish women emerged (Brook 2006: 205). The Jewess moved to the forefront increasingly to occupy the space once reserved only for the Jew onscreen. Even Allen began to deviate from his routine of representations. *New York Stories* presents the unusual image of the nowhere-explicitly defined Jewess, Treva Marx (Julie Kavner), to whom Sheldon (Allen) is engaged by the end of the film (much to his Mother's satisfaction). And in his *Deconstructing Harry*, a Jewess (Kirstie Alley) is seen to be sexually attractive, available, adventurous and endogamous. In both of these instances, Allen's previous constructions of the Jewess are reversed to produce more rounded images that undermine his familiar, stereotypical dichotomy.

Gentle JAPs or *schlemiel*-isation

The stereotype of the JAP may still persist, but it is evolving in contemporary cinema. As the Jew becomes increasingly de-skilled and de-professionalised on film, female *Yiddische kopf* is highlighted. Where the Jewess on film once had to disguise her intelligence and mimic masculinity, as in *Yentl*, now she can be openly and explicitly identified as smart. In contemporary cinema 'there seem to be no "dumb" Jewish women' (Gilman 1996: 180). The Jewess is professional, economically comfortable, middle class, well to do, and her parents and family live in suburban affluence.

Furthermore, these female-focused films 'have resisted the Jewess's systematic exclusion from representation by reclaiming Woody Allen territory and swapping the roles of the male *schlemiel* and JAP' (Johnston 2006: 216). The JAP may be the reverse or mirror-image of the *schlemiel* – both are sexually neurotic (Biale 1997: 207) – but where we were typically given access to the inner thoughts of the *schlemiel*, the JAP was only viewed extrinsically. In the post-1990 period, however, not only the JAP in particular but also the Jewess in general is entering the space once reserved exclusively for the *schlemiel* and we *sympathetically* view her inner conflicts, 'while the Jewish male is either objectified or excluded altogether as an object of desire' (Johnston 2006: 216). She is becoming normalised.

The JAP character is embraced in a form of reversal and empowerment. In *Sex and the City* (dir. Michael Patrick King, 2008) Carrie (Sarah Jessica Parker) is not explicitly Jewish but clearly resembles an Allenesque *schlemiel*, in that she represents the female mirror-image of an Upper East Side, neurotic, insecure, hyper-reflective writer-protagonist, obsessed with relationships, with a tendency to date non-Jews and who directly addresses the camera (Grochowski 2004: 153). The title character in *Amy's O* (dir. Julie Davis, 2001), for example, 'does not transcend the JAP stereotype; she assumes it' (Johnston 2006: 219). In a direct address to camera at the outset of the film, Amy identifies her chief worry as the cellulite spreading from her bottom to her thighs. She fears, for example, that the man she is dating does not return her calls because of her 'big fat Jewish ass'. But unlike the JAP, Amy is not so much frigid as asexual. She fashions herself into a 'sexorectic', someone who has sworn off men and actively decided to be celibate. She even pens a self-help book entitled *Why Love Doesn't Work*, which makes her into a celebrity and a 'feminist icon'. At the same time, she fantasises about being ravished by a 'clean, good-looking, and Jewish' man. That someone is definitely a man, for she turns away and wipes her mouth in disgust when her lesbian literary agent kisses her. After an interview with Matthew Starr (Nick Chinlund), a misogynist shock-jock radio host, they start dating and, doing an abrupt about-face, Amy confesses to being 'misguided, horny, and just a hopeless romantic looking to connect'. While the film may suggest that 'her self-imposed celibacy, her professional success, and her feminist stance are all the result of a bad breakup, and the superficiality of her convictions (if not her homophobia) is underscored by the ease with which she abandons her feminist principles' (Johnston 2006: 219), Amy is given agency in determining her future.

This more modern JAP is not as pernicious as her earlier incarnations. In *Clueless* (dir. Amy Heckerling, 1995), Cher Horowitz (Alicia Silverstone) is a self-absorbed, popular, over-privileged neoliberal Beverly Hills high-school student (Byers 2009). 'A virgin who can't drive', she is spoilt, fashion-conscious and shallow. She is obsessed with clothes, shopping, status and style. As played by the blonde and blue-eyed Silverstone, Cher does not even 'look' Jewish, but the film hints that plastic surgery is common among high-school girls in Beverly Hills; indeed, it is revealed that Cher's mother died in a cosmetic surgery accident when Cher was young. Cher's Jewishness is established by the actor playing her (who is Jewish), as well as her lawyer father Mel (Dan Hedaya) from whom she gets 'her Jewish name, her entitlement, her money, and her questionable morals' (Byers 2009: 49). As Stratton points out, 'Cher is Jewish. Her consumerism is identified as an aspect of her Jewish American Princess personality' (2008: 267 n.34). At the same time, however, Cher is a sweet do-gooder with a good heart and likes to help the less fortunate (albeit interpreting 'less fortunate' as the fashion-challenged).

Jessica Stein in *Kissing Jessica Stein* (dir. Charles Herman-Wurmfeld, 2001) is a neurotic, New York Jewish princess who, like Cher, is 'clueless', blind to her own privileged situation (Byers 2009: 45). Blonde like Silverstone, Jessica's *physiognomic* Jewishness is also not immediately apparent. At the same time, she is highly intellectual and defined not just by her ethnicity. The film opens in synagogue, where Jessica is seated between her *kvetching* mother and grandmother during the Yom Kippur (Day of Atonement) service. As the women's voices rise in pitch Jessica exasperatedly shouts, 'Would you shut up? I'm atoning.' As Michele Byers states, 'this opening positions Jessica as a new kind of JAP, one who is fluent in a discourse of moral value seen to be absent from, and unknown to, her foremothers' (2009: 45). Norah Silverberg (Kat Dennings) in *Nick and Norah's Infinite Playlist* (dir. Peter Sollett, 2008) fits into a similar pattern. Not only is she explicitly identified as Jewish, but also willingly expresses her enthusiasm for her heritage and background. Small hints are given throughout the film regarding Norah's Jewishness and identification with Judaism, even as it is not explicitly revealed until a pivotal moment. She asserts that being Jewish is just as much a part of her, if not more so, than anything else and that it is a deeply invested part of her identity. The film also meta-critically comments on previous characterisations of the Jewess to describe her, ironically in this context, as a 'frigid, jealous JAP [...] who was a complete bitch'. In these varied characters, therefore, as Byers concludes, 'JAPpiness is gentled' (2009: 45) and, as a consequence, is also normalised.

JAPs with attitude

At the same time as the new JAP is being gentled, she is also manifesting *attitude*. This reflects the attempts to recuperate the stereotype, such as *Heeb* magazine's call to its readers to 'liberate your inner JAP' in 2004 (quoted in Itzkovitz 2006: 240), and Alana Newhouse, the arts and culture editor of *The Forward*, publicly 'outing' herself as a JAP the following year (Byers 2009: 35). In *Saving Silverman* (dir. Dennis Dugan, 2001) Judith Fessbeggler (Amanda Peet) is, on the surface, a JAP. She is described as a 'hardcore bitch': controlling, domineering and manipulative. Judith completely dominates her boyfriend Darren Silverman (Jason Biggs) from the outset. At their first meeting, she orders his drink for him – an effeminate gin and tonic – while she demands a manly neat Scotch. She then proceeds to take over his life: she forbids Darren to see his friends, threatening to remove his 'masturbation privileges' if he does. She demands that he quit his Neil Diamond tribute band (surely a sign of queering if ever there was one), get bottom implants, burn his albums, wax her legs and attend relationship counselling under her care. As she puts it, 'Darren's mine [...] I own him. He does whatever I say. I'm in complete control of him. He's my puppet and I'm his puppet master.' As a final sign of submission he even proposes to take her last name. Sexually Judith is frigid – six weeks into their relationship it is still not yet consummated. When she finally grants Darren his wish to have sex, she is acutely selfish and inconsiderate – he performs oral sex on her but she does not reciprocate. Instead, she permits him to masturbate while she turns out the light and rolls over to sleep. Thus, so far, so JAP.

Judith is further coded as the masculinised or 'manly Jewess' in the film (Pellegrini 1997: 119). She is a brunette, connoting a 'tempestuous and sexual' nature (Kuhn and Radstone 1994: 47).[11] She is physically strong, and knows self-defence, kicking in the bathroom door when her home is invaded. She makes men *sweat*. Yet, in a seeming contradiction, she is also depicted as sexy and shown wearing multiple low-cut tops and dresses depicting her ample décolletage. Darren's friends describe the contradiction by comparing her only to male anti-heroes: 'Our enemy is wicked. She's Freddie Kruger, Damien, Darth Vader, the Emperor [...] but with really great tits.' Since female toughness cannot be a threat or too challenging, as it is transgressive and dangerous, it must be diluted and given a more feminine appearance (Inness 2004: 12). Judith is thus simultaneously sexualised and objectified yet masculinised as the monstrous female in their comparison with these murderous and dark 'Others'.

Although Judith is nowhere explicitly identified as Jewish, we can read her as conceptually or symbolically Jewish for a number of reasons. Her surname certainly suggests an ethnic Jewishness, while her given name connects to that of her biblical namesake – the Jewish heroine who slaughtered Holofernes after getting him drunk. She is of superior intelligence, a career woman, able to outwit her much dumber male rivals, Darren's friends ('She used her super-intellect on me, man. She's like Hannibal Lecter.') and is a psychologist, which since the 1960s has became a stereotypically Jewish cinematic profession and even more so from the beginning of the twenty-first century as more and more Jews became psychoanalysts in reality. In a conflation of her real-life persona with her onscreen performance, Jewish actress Peet plays Judith. And finally, and most conclusively in cinematic terms, she is dumped in favour of the *shiksa*.

Karen Hill (Lorraine Bracco) in *Goodfellas* (dir. Martin Scorsese, 1990) also reverses 'many of the conventions embodied by previous female characters' (Yaquinto 2004: 220). Superficially, she is a 1960s New York JAP. Middle-class, dark-haired, rich, with a distinctive nasal accent, Karen still lives with her parents (even after she marries), who are affluent country-club members. Her mother is domineering, nagging and overbearing. Yet, beneath appearances, Karen's character departs significantly from the JAP stereotype. She dates and then marries Gentile Italian mobster Henry Hill (Ray Liotta). She has her own voiceover narrative, giving her more agency than is typical for JAPs (or mob wives for that matter). By being allowed to talk, and thus assist in narrating the story, she is placed in 'an empowering position never before accorded a female character in a gangster story', let alone a Jewish one. 'Her voiceovers put her in the subject position, and we hear the same intoxicating greed in her that we find in Henry and the other wiseguys. We witness the underworld as she does' (Yaquinto 2004: 220). Indeed, when Henry gives her a bloodied gun to hide, which he has used to smash in a Jew's face, she admits to a certain *frisson*. 'I know there are women, like my best friends, who would have gotten out of there the minute their boyfriend gave them a gun to hide. But I didn't. I got to admit the truth. It turned me on.' A jump cut then portrays a joyous Henry and Karen breaking a glass under a traditional *chuppah* (wedding canopy) with cries of 'Mazel tov!'

Once married and a mother, Karen is Henry's partner in crime, fascinated with and complicit in his lifestyle. She participates in his criminal activities, trafficking and hiding drugs, money and guns for him on demand, even smuggling contraband items to him when he is sent to prison. During a raid by federal agents on their house, she calmly watches the television[12] as they search her house, because it is such a routine activity (Mizejewski 2008: 36). 'Karen manages to subvert traditional portrayals of Mob wives, which paint them as victims whose toughness cannot be deployed to serve a personal agenda, only to protect their family. But Karen proves otherwise'

(Yaquinto 2004: 220). Actress Bracco suggests, 'it was much more than the stereotypical mama-in-the-kitchen thing' (Yaquinto 2004: 229 n.33). As JAP and then Mother, Karen is the 'bad girl who enjoys danger, sex, and drugs' (quoted in Yaquinto 2004: 220).

Finally, in *Hostel II* (dir. Eli Roth, 2007) Beth Salinger (Lauren German) is another JAP with attitude. Again, like Judith above, although she is nowhere explicitly identified as Jewish, the viewer is given the possibility of reading Beth as a Jewess – looks, intellect, hairstyle, speech patterns and accents, anxieties, neuroses, behaviour and name – but not with certainty. Reading Beth as Jewish requires that knowledge of the complex of largely unconscious codes that cross-check each other, allowing the reader to decode Jewishness through aural, visual, emotional or genre signifiers. Thus, where Jews or those who know the codes will interpret these elements of performance as Jewish, general audiences may not recognise them as markers of Jewish difference (Bial 2005: 70, 152). This allows Rikke Schubart (forthcoming) to describe Beth as a 'Valkirye'. Both of Beth's names suggest her Jewishness: Beth is the diminutive of Elizabeth, the Greek translation of the biblical name Elisheva, which in Hebrew means either 'my God is an oath' or 'my God is abundance', while Salinger associates her with the famous Jewish author of the same name. She is wealthy – rich enough to spend time off, travelling in Europe with her two friends, Lorna (Heather Matarazzo) and Whitney (Bijou Phillips), and learning in a leisurely way to paint in Italy. When she is persuaded to visit a small

Beth Salinger in *Hostel II*.

Slovakian spa town – unaware that it is a trap to lure her and her friends to a disused factory in which rich individuals pay to torture and kill foreign tourists – she agrees because money and time are no barrier. She is a brunette. Sexually, she is not frigid but stands somewhere between the promiscuous Whitney and the chaste Lorna.

However, unlike the JAP, Beth is sensitive, unselfish and, above all, smart. She genuinely cares about her friends' welfare. When Lorna and Whitney are kidnapped they both panic and plead and beg for their lives, to no avail. In contrast, when Beth realises Stuart (Roger Bart) has paid to kill her, she uses her *Yiddische kopf* to talk her way out of and reverse the situation. Using a combination of comforting ('No, you're a good person'), empathy ('I'm not your wife. She doesn't understand you. Not like I do') and role-playing as masochistic prey to his sadistic torturer ('Are you scared? You fucking better be,' Stuart demands. 'I am. I like it,' she responds), Beth induces Stuart into releasing her from the chair to which she is shackled ('I was hoping you would kiss me. I wanted you to kiss me. I thought about you all night').

While she is rich like the JAP, unlike her, she uses her money not to adorn her body in this instance but to negotiate her way out of a life-threatening situation. 'I wanna buy my way out of here!' When told 'You can't afford it,' she responds, 'Don't tell me what I can't afford. There's nothing I can't afford. I could buy and sell everyone in this room.' Beth is then asked, 'You going to call your parents for money?' suggesting that she is a rich princess. However, her response dispels any such notion: 'No, motherfucker, it's *my* money. Just get me a PDA, a SWIFT number and a recipient name. I have accounts in Switzerland, Luxembourg, and the Isle of Man. Just *name* your fucking price! Trust me, I got it'. And where Beth's body is adorned it as not as a result of self-beautification. As dictated by the terms of the contract, in order to leave the factory alive, she agrees to a tattoo of a bloodhound on her lower back. Although the close-up on her face, which moves in to focus on the needle, suggests a sexually submissive position, as if she is being penetrated from behind, which, figuratively speaking, she is, reinforced by the sinister non-diegetic music, this sequence is one of empowerment. Without complaining, Beth grits her teeth and *sweats* through the ordeal. Beth thus overturns the paradigm of the JAP, who does not sweat and is passive, to become the tattooed Jewess with Attitude (and who will be seen again in Chapter 5).

The Jewish female gaze

Another sign of this new confidence emerging among female Jewish directors, screenwriters and actresses in the post-1990 period is that the Jewess is increasingly the author rather than the subject of the gaze. The 1998 British film *The Governess* directed by young British-Jewish filmmaker Sandra Goldbacher and starring Jewish actress Minnie Driver stands out in the history of cinematic representation of the Jewess/*belle juive* in this respect. Set in eighteenth-century London, its protagonist Rosina da Silva is a strong and sophisticated Jewess with Attitude. Living a comfortable and wealthy Jewish life in the East End, Rosina is religiously defined: the opening sound of the film is the recitation of the *Shema*, the key Jewish prayer recited twice daily, accompanied by the image of a *tallit* – a Jewish prayer shawl. And notably, she is Sephardic, the daughter of an Italian Jew, in a medium that tends to elide all intra-Jewish difference, often collapsing it into Ashkenazi whiteness.

Rosina presents an alternative model of representation of the Jewess (I will explore her sexuality in the following chapter). In the words of Judith Lewin, she is 'Jewish, but also unorthodox, rebellious', as well as 'experimental, active, liberated (fun, radical, modern, and anachronistic)' (2008a: 90, 89). Helene Meyers described her as 'high-spirited, theatrical, and independent', as well as 'cosmopolitan' (2008: 106, 109). Contrary to convention (on two counts), she aspires to be, like her Aunt Sofka, an actress who never married. However, when her father is murdered, her mother tries to convince her to marry, thus securing the family's financial future. Rosina refuses, and rejects the traditional path, abandoning her dream to become an actress. Reinventing herself as 'Mary Blackchurch', she removes her distinguishing Jewish hat, clothing and hairstyle and replaces them with monochrome clothes and glasses in order to mimic a Gentile identity. In doing so, she ironically adopts a 'white' name that alludes to, and hence reinforces, her historical blackness. She takes a job as a governess on Skye in the home of the Cavendish family, where she assists the head of the household (Tom Wilkinson) with his photographic experimentation.

Rosina is associated with colour where Gentiles are not. Her Jewish name invokes the colour red. The interior shots of the da Silva household are warm and lively, characterised by deep reds and gold, in comparison to the washed-out colours of the Cavendish household. The reds allude to

Rosina's concealed identity: in sixteenth-century Venice Jews were forced to wear red, as a distinguishing mark, a law changed to yellow when it became clear that it made them look too much like cardinals (Hughes 1986, Bradshaw 2011). When Rosina first arrives on Skye, she asks herself, 'I'm not like them, how will I ever pass?' In order to do so, Rosina must suppress the colour red, and it is only glimpsed in private thereafter. When she opens her trunk in the safety of her bedroom, for example, we see 'the fiery reds of her shawls, the colour of her appetite', which contrast 'to the cold, green-grey tones of the country home of the Cavendish family [and] As she takes on a more proactive role in assisting Mr Cavendish in his photographic experiments, warm colours move into his cold workshop realm' (Wood 2007: 138).

However, Rosina's otherness is not entirely suppressed. In a sly allusion to her orientalism and blackness, she assembles a still life in Cavendish's studio consisting of a Turkish rug, fruit and dark cherries. The colour and nature of the latter item hints at her religious-ethnic identity as well as her blossoming sexuality and latent desires as she falls for Cavendish. Invoking her *conversos*

Rosina da Silva in *The Governess*.

(Spanish: lit. 'converts') ancestors, those Jews who were outwardly Christian but remained privately Jewish, Rosina also secretly practices her hidden Judaism, observing the Passover Seder within the privacy of her bedroom. In doing so, she appropriates and wears the *tallit*, the marker of a married Jew, its black-and-white stripes symbolising her liminal Jewish status in a Gentile household, as she attempts to publicly downplay her historical blackness in order to pass as white. As Meyers points out, 'the position of governess is one of structural ambivalence – neither a member of the family nor quite a servant, the governess mediates between the world of children and the word of adults' (2008: 107). In this way, Rosina thus stands as a metonym for an ambivalent English Jewishness that is not entirely at home in Britain or with itself because it cannot fully pass.

Furthermore, *The Governess* is shot as if deliberately engaging with Laura Mulvey's seminal notion of the male gaze (1975), frequently placing the audience and the male protagonist as the object of her attention. As the film opens, a high-angle shot in the synagogue of praying men privileges her point of view, which we share throughout the narrative. Later in the film, in 'a reversal of the static "woman at the window" shots identified as typical of costume drama, Rosina observes her employer entering and leaving his workshop and races through the house and outside to gain entry to it' (Wood 2007: 138). She 'is licensed to actively look at the world rather than to be looked at. There are many shots of her eyes gazing to camera and Cavendish's camera's lens, and point-of-view shots of her stroking Cavendish's soft, hairy chest foreground her desire' (Wood 2007: 138). Indeed, it is the photograph she takes of his naked body resting after lovemaking that leads to her eventual expulsion from the house (combined with the revelation of her Jewishness). In these ways, Rosina constructs a 'Jewish gaze' (Meyers 2008: 106).

In addition, Rosina is at the centre of the narrative, and she drives the action. As a marker of this, she is a blur of activity in contrast to the stereotypically static female roles in costume drama. As Mary Wood observes, 'Immobility provides a metaphor for women's disempowerment under patriarchy, whereas Rosina embodies female aspirations for autonomy and self-assertion' (2007: 138). She initiates sex with Cavendish and she is an active partner in their love affair. Rosina's gender, ethnicity and religion do not prevent her from engaging in scientific and intellectual endeavour at a time when such opportunities were restricted for a woman, let alone a

Jewess. She discusses science with Cavendish and takes a proactive role in assisting him in his photographic experiments. Her independence, autonomy and blossoming sexuality are reinforced by the clear contrast she provides to Mrs Cavendish (Harriet Walter), who 'is distinguished by her immobility within the house, by her soft, ringletted hairstyle and the display of her body in excessively low-cut dresses' (Wood 2007: 138). Ultimately, Rosina leaves the household, discards her mimicry as 'Mary Blackchurch' and reclaims her Jewishness by re-dressing as a Jewess. She returns to London where, having appropriated the technology of photography she has helped to develop, sets up her own studio. Cavendish visits, declares his submission to her will, but is rejected. In contrast, Rosina is financially independent, autonomous and famous for her portraits of the Jewish people. She thus ends the film with agency, a Jewess with Attitude.

Undercover agents

Contemporary cinema reverses previous paradigms to portray a variety of Jewesses with Attitude who are far from passive or marginalised into domestic space. In *Aimée & Jaguar* (dir. Max Färberböck, 1999), Felice Schragenheim (Maria Schrader) is a Jewess hiding her identity in Berlin during the final two years of the Second World War. As Felice Schrader, she works for a Nazi newspaper while passing secret documents to the underground. She is strong, sexy, sensual, reckless and not averse to taking risks. 'She might work for the underground, but she consumes life to the fullest' (Koepnick 2002: 63). Similarly, in *Zwartboek/Black Book*, even though she asks 'What's my role in this boy's club?', Rachel Stein (Carice van Houten) is a spirited young Jewish cabaret singer in occupied Holland towards the end of the Second World War. Escaping the murder of her family by the Nazis, Rachel refuses to run, hide or await her own fate, and seeks to avenge their deaths. Not only is her continued existence an act of Jewish rebellion, but also she joins the anti-Nazi Dutch Resistance, concealing her identity by adopting the pseudonym of Ellis de Vries. Crucially, in terms of her appearance, she also dyes her hair blonde, which allows her to mimic a non-Jewess and pass as Gentile. Unlike those Jewesses who dye their hair blonde for cosmetic reasons, that is to fit a perceived ideal of Anglo-Saxon femininity, Rachel does so out of necessity rather than for adornment or beautification. In this way she effortlessly moves from Jewish brunette to Aryan blonde, from Rachel Stein to Ellis de Vries, and from Dutch Jewess to Dutch Gentile to Israeli Jewess by the end of the film. She becomes to some extent an attractive version of a real-life Zelig – a curiously nondescript and chameleonic Jewish character who is discovered for his remarkable ability to transform himself to resemble anyone he is near, as depicted in the film *Zelig* (dir. Woody Allen, 1983).

As the events are told in flashback, Rachel's memory and subjectivity are privileged from the outset. She is not merely the object of the gaze. Since she is the heroine she is not merely passive, and drives the accelerating, hairpin narrative of an action-packed thriller forward. At one point she is smuggled past German soldiers made up as a corpse and lying in a coffin. During a train journey with a fellow Resistance member she shows her audacity as she chooses to share a train compartment with (unbeknownst to her) the head of the regional Gestapo, Ludwig Müntze (Sebastian Koch), in order to ensure that the soldiers patrolling the train will not search her. Furthermore, when asked by her comrades, 'How far are you prepared to go?' she answers as far as is necessary. Confronted with the specific question of what she will do in order to get information for the Resistance from Müntze, Rachel agrees to go 'as far as he wants to go'. Thus, 'Rachel is a complex character, an indomitable survivor, with agency and desire, the very antithesis of a passive victim of Nazi persecution [...] Neither heroine nor whore, she defies easy categorisation', representing a 'significant departure' and 'turning point' in the post-1990s portrayal of the Jewess (Condron 2008).

A somewhat similar character is Shoshanna Dreyfus (Mélanie Laurent) in *Inglourious Basterds* (dir. Quentin Tarantino, 2009).[13] Like Rachel, she is another young brunette Jewess who is the only survivor of a murdered family and whose continued existence is itself an act of resistance. Four years later, and hiding in plain sight as Emmanuelle Mimieux, Shoshanna (also like Rachel) is now blonde, allowing her to pass, her alias evoking the French ('*mimier*') and English terms for mimic.[14] Financially independent, she is the proprietor of her own art-deco cinema in occupied Paris. Beautiful and sexy, her assumed name simultaneously evokes the series of French soft-core erotic movies based on the character with the same name while alluding to her Jewish origins (the name literally translates as 'God is with us'). Shoshanna has a black French lover, as well as being the object of desire of Fredrick Zoller (Daniel Brühl), a young Nazi war hero.

Shoshanna embodies the New Jewess with Attitude. Despite the film's title, referring to a group of American GIs who take intemperate revenge on Germans and Nazis alike, she takes up more screen time. Goebbels (Sylvester Groth) pressures Shoshanna to host the gala premiere of his new propaganda film that, in turn, becomes central to a plot to avenge her family. The sequence that immediately precedes Shoshanna's revenge (explored in more detail in Chapter 5) emphasises the distance between Shoshanna and the stereotypical princess. We watch her preparations as she prepares to mingle among the Nazis at the premiere. Wearing a tight-fitting red (alluding to her masked identity) dress, Shoshanna applies red lipstick, rouge and nail polish, before loading bullets into the magazine of a gun. Her makeup is not mere adornment or beautification. Her maquillage is not simply a disguise. As a form of mimicry, it allows her to pass freely among the Nazis whom she is hosting at her cinema, but it is also transformed into war paint, and the way she applies it resembles that of a commando putting on camouflage. Four successive shots cement this imagery of Shoshanna donning a costume as she mimics the role of gracious pro-Nazi hostess. At the same time, the shots compare her to the double-agent Bridget von Hammersmark (Diane Kruger), while reflecting Shoshanna's face in the middle of a Nazi swastika. As Allen H. Redmon (2010) observes, 'The sequence of images performs Shosanna's very progression in the film as she moves from victim to duplicitous other

Shoshanna Dreyfus in *Inglourious Basterds*.

before finally transforming herself into the very thing against which she seeks revenge' – a Jewess with Attitude.

The New Jewish Mother

Even the stubbornly entrenched stereotype of the Jewish Mother, which proved almost impermeable to change in the past, is reversed in contemporary cinema to introduce greater variety. A more loving and understanding mother, resembling the pre-war *Yiddische mama*, replaces the manipulative and repulsive post-war Jewish Mother of films such as *Next Stop, Greenwich Village* (dir. Paul Mazursky, 1976). This builds upon earlier such representations as Maude (Ruth Gordon) in *Harold and Maude* (dir. Hal Ashby, 1971) who, although more grandmotherly than motherly, is a fun-loving, free-spirited, lively, septuagenarian Holocaust survivor who has an affair with a young man. Israeli Prime Minister Golda Meir (Lynn Cohen) in *Munich* is a positive matriarchal figure, a mother to the nation. In *Kissing Jessica Stein*, when Jessica is inconsolable over the departure of her girlfriend, her mother (Tovah Feldshuh) tries to comfort her with the words, 'She's a very nice girl'. Because she 'loves her daughter – lesbian or not', Furnish comments, 'she offers a new norm for the Jewish mother' (2005: 141). When the lesbian Rachel comes out to her parents in *A Family Affair* (dir. Helen Lesnick, 2001), her mother Leah (Arlene Golonka) initially sits *shiva* (seven-day mourning period) for her, thus conforming to type. However, she eventually becomes reconciled to her daughter's sexuality, and applying her New Jewish Mother instincts she enthusiastically embraces gay rights, becoming an activist, supporter and member of the local chapter of the Parents and Friends of Lesbians and Gays, insisting on referring to herself as 'non-gay' rather than 'straight'. Not only does she guilt Rachel into attending a gay pride parade, but also sets her up with 'Ms. Rightowitz' Christine Peterson (Erica Shaffer).

Roz Focker (Barbra Streisand) in *Meet the Fockers* and *Little Fockers* (dir. Paul Weitz, 2010) embodies this new caring Jewish Mother *par excellence.* Roz 'transcends typical gender and Jewish roles' (Baskind 2007: 7). She is a liberated, sexual, Jewish, funky, charismatic, loving, horny earth mother, living in the heart of Cuban Miami (Coconut Grove) rather than typically Jewish Boca Raton or Boynton Beach. Although professional, she is, atypically for the stock Jewess character, a sex therapist specialising in senior sexuality. She is also the primary breadwinner. Her husband is the stay-at-home father who does the cooking, as she is unable to 'even fry an egg'. Her house is filled with phallic statues and books on sex, much to the embarrassment of her son. Unlike so many of her filmic foremothers, Roz is thrilled by her son's impending wedding to a non-Jewish woman, and is not in the least bit concerned that he is 'marrying out'. Rather, she worries about the quality of their sex life, as well as that of her prospective in-laws.

Like Roz, Bobbie Markowitz (Bette Midler) in *The Stepford Wives* (dir. Frank Oz, 2004) is the antithesis of the Jewish Mother. As a Jewess among a suburb of identikit WASP blondes, she is defiantly subversive. The town misfit, she is a quirky, kooky writer who penned a bestselling book about her relationship with her mother entitled, *I Love You But Please Die*. She is poor at cooking, cleaning (her house is a pigsty, unlike every other one in Stepford, which is spotlessly clean) and taking care of her children. She is also marked by her Jewish difference. Indeed, Bobbie revels in her ethnic/religious otherness. During a discussion about Chanukah that involves pine cones she articulates this otherness: 'I could just use hundreds of pine cones to spell out the words "Big Jew" in letters 15 feet tall, on the snow in my front yard.' She takes the discussion one step further by introducing a hitherto absent sexual element. Responding to the suggestion 'I'm going to use a pine cone as the baby Jesus this year,' she says, 'And I'm going to attach a pine cone to my vibrator and have a really merry Christmas.'

Sara Goldfarb (Ellen Burstyn) in *Requiem for a Dream* (dir. Darren Aronofsky, 2000) is an even more unusual Jewish Mother. Superficially, she resembles her forebears by protecting her heroin-addicted son, continually allowing him to pawn her TV set so he can buy drugs. A lonely widow, she herself becomes addicted to watching television and diet pills containing amphetamines and barbiturates in an attempt to lose weight for her hoped-for appearance on a health-related television game show. Failing to see immediate physical results, Sara increases her dosage and begins to experience terrifying hallucinations involving her refrigerator, which taunts her about her inability to stop eating, and the television set, in which the game show hosts enter her living-room and teases her about her weight. Ultimately, Sara becomes delusional, unable to distinguish between reality and fantasy, and is institutionalised and subject to electroconvulsive therapy. Her own state parallels that of her son, whom she is unable to protect, and his arm is amputated as a result of an infected needle.

Conclusion

The New Jewess is not simply confined to the selfless, self-abnegating, overbearing and neurotic Jewish Mother or the materialistic and passive JAP. Neither is she the sexualised, raped and victimised *belle juive*. She is not simply defined in relation to the Jew, nor blamed for his problems. And she is not always a female *schlemiel* or *nebbish*. The advent of the New Jewish Mother alongside the gentle JAP and Jewess with Attitude presents a clear sea change, attempting, in the words of Hiller (2009), 'to flip the Jewess myth on its ear'. As 'the radiant Jewish female' defined by 'her comeliness and willingness', she does not simply serve 'to enhance and elevate hegemonic, Christian beauty', but exists in her own right. Thus, this New Jewess in contemporary cinema does not exist merely as a screen for the projections about the anxieties of passing from blackness to whiteness, as these anxieties are being wiped away and a new generation of female Jewish studio personnel, writers, directors and actresses moves to the forefront. As I pointed out in my introduction, stereotypes change when the cultural patterns on which they are based are becoming out of date. Because stereotypes of the Jewess were in part bound to the process of acculturation, as Jews became more assimilated the need for such negative portrayals arguably abated. Furthermore, film stereotypes change as real women's lives change, and the Jewess cannot be represented in the same old stereotypical ways as previously. Contemporary Jewish feminism, combined with the absence of significant antisemitism, as Hyman predicted, muted the gender politics of Jewish identity (1995: 168). What is clear is that new character-types are emerging in cinema which do not simply conform to previous notions of the Jewess, but begin to introduce a more variegated spectrum, and are pointing towards greater normalisation.

CHAPTER 3

Sex

Introduction

Since Jewish sexuality overlaps with the representations outlined in the previous two chapters, it has been similarly subjected to a series of self-images and stereotypes some of which date back to antiquity. Alongside the archetypal in-group-created variations of the Jew as the *schlemiel*, *nebbishy*, neurotic, lacking, queer, impotent and sissy (what the film *Being Ron Jeremy* [dir. Brian Berke, 2003] refers to as 'skinny horny needy Jews with glasses'), there is the outside-constructed and surprisingly sexually oriented Jew, who is portrayed as predatory, sleazy, sex-obsessed, repellent and repulsive. This Jew was the product of the antisemitic imagination, circulated through Christian theology, medieval anti-Jewish polemics, religious art and latterly antisemitic propaganda. In pre-modern times, for example, the Jew was 'primitive, more fully sexual, impulsive and hyperphallic', as well as 'unmanly, weak, effeminate or otherwise outside the norm of properly assertive masculinity' (Freedman 2005: 137). He was, simultaneously, a sexually predatory monster (the Jew-Devil) and a castrated effeminate (the Jew-Sissy) (Biberman 2004). In the antisemitic literature of the late nineteenth century, much of which was rooted in medieval anti-Jewish polemics, Jews were 'either seen as debased lechers yearning for Christian girls (preferably virgins) or as men-women' (Freedman 2005: 137). This 'cultural contradiction was ameliorated when the two merged into a new character type: the Jewish pervert, a figure that conjoined the will-to-power of the hyperaggressive Jewish male with sexual nonnormativity of the feminised Jewish man' (Freedman 2005: 137). Such a figure appeared in the notorious Nazi propaganda film *Jud Süss*, embodied by the 'seductive and dangerous' Joseph Süss Oppenheimer (Ferdinand Marian) (Koepnick 2002: 62).

As for the Jewess, as seen in the previous chapter, the Jewish Mother and the JAP were represented *from the inside*, as sexually neurotic, unattractive and frigid (Biale 1997: 207). As Prell puts it, 'for every unerotic woman there is a Jewish man who is powerless, dominated, and unable to find sexual satisfaction with his Jewish wife or girlfriend' (Prell 1996: 74). The JAP, in particular, is passive, sexually un-alluring, unresponsive and non-childbearing, part of the tradition of what Prell calls 'De-eroticised Jewish women' (1996: 74) or 'ugly old kikes' (Gershenson 2008: 178), both playing into the unfortunate stereotype of the undesirability of the Jewess perpetuated by Jews and non-Jews alike (Berger 1996: 102). It is suggested that 'Nice Jewish Girls' do not engage in sex before marriage (or afterwards, even according to Woody Allen). Yet, at the same time the Jewess was viewed *from the outside* as exotic, as *la belle juive*. Jon Stratton points out how in parallel with other 'Othered women', such as 'the "oriental" woman with whom she was discursively linked', the Jewess/*la belle juive* 'tended to be constructed as highly sexed and desirable' (2000: 56), carrying with her a very special sexual signification of magnetic eroticism. Nonetheless, all of these images and stereotypes share a history of the suppression of the representation of the female Jewish form.

This chapter will explore how contemporary cinema not only recycles and reverses many of these sexual stereotypes, but also begins to introduce a spectrum of sexually defined and sexually active Jews that challenges previous binaries. What is particularly noticeable in the post-1990 period is that, unlike the past, representations of Jews as hyper-sexual predators or as beautiful Jewesses do not simply emanate from the non-Jewish outside but rather from inside, from Jews themselves. It is a sign of increased confidence that Jewish filmmakers are unafraid to touch what could be perceived as potentially troubling subject matter, including representing the Jewish body more explicitly than hitherto. As a form of pleasure – *Jewissance* – and as an example of reverse stereotypes, this trend encompasses both the younger generation of filmmakers, actors, actresses and screenwriters

I mentioned previously, and an older strata of Jewish film personnel who, in the last two decades, have come out not only as much more Jewish than hitherto but also as much more explicitly sexual.

Perverts, pornographers and porn stars

As a clear illustration of this change in the depiction of Jewish sexuality in contemporary cinema, even Woody Allen's sensibility changed after 1990, becoming increasingly perverse, darker and misogynist, encapsulated in the words from his film *Deconstructing Harry* as 'cynicism, sarcasm, nihilism and orgasm'. Sam B. Girgus detected a new 'fascination' with sexual activity in Allen's films, manifesting a 'new pornographic sensibility towards the representation of sexuality' and constituting a 'radical departure from Allen's distinct, even signature, style of treating sex in previous films'. Girgus singles out *Deconstructing Harry* in particular for its 'sadism and masochism, faceless service, domination, subservience, self-deprecation, and mechanised and routinised pleasuring, all usually at special cost to the dignity and respect for women' (2002: 162, 158). For example, the eponymous antihero gives specific instructions to a prostitute, mimicking the language of hardcore porn: 'Tie me up! Hit me! Blow job!' In another sequence, he convinces his lover to give him a blow job at her father's funeral. Similarly, Leslie (Julia Louis-Dreyfus) performs oral sex on Ken (Richard Benjamin) before proceeding to full intercourse as they keep watch from the window on the guests at a barbecue taking place in the back garden, among whom is Ken's wife, who is Leslie's sister. Leslie's blind grandmother even makes an unanticipated appearance *in media res*.

Like Harry, the character of Victor Ziegler (Sydney Pollack) in Jewish director Stanley Kubrick's final film *Eyes Wide Shut* (1999) is the embodiment of a 'menacing hypersexuality' (Kaplan 2010). Gene D. Phillips and Rodney Hill describe Ziegler as 'sinister',[15] while James Naremore refers to him as 'the most morally corrupt character' (2007: 227) and Phillips and Hill describe his 'unambiguously corrupt nature' (2002: 105). Randy Rasmussen calls him an 'evil' and 'satanic temptor and manipulator, motivated purely by self-interest' (2005: 353). Jonathan Rosenbaum notes that Ziegler is the only thoroughly evil character in the film, although his evil comes 'wrapped in impeccable manners' (2006: 249). Strangely, however, only two scholars have noticed that he can be read as Jewish (Naremore 2007, Kaplan 2010). Naremore comments, 'I'm not sure what to make of the irony that the character who is coded as Jewish [...] is also the most morally corrupt character' (2007: 227). I will argue that 'a hidden Jewish substratum undergirding the film', despite the absence of any such 'ethnic' designation (Shohat 1991: 220), can be detected here. The ability to read Ziegler thus requires knowledge of those Jewish moments I mentioned in my introduction and which will be explored more fully in my final chapter. Suffice to state here that Ziegler is not only played by Jewish actor Sydney Pollack, but also has a recognisably Jewish name, looks, physiognomy, location and profession.

Only the second time we meet Ziegler, he is semi-naked, emphasising his hirsuteness[16] and oversized glasses, having just had drug-fuelled sex with a semi-conscious prostitute, clad only in high heels and a pearl necklace, in his spacious bathroom (which is decorated with very sexually explicit artwork) during his own party (discussed in more detail in Chapter 8). Later, although we never actually see his face (he subsequently confirms his presence), Ziegler orchestrates and attends such *goyim naches* as a highly ritualised, quasi-religious masked orgy during which hired prostitutes, dressed only in masks, g-strings and high heels, participate in the cult-like ceremony, as well as having sex with the guests. And when an uninvited outsider infiltrates the orgy, Ziegler is only concerned with protecting the identity and reputation of its guests, rather than the legality, morality and ethics of the event itself. Ziegler is not a *mensch*. Indeed, Ziegler views women as sex objects: he callously describes a prostitute at the orgy, who later turns up dead, as merely the 'hooker' with 'the great tits who ODed in my bathroom' and 'got her brains fucked out'.

Another erstwhile Jewish performer/director that 'came out' as more Jewish in a sexual fashion is porn star Ron Jeremy. Although Jeremy has been a fixture of the adult film industry since the 1970s, only in 2001 did he present himself as Jewish in a mainstream cinema documentary about his life entitled *Pornstar: The Legend of Ron Jeremy* (dir. Scott J. Gill, 2001). Far from shying away from his Jewishness, Jeremy's pride in his ethnicity was highlighted from the outset, including material discussing his bar mitzvah. At the same time, Jeremy's celebrity status as the biggest, in all senses of the word, male porn star is celebrated, as indicated by the inclusion of the term 'legend' in the film's subtitle. This standing allowed Jeremy to make a number of crossover appearances into mainstream cinema, frequently cameoing as himself in a number of films, including the parodies *Orgazmo* (dir. Trey Parker, 1997), *Being Ron Jeremy* and *One-Eyed Monster*, which explicitly draw and capitalise upon his porn-star persona, making almost no distinction between Jeremy the person and Jeremy the porn star.

His longevity in the adult industry aside (he began his porn career in the 1970s) Jeremy is a highly unusual porn star in that he is not conventionally attractive. Described in *Pornstar* as 'small, fat and very hairy', his overweight and unkempt body earned him the nickname 'the Hedgehog'. Although presented in erotic scenarios, his body is the obverse of the normative models of masculine sexual attractiveness, of *goyim naches*. One scholar even described him as 'repulsive' (Shelton 2002: 119). Nonetheless, in a form of mockery and reversal of the antisemitic imagining of the Jew as corpulent and hirsute, Jeremy refuses to lose weight or shave, instead celebrating his non-normative non-*goyische* body. He is also represented as a *mensch*. And, in turn, this very normality has helped Jeremy's cinematic Jewish body to achieve iconic status. In part this is due to his positioning in erotic films, his longevity in the industry, as well as his above-average-sized penis, but no doubt it is mainly due to his collapsing of the boundaries between porn's hyper-masculine excess and the average, everyday male physique. As Gill's film states, he is 'a hero for the common man'.

In this way, an older generation of Jewish filmmakers and actors, here Allen, Kubrick and Jeremy, arguably not only increased the Jewishness of their work, but updated it to match the new post-1990 sensibility by defining it in increasingly sexualised (and pornographic) terms. If his viewers did not already know it, *Pornstar* outed Ron as a proud Jew, cementing the link between pornography and Jewishness. A similar link is found in Paul Thomas Anderson's somewhat affectionate evocation of the so-called 'golden age' of the porn industry, *Boogie Nights* (1997), in which the central character Jack Horner (Burt Reynolds) is an adult-film director with a heart, a character modelled on the notorious Jewish pornographer Reuben Sturman. Anderson's sympathetic portrayal of Sturman as a caring paternal figure humanises and normalises this Jewish pornographer if not explicitly drawing attention to his ethnicity.

Sex-obsessed Jews

In line with this trend, the younger generation of Jewish filmmakers is also producing more sex-obsessed Jews. This is especially true of Adam Sandler's various characters and Judd Apatow's Jew Tang Clan. As we have already seen in Chapter 1, the *American Pie* trilogy followed the hapless Jim on his journey from high-school virgin to married man and his various attempts, both successful and otherwise, to get laid. In *A Price Above Rubies* (dir. Boaz Yakin, 1998), Sender Horowitz (Christopher Eccleston) is a 'sexual predator' who persuades his sister-in-law to 'accept' being raped by him in return for a job (Wright 2009: 101). The Jewish father in *Transamerica* is described by his wife as a 'sex maniac'. Jewish Boxer Max Baer (Craig Bierko) in *Cinderella Man* (dir. Ron Howard, 2005) is so oversexed that he spends the night before his fight with non-Jew James Braddock (Russell Crowe) partying with two women. Unsatisfied, Baer even hits on Braddock's wife Mae (Renée Zellweger).

Adam Sandler often plays a Jew who possesses near superhuman physical prowess. Chuck Levine in *I Now Pronounce You Chuck and Larry* is a self-confessed 'whore'. He is a raunchy, horny, successful stud, a red-blooded sex maniac who is ridiculously popular with the ladies and regularly has group sex featuring multiple partners (five at one count, including his accident-and-emergency doctor, who later appears semi-naked in his bedroom). Sandler is similarly hyper-potent as comedian George Simmons in *Funny People*. Finally, his Zohan Dvir in *You Don't Mess with the Zohan* is another oversexed Jew. An Israeli super-agent-cum-hairdresser, Zohan offers a unique selling point. He not only provides a decent haircut and style, making it 'silky smooth', but also a rather unusual aftercare package, servicing a series of senior ladies who come to his salon for a style and cut, but giving them an extra finish that they had not anticipated.

The films of Judd Apatow and his Jew Tang Clan in particular depict a series of sex-obsessed Jews. In *The 40-Year-Old Virgin*, we learn that Cal is Jewish when he reveals, 'I touched a guy's balls in Hebrew School once.' Thus, his religious/ethnic identity is simultaneously defined in sexual terms. Cal is shown to be sexually adventurous, enthusiastically getting into the tub with a woman described as 'a freak' and 'scaring the shit out of me'. Elsewhere in the film, Jewish teenager Seth (Loren Berman) and his father (Jeff Kahn) are attending a session on family planning/sexual information.

During a group discussion about different forms of non-penetrative sexual 'outercourse', such as 'body rubbing, dry humping, masturbation, mutual masturbation, deep kissing, erotic massage, oral sex play', Seth volunteers, 'Sounds like my Friday night.' In *Knocked Up*, Ben Stone and his Jewish friends are engaged in a project compiling a website ('Flesh of the Stars') listing films depicting star nudity. Here, though, they talk more about sex than actually having it, even if a drunken one-night stand leads to Ben impregnating a *shiksa* he met at a nightclub. Sex is even more radically foregrounded in *Superbad* (dir. Greg Mottola, 2007), which follows a similar narrative trajectory to *American Pie* in its shadowing of three Jewish teenagers' attempts to lose their virginity, but whose language is much more obscene. The film opens with a long, serious, detailed and matter-of-fact dialogue about hardcore pornography between the two Jewish protagonists. This explicit and sex-fixated language continues in a similar vein throughout the film. Likewise, *Funny People*, which depicts the sex lives of a group of Jewish stand-up comics, is literally peppered with sex, penis and testicle jokes.

Another sign of increased confidence of the younger generation of Jewish directors, screenwriters and actors is not only their increased openness about the consumption of hardcore pornography but also their drawing attention to it in their films. Jim in *American Pie* and *American Pie 2* is seen consuming adult material, as is Darren in *Saving Silverman* (although here it is not out of choice). Archie Moses (Adam Sandler) in *Bulletproof* (dir. Ernest R. Dickerson, 1996) is a self-proclaimed adult-film aficionado. The Wiseman brothers in *A Mighty Wind* (dir. Christopher Guest, 2003) open a sex emporium. In *Being Ron Jeremy*, Brian Pickles (Brian Berke) is shown returning a pile of some dozen porn videos after one 'busy' weekend. Indeed, it is in a faulty peep show booth that he discovers a secret tunnel that leads inside Ron Jeremy's head. In *Harold & Kumar Go to White Castle/Get the Munchies*, Rosenberg and Goldstein refuse to go out because they are staying in to watch nudity on television, prompting Kumar to ask, 'Is that all you Jews ever think about? Tits?' Meanwhile Goldstein wears a T-shirt emblazoned with the words, 'Ass – the other vagina'. Thus we are witnessing two new trends in contemporary cinema, particularly in the United States, in which porn stars are becoming increasingly open about their Jewishness, while male Jewish directors, actors and screenwriters are likewise becoming more open about their sexual and pornographic obsessions. Both growing Jewish confidence in the post-1990 era and the increasing creep of pornography and its stars (such as Jeremy) into mainstream cinema undoubtedly helped to fuel this development.

The erotic and exotic Jewess

'Finally: Jewish women have sex on the screen', Aviva Kempner triumphantly called out in 1999 (38). Insider images of the Jewess prior to 1990 tended to depict her as a wholly undesirable and/or frigid partner, who is usually, if even looked at in the first place, rejected in favour of the *shiksa*. However, reflecting the increased visibility of Jewish women writers, actresses, filmmakers and other industry personnel during the post-1990 period, meaning that many films are written and often directed by, as well as starring, Jewish women, female Jewish desire is central to many contemporary films, which often feature young, free-spirited and liberated Jewesses who express their sexual selves in increasingly explicit (verbally and visually) terms. In *Amy's O*, for example, the very title foregrounding the Jewess's sexual pleasure (the 'O' standing for 'orgasm'), Amy publicly admits, 'I don't think I'm a lesbian because when I fantasise, I fantasise about sucking dick'. Emily Lewin (Kristen Stewart) in *Adventureland* (dir. Greg Mottola, 2009) is a very sexy, desirable Jewess, shown in two simultaneous relationships, both with non-Jews.

Kissing Jessica Stein is a reworking of a familiar theme of the Jewess trying to find an appropriate partner. A comic montage sequence near the beginning of the film depicts a series of disastrous first dates with (presumably) Jewish men in which, argues Tamar Jeffers McDonald, Jessica is established as 'bright but brittle and neurotic, yearning for love but too frightened of rejection to be approachable', as well as 'desperate' (2007: 80). This is a somewhat unfair assessment, as it is the men who are represented as inappropriate, displaying a series of unattractive traits and tics. Yet Jessica does not display much sexual desire or drive. Her mother complains that she has not dated in a year. Disillusioned with the range of Jews on offer, she embarks on a friendship with *shiksa* Helen (Heather Juergensen) that forays into a lesbian relationship and romance. However, Jessica is impeded by her constant self-abnegation and self-consciousness. She finds it very difficult to admit her feelings, and is unable to have the passionate sexual relationship Helen desires. She never makes noise during sex; Helen complains that she is 'so quiet'. When Helen asks Jessica about her therapist's response to their relationship, Jessica is horrified: 'I don't talk about it with my therapist! It's private!' Although the film 'elects a conservative ending' (McDonald 2007: 81) by matching Jessica with her male boss, Josh (Scott Cohen), rather than Helen, by putting female desire at the centre of the narrative and having her couple with another Jew, the film actually reverses the dominant paradigm and is thus far from conservative in Jewish terms, if far from being outright revolutionary either.

The British film *The Governess* certainly presents an alternative model of Jewish sexuality to the mainstream American fare mentioned previously. Although it does replicate the older stereotype of *la belle juive*, it is constructed from the inside, by a British Jewess (Sandra Goldbacher), rather than from the non-Jewish outside. 'Rosina's rather anachronistically liberated way of Jewishness,' argues Antje Ascheid (2006), 'helps the narrative to free her from the conventions of Gentile Victoriana that stress sexual repression and the inability to express erotic desire directly'. Rosina's Jewishness is defined in sexual terms. When in synagogue, 'Her gaze at the men below foregrounds her sexual curiosity' (Ascheid 2006). As she leaves, dressed in exotic, Sephardic clothing (including a black fez), she passes in front of a poster for the 'first appearance of Rachel La Grande Tragedienne – Jewess and Jewel of Paris', while simultaneously she is shouted at ('Jew girl') by some prostitutes, one of whom offers her 'lessons' by baring her breasts. The naming of her ethnicity and religion, the advertisement for an actress and the London prostitutes all serve to cement the link between these identities. Certainly, as we learn later, Rosina aspires to be an actress herself, and her riposte to the prostitutes by opening her shawl to flash her own covered chest hints at a cosmopolitan-ness beyond her specific milieu. This openness, curiosity and worldliness is underscored when she recounts the encounter with the prostitutes to her sister Rebecca (Emma Bird), which includes a frank discussion about whether prostitutes enjoy 'drinking semen'. Rosina and Rebecca are simultaneously sexually naïve and innocent yet frank, 'signalling their otherness in relation to repression and silence of the upper-class English' (Wood 2007: 138).

Rosina is certainly a sexual nonconformist. She is willing to kiss her betrothed before marriage, and defends her action with a flourish: 'Actresses care not for such convention.' When she takes up her position as a governess on Skye, it is she who makes the first moves to seduce her employer, Charles

Cavendish. Sex between them is initiated when Rosina says, in the context of a photo session, 'I dreamt of a beautiful picture we could make of Salomé.' She then proceeds to remove her outer garments, but does not undress further; indeed, she covers herself with a white veil, adding, 'I have heard it said that the ancient Hebrews used to express love for each other entirely covered.' In this way, Rosina models herself on 'exotic Jewish sexual projections' (Lewin 2008a: 96), performing Queen Esther and Salomé. Charles's son Henry (Jonathan Rhys Meyers) also falls for Rosina; but where his father loves her in spite of her Jewishness, Henry does so because of it, for she represents a fetishised, exotic Other (Meyers 2008: 107). 'This is the Jewess figure as overwhelmingly sensual and carnal,' concludes Lewin (2008a: 92).

The highly sexed, desirable and erotically magnetic Jewess certainly occurs across a number of films, particularly as viewed from the perspective of the non-Jew. In *Schindler's List*, Amon Goeth (Ralph Fiennes) states, 'They cast a spell, you know, the Jews. When you work closely with them, like I do, you see this. They have this power. It's like a virus. Some of the men are infected with this virus.' Despite his vicious antisemitism, Goeth is attracted to Jewish concentration-camp inmate Helen Hirsch (Embeth Davidtz). The camera shoots her from the front, sexualising and eroticising her body, her breasts clearly visible through her negligible shirt. Although Goeth desires her, he is clearly troubled by, and hence questions, his impulses, not least because they contradict Nazi racial doctrine: 'Is this the face of a rat? Are these the eyes of a rat?' Parodying Shakespeare, he concludes, 'Hath not a rat eyes?' 'I feel for you, Helen,' he tells her. 'No I don't think so. You're a Jewish bitch. You nearly talked me into it, didn't you?' Goeth then beats Helen up, which Spielberg crosscuts with images of a Jewish wedding inside the camp, to contrast murderous *goyim naches* with a more loving *Yiddishkeit*. Meanwhile, German factory owner Oskar Schindler (Liam Neeson) is arrested for violating the race and settlement act when he kisses a Jewess in public. During his interrogation, reflecting the notion of the Jewess as sexually diseased, Schindler is asked, 'Did your prick fall off?' The absurdity of such a notion to contemporary ears serves to highlight yet mock Nazi antisemitism.

In the Dutch film *Zwartboek/Black Book*, Rachel Stein is the attractive and sexually active *belle juive*. 'Men fall for you easily, it seems,' Rachel is told, and indeed they do. Gestapo officer Müntze, for example, falls 'head over heels for her', even when he knows she is Jewish. Rachel 'seems to have few scruples when it comes to intimate liaison with the enemy, flashing her legs early on at a group of German soldiers as she hitches a ride on a bicycle' (Williams 2007). When asked by her comrades, 'How far are you prepared to go?', she answers as far as is necessary, 'for Queen and Country!' Williams (2007) comments, 'Ironic as this may be, it's hard to know whether her willingness is purely altruistic.' By cabaret singing for the Nazis, Rachel's career allows her to 'go undercover', in both senses of the term, providing the opportunity for her to seduce Müntze and initiate sex with him. Although Rachel sleeps with Müntze at the request of the Resistance, it is never clearly revealed how far she considers this a personal sacrifice.

Simply by appearing in the film, it could be argued, Rachel is eroticised as an object of desire, as Verhoeven is renowned for his inclination to include voyeuristic and gratuitous nudity, as well as graphic sex, in such films as his 1992 *Basic Instinct* and 1995 *Showgirls*. *Zwartboek/Black Book* contains similar explicit imagery and unusual sequences of the naked Jewess's body. In a homage to that infamous shot in *Basic Instinct*, where Sharon Stone's genitalia can be glimpsed, we see an extreme close-up of Rachel's pubis for several seconds before voyeuristically witnessing her, from behind but reflected in a mirror, dying[17] her pubic hair blonde as she transforms herself from brunette Jewess to blonde Gentile Ellis de Vries. Such a shot of the

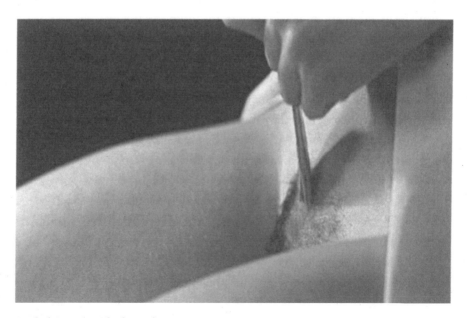

Rachel Stein in *Black Book*.

Jewess's pubic area is still rare in mainstream cinema, which shies away from depicting her genitalia, even breasts, outside the Holocaust genre. If the circumcised Jewish penis is invoked frequently in contemporary cinema, the Jewess's genitalia are not (beyond swearwords). This taps into an older discourse, one dating back to Renaissance Italy at least, where earrings became the identifying mark of the Jewess (and prostitutes), standing in for the lack of circumcision, designed to distinguish her from the virtuous Christian, who was forbidden their use by the provisions of the sumptuary laws (Bonfil 1994, Hughes 1986).

Verna Bernbaum (Marcia Gay Harden) in *Miller's Crossing* (dir. Joel Coen, 1990) is a Jewess defined solely by her manipulative sexuality, which enables her to survive the Depression-era world of gangsters and their molls in which the film is set. We first meet her in her bedroom, scantily dressed, before she proceeds to seduce Tom (Gabriel Byrne). Tom's boss Leo (Albert Finney), with whom she is also sleeping, thinks that Verna is the 'original Miss Jesus', suggesting that Verna not only seduced him, but also masked her aims and character beneath an aura of innocence. Tom, on the other hand, calls her a 'tramp', indicating that he sees through her sexual wiles and realises he is pawn in her game. Even Verna's brother, Bernie (John Turturro), whom she is protecting, is less than impressed, 'She'll sleep with anyone – you know that. She even tried to teach me a thing or two about bed artistry. Can you believe that? My own sister... She's a sick twist alright.'[18]

Drawing upon a much older antisemitic discourse, collapsing the Jewess and the prostitute (Hughes 1986), heroin-addicted Marion Silver (Jennifer Connelly) in *Requiem for a Dream* resorts to prostitution to fuel her drug habit. In *When Do We Eat?* Nikki (Shiri Appleby) is a professional sex worker. Jewish porn star Nina Hartley features, as herself, in a cameo role in *Boogie Nights*. She is always shown naked, unabashedly mid-coitus with a variety of strangers, but never her husband. She not once shows a hint of remorse at her multiple, and often public, infidelities. The picture of the Jewess that emerges in the films in this section therefore deviates from the normative codes of Jewish cinematic sexuality. Increasingly, the Jewess is shown having sex, and her body is revealed by a nudity that was hitherto rare. In so doing, such depictions mimic, mock and reverse some of the worst antisemitic tropes of the Jewess as a wanton, manipulative, deviant, hyper-sexual and incestuous prostitute.

Nina Hartley in *Boogie Nights.*

Endogamy vs exogamy

Diaspora Jews are rarely found coupling with each other cinematically prior to 1990. Consequently, exogamy, or intermarriage, is a fairly standard device in cinema, as the Jew gravitates towards the *shiksa*, rejecting and stigmatising the Jewess as a JAP, who is then blamed for this very process. There are three reasons for this cinematic exogamy. First, many Jewish directors perceived themselves in secular, ethnic terms, and few of them observed any form of Judaism. Second, it is a metaphor for 'assimilation' (Fiedler 1984), and representations of the Jew with the *shiksa* are 'reassuringly assimilatory for the dominant culture' (Stratton 2000: 295). Finally, these relationships are also reassuring for the Jew, especially when the women are middle class, as 'the visible, romantic reward for "making it," the certification that all barriers had been scaled' (Whitfield 1986: 326). Conversely, the Jew marrying the Jewess, on the other hand, is threatening to that same culture because the Jewess presents a threat to the dominant culture, as the children of any relationship, whether with Jew or Gentile, are *halachically* Jewish, and the husband and children may become more culturally Jewish, as a result. 'In other words, where Jewish men dating and marrying out connotes an increasing social cohesion [...] Jewish women whether marrying in or out are more threatening to that hegemony' (Stratton 2000: 295).

Two new trends are observable in contemporary cinema. The range of non-Jewish partners is broadening beyond the stereotypical Meg Ryan-*shiksa*, as befitting an increasing acceptance of cultural pluralism and multiculturalism in the post-1990 period, to embrace a wider range of other ethnic groups than hitherto. And exogamy's antonym – endogamy, or in-group coupling – is increasing onscreen, even embracing some older filmmakers for whom it was previously a taboo topic.

American Jews are not only shown in a variety of exogamous relationships (attested to by the growing number of multi-faith weddings onscreen), but also these are newly coded in terms of the race and/or ethnicity of the non-Jewish partner. In *Keeping the Faith* (dir. Edward Norton, 2000), the stock character of the sympathetic barman turns out to be a half-Punjabi 'Sikh Catholic Muslim with Jewish in-laws'. *27 Dresses* (dir. Anne Fletcher, 2008) features a 'traditional' Indian–Jewish wedding. In *The Social Network* (dir. David Fincher, 2010), Jewish students Mark Zuckerberg (Jesse Eisenberg) and Eduardo Saverin (Andrew Garfield) sleep with fellow Asian students Christy (Brenda Song) and Alice (Malese Jow). Sonia in *Price Above Rubies*, David Kleinfeld (Sean Penn) in *Carlito's Way* (dir. Brian De Palma, 1993) and Jennifer (Meredith Scott Lynn) in *When Do We Eat?* have Latin lovers. Greg Focker loses his virginity to his family's much older Latina maid, and his parents are proud of it! Félix in *Métisse* is seeing a mixed-race woman. When Marion in *Requiem for a Dream* resorts to prostitution she is shown with a black man. Shoshanna in *Inglourious Basterds* also has a black lover. In *Liberty Heights* (dir. Barry Levinson, 1999), while Melvin Kurtzman (Adrien Brody) falls in love with a blonde WASP (Carolyn Murphy), his younger brother Ben (Ben Foster) is attracted to a black girl, Sylvia (Rebekah Johnson), to the scandalised reaction of both families. *Zebra Head/The Colour of Love* (dir. Anthony Drazan, 1992) takes place in Detroit, where a Jewish teenager named Zack (Michael Rapaport) dates a black girl called Nikki (N'Bushe Wright), much to the consternation of both their families and their high-school circles. And *Marci X* (dir. Richard Benjamin, 2003) and *Bringing Down the House* (dir. Adam Shankman, 2003) are very rare creatures: interracial Black–Jewish comedies.

This new cinematic exogamy extends beyond the United States. The Israeli Zohan has a Romeo and Juliet-style romance with a Palestinian-American woman. *Train of Life* (dir. Radu Mihaileanu, 1998) and *The Man*

Who Cried (dir. Sally Potter, 2000) both feature romances between Gypsies and Jews. *Solomon and Gaenor,* another Romeo and Juliet-like drama set in the Welsh Valleys in 1911, focuses on a love affair between the Jewish Solomon Levinsky (Ioan Gruffudd) and Welsh Gaenor Rees (Nia Roberts). (It is one, if not the only, film, to feature Welsh, Yiddish and English in the dialogue.) Ruth Wiseman (Emily Woof) in Morrison's 2003 follow-up film *Wondrous Oblivion* is a young, neglected German-born Jewish housewife married to a much older man (Stanley Townsend) in 1960s working-class South London when a Jamaican family moves into the house next door, to the horror of the other English residents. As her son David (Sam Smith) cautiously becomes friendly with the new neighbours, two simultaneous relationships develop between David and Judy Samuel (Leonie Elliott), and Ruth and Dennis Samuel (Delroy Lindo), the father of the family.

Exogamy may still be a celluloid cornerstone, but contemporary cinema is increasingly depicting in-group sex and marriage, reflecting a younger post-assimilatory generation of Jews who are less anxious about the need to acculturate. The refusal to marry or couple outside the community is a repudiation of the impulse to erase those distinctive qualities that make the Jew/ess an appealing partner in the first place. It is a symbolic rejection of *goyim naches.* Indeed, since endogamy perpetuates Jewish identity as separateness, it is a mark of Jewish confidence. *Then She Found Me* (dir. Helen Hunt, 2007) shows a Jewish couple making love in the back seat of a car in the street in broad daylight, fully dressed, but with no concern for anyone who may be passing. Norah in *Nick and Norah's Infinite Playlist* has an on-off relationship with the Israeli Tal (Jay Baruchel). *The Birdcage* (dir. Mike Nicholls, 1996) features a gay Jewish couple. *Meet the Fockers, When Do We Eat?, La fille du RER/The Girl on the Train* (dir. André Téchiné, 2009), *L'homme est une femme comme les autres/Man is a Woman* (dir. Jean-Jacques Zilbermann, 1998) provide further cinematic depictions of endogamous coupling. In *L'homme est une femme comme les autres/Man is a Woman,* we even see Simon Eskanazy (Antoine de Caunes) stand naked with his back to the camera as he is fellated by his wife Rosalie (Elsa Zylberstein), wearing nothing but his *kippah* (skull cap). At the end of *Clueless,* Cher chooses her Jewish step-brother Josh (Paul Rudd) rather than a man named 'Christian' (Justin Walker). And Bernie's claim in *Miller's Crossing* that his sister taught him something about 'the bedroom arts' introduces endogamous incest. This is replicated in the British film *Song of Songs* (dir.

Josh Appignanesi, 2005), where some sort of unseen but clearly implied incestuous and sadomasochistic relationship has occurred between its Jewish sibling protagonists.

The sex sequences in *Munich* are an advert for endogamy. As Avner (Eric Bana) and Daphna (Ayelet Zurer) make love, their beautiful almost naked bodies are on display. Her face is shown in close-up, sweating and panting, as she achieves orgasm. On finishing, he asks her, 'How late into pregnancy are you supposed to stop having sex?' This sequence of two, young, beautiful Jews making love is striking, almost idealised in its portrayal, reversing previous portrayals and/or the repression of endogamous Jewish sexuality in film.

Other endogamous Jews can be found in *Deconstructing Harry*, *Meet the Fockers*, *A Price Above Rubies*, *Kadosh/Sacred* (dir. Amos Gitai, 1998) and *Two Lovers* (dir. James Gray, 2008) to mention just a few. In *A Serious Man*, Larry Gopnik imagines himself with his sultry Jewish neighbour (Amy Landecker). In *Jakob the Liar* (dir. Peter Kassovitz, 1999), Mischa (Liev Schreiber) and Rosa (Nina Siemaszko) poignantly make love within the ghetto's confines during the Shoah. *The Hebrew Hammer* also reverses the Jew–*shiksa* paradigm by depicting its hero, Mordechai Jefferson Carver (Adam Goldberg), a Jewish stud, with a sexy, attractive Jewess, Esther Bloomenbergensteinenthal (Judy Greer), who calls him a 'Semitic stallion'. He brings her to orgasm with the words, 'I want to have lots of children by you. I want to get a good-paying, stable job. I want for our children to go to private schools [...] Also, on a daily basis, I want you to tell me what to do, where to do it and how I should live my life.' These films, in the words of

Avner and Daphna in *Munich*.

David Biale, 'represent a clear development in the willingness of filmmakers to portray erotic attraction between Jews. In making that statement, all these films dissent from the dominant discourse that continues to be drawn to eroticising the Other rather than the Self' (1997: 222). Furthermore, unlike the films that Biale analysed to make his statement (*The Way We Were*, *Crossing Delancey*), these films are located in the Americanised middle-class present rather than the politically radical or working-class past.

Even older directors like Woody Allen include several such couplings, having typically rejected them previously. For example, in his *Deconstructing Harry*, in a fictionalised account fantasised by the film's eponymous antihero, Leslie and Ken make love. As they do so, Leslie's blind grandmother makes an unanticipated appearance. Although she cannot see what is transpiring, she can hear the couple's increasing excitement, leading to a ludicrous conversational exchange that infuses the whole Jewish sexual coupling with comedy, no doubt reflecting Allen's view of the value of keeping it within the faith. In another of Harry's novels, he caricatures his Jewish ex-wife, Joan (Kirstie Alley), as 'Jewish with a vengeance', 'like a born again Christian but a Jew' who recites a blessing over everything: wine, the *challah* (Hebrew: bread eaten on the Sabbath and festivals), candles and her husband's penis before performing fellatio, using the Hebrew words '*borei pri ha* blow job' (literally translating as 'He who creates the fruit of the blow job'), mixing prayer, profanity, pornography and perversity (Girgus 2002: 162) in a way that echoes Walter's '*shomer* fucking *shabbes*' in *The Big Lebowski* (see Chapter 6). At the same time, perhaps unwittingly, by having a Jewess performing fellatio (and several times at that, as well as tolerating her husband's 'perversions', namely the need to be tied up and to watch her with other women) Allen overturns previous constructions of the JAP, who resolutely resists such acts. These scenes are nevertheless examples of rare endogamous Jewish coupling in Allen's oeuvre.

Furthermore, the Jewess is increasingly represented as an active agent in the process of miscegenation. In the Jewess-centred films I mentioned earlier, she is empowered either to reject altogether the Jew, who is represented as neither a sexually attractive nor available partner, or to be more selective about the Jew she chooses. The Jewess is shown intermarrying out of genuine love for her Gentile partner, while the Jew, in contrast, is motivated only by professional mobility and a desire to overcome obstacles to his social advancement. The Jewess who intentionally falls in love with a non-Jew on film further reflects the changing situation in which the secularised Jewess, no longer being confined to domestic or religiously segregated contexts, has more opportunities to meet and mingle with Gentile men. A cause of this shift may be the trend that Jewish women throughout the Western world have recently caught up with Jewish men in terms of intermarriage (Hyman 1995: 19–20).

Rainbow Jews

Another sign of the post-1990s paradigm shift and increased confidence is the growth in the number of non-normative Jewish sexualities across the spectrum of gender, sexual preference, religious identity and age. It points to a greater inclusiveness by representing those 'outside' normative Judaism. Jews in contemporary cinema are increasingly outing themselves as gay. Israel witnessed a number of films, in particular *Yossi Jagger*, *Walk on Water* (dir. Eytan Fox, 2004), *The Bubble* and *Eyes Wide Open* (dir. Haim Tabakman, 2009). Several documentaries on the subject were released, including *Treyf* (dirs Alisa Lebow and Cynthia Madansky, 1998) and *Trembling Before G-d* (dir. Sandi Simcha Dubowski, 2001).

In addition to *Miller's Crossing*, *Knocked Up*, *The History Boys* and *I Now Pronounce You Chuck and Larry* (in which the lead Jewish character only mimics homosexuality but still participates in a gay Jewish wedding), we encounter the gay characters of 'Yitzchok the fairy' (Michael Rubenfeld) in *Lucky Number Slevin* (dir. Paul McGuigan, 2006), Harvey Milk (Sean Penn) in *Milk* (dir. Gus Van Sant, 2008), Allen Ginsberg (James Franco) in *Howl* (dirs Rob Epstein and Jeffrey Friedman, 2010) and Elliot Teichberg (Demetri Martin) in *Taking Woodstock* (dir. Ang Lee, 2009). In the opening sequence of *L'homme est une femme comme les autres/Man is a Woman* the camera tracks Simon as he cruises in a gay sauna to a soundtrack of *klezmer*, thus subverting our genre expectations, as such music is typically used to code a folksy *heimische* (homey) Jewishness (Aaron 2004: 98–99). Simon's uncle offers him a large sum of money to marry a Jewess in order to continue the family name. Simon thus mimics heterosexuality, but this proves difficult when he meets his fiancée's brother and learns that the young man is himself, in a mirrored manoeuvre, mimicking *haredism* to hide his secularism (and implied homosexuality). In the Swedish film *Freud flyttar hemifrån/Freud Leaving Home* (dir. Susanne Bier, 1991), David Cohen (Philip Zandén) is gay, living in Miami with his partner Mike. His family find it hard to accept his homosexuality. His father (Palle Granditsky) tells him to stop dancing around at Disney World like a 'ridiculous fag' ('But I am a ridiculous fag,' David replies) and his sister (Jessica Zandén) comments, 'That Mike at least looks Jewish, but a little too pretty, don't you think, Mom?' – 'an ironic twist on Jewish concern about intermarriage' (Wright 1998: 373). Finally, the US adaptation (*The Birdcage*) of the French film *La cage aux folles* (dir. Edouard Molinaro, 1978) transforms its protagonists from French to Jewish-American gays. In doing so, *The Birdcage* injects a Jewishness that was missing from the original film. Armand (Robin Williams) and Albert Goldman (Nathan Lane) are a homosexual nightclub owner and transvestite diva respectively, thus aligning 'Jews with gays as perennial foreigners in American culture' (Desser and Friedman 2004: 291). They agree to conceal their gay and Jewish identities, pretending to be and mimicking straight Christianity for the sake of their son's future marriage. Albert even mimics Val's birth mother.

If the gay Jew is more in evidence since 1990, so is the lesbian Jewess becoming increasingly prominent. Jessica Stein might be more 'queer' (in the sexual rather than Jewish sense) than lesbian, but contemporary cinema increasingly includes and even focuses on Jewish lesbianism. *Amy's O* includes a lesbian literary agent. *What's Cooking?* (dir. Gurinder Chadha, 2000) features a lesbian Jewish relationship. At the outset of *A Family Affair*, which 'has the feel of a lesbian Woody Allen film' (Friedman 2007: 154), in direct address to the camera, Rachel Rosen reveals that, 'I've known I was gay ever since I was DNA.' The film then takes on a typical narrative trajectory in which Rachel rejects her former *Jewish* lover Reggie Abravanel (Michele Greene) in favour of wholesome guileless Gentile Christine who, in turn, announces her desire to convert to Judaism. Rachel, however, gets cold feet, having nightmarish visions of Christine as a *haredi* wife making *kreplach* (meat-filled dumplings). Nonetheless, the film ends with a traditional Jewish wedding officiated by a lesbian rabbi. *Aimée & Jaguar* depicts a passionate undercover lesbian affair in which Felice Schragenheim, an elegant, clever Jewish lesbian, is working undercover for a Nazi newspaper so she can get things to the underground in Berlin, and falls in love with Lilly Wust (Juliane Köhler), a Nazi photographer (Insdorf 2003: 330). As the Jewess masquerading as Gentile, Felice is defined by her attractiveness, sensuality and eroticism. Another German film, *Alles auf Zucker!/Go for Zucker!*, features a lesbian Jewess Jana Zuckermann (Anja Franke). Contemporary cinema is thus ahead of the curve in normalising lesbian Jewesses by putting them at the forefront of film than hitherto.

Senior sexuality

In line with the changes outlined above, contemporary cinema is widening the range of available Jewish sexualities beyond the young Jew. Building upon the aforementioned Maude in *Harold and Maude*, post-1990 films are, for example, increasingly sexualising the older Jewess. In *American Pie: The Wedding* Jim's grandmother (Angela Paton) undergoes a transformation from the traditional representation of the Jewess (as an 'ugly old kike') into a giggly lover. When we first meet her, she presents a stereotypical relative who is upset that her grandson is marrying a non-Jew; after peering closely at Michelle, she cries, 'Not Jewish! No wedding Jimmy. No wedding. *Goyeh* [non-Jewess]!' Further into the film, however, Stifler, believing her to be someone else, mistakenly makes love to her. Rather than objecting, she urges him to carry on. Indeed, when he is interrupted, she implores him to 'focus, focus'. At the wedding itself, she is a picture of guilt-free happiness, not because she accepts the union, but rather as a result of Stifler's amorous attentions. Jim's dad remarks, 'Look at the smile on my mother's face. Do you know how long she's been waiting for a day like this?'

You Don't Mess with the Zohan takes this concept even further, as Zohan sexually satisfies a series of middle-aged and elderly Jewesses in the back room of his hair salon. Eventually, as the word spreads, there is a line of such women, including the infirm, queuing up around the block to take advantage of his skills. Zohan makes these women look and feel desirable as he peppers them with compliments, 'Mrs Skitzer, you have the ass and tits of a schoolgirl and everybody knows it' being a typical line. He also *schtups* his American *schlemiel* friend's middle-aged Jewish mother (Lainie Kazan). Similarly, Roz Focker teaches senior sex-therapy classes and is shown engaged in guilt-free lovemaking with her husband.

Even in their mockery, the examples in this section potentially offer a transgressive eroticisation of the Jewess in contemporary cinema. The Jewish matriarch may have long been revered, but rarely had she before been so sexualised on film, reversing the maternal – frigid binary, and normalising her.

Hot *haredim*

Even *haredim* have come in for similar treatment, leading to an unprecedented eroticisation of the *haredi* in contemporary cinema. In *Orgazmo*, two *haredim* are depicted in the throes of orgasm as they stroll down the street. *The Hebrew Hammer* seeks to 'construct a more virile Jewish masculinity' (Brook 2006: 206) in which Carver, who dresses as a cross between Shaft and a *haredi*, is defined sexually. The first thing we learn about him is that he is 'the sex machine to all the chicks'. His mother (Nora Dunn) tells his date, 'You know there's a reason they call him the Hebrew Hammer,' before asking her to 'Take his mind off his work. Maybe a blowjob here and there'. In *The Girlfriend Experience* (dir. Steven Soderbergh, 2009), a *haredi* jeweller visits a high-class Manhattan hooker. The Israeli film *Kadosh/Sacred* provides an unprecedented representation of the marital and sexual lives of the *haredim* in Mea Shearim, Jerusalem, including a disturbing scene of marital rape. Together with the sequence in *A Price Above Rubies* mentioned earlier, in which Sonia Horowitz (Renée Zellweger) is seduced by her brother-in-law Sender, 'but reads more like rape than seduction' (Rubel 2010: 85), these two films are particularly notable for depicting *haredim* engaged in sex, in a way that previous films shied away from.

In *A Stranger Among Us* (dir. Sidney Lumet, 1992) the *haredi* becomes the object of sexual desire, a previously rare depiction in mainstream cinema. Ariel (Eric Thal), the son of the Hasidic *rebbe* (Yiddish: a charismastic religious leader of a Hasidic sect, derived from the Hebrew word Rabbi) may be the embodiment of the queer, diaspora Jew, but he is represented as attractive. He is, in the words of Laurence Roth, a 'beefcake Hassid' with a 'Hollywood handsome face' (2004: 180, 179). The non-Jewish heroine, Emily Eden (Melanie Griffith) is sent to investigate a murder within the *haredi* world, where she meets Ariel. She is attracted to him. This is a double reversal of the typical cinematic paradigm, for not only does she pursue him, rather than the other way around, but also he ultimately rejects her in favour of a Jewess. In one sequence, Eden discovers Ariel reading a Kabbalistic text on sex, a lure she cannot resist. In order to blend in and not to upset any sensibilities,

Eden adopts *haredi* guise. Returning to a meeting at the police precinct, she forgets to remove her *haredi* dress. Clad in a modest dark-blue dress and topped by a wig-like hairdo, the reactions from her male colleagues reveal 'the seductiveness of Jewish bodies' (Roth 2004: 182). All the men ogle Eden, and they tell her she looks 'radiant' and like a 'lady'. Ironically, Eden's new identity is a turn-on for the self-hating, secular Jew Levine (John Pankow). 'You still got a great ass, Eden,' he tells her (Roth 2004: 182). Such a representation, in which a *haredi* female, *qua haredi* female, is depicted as sexual and attractive either to secular, non-*haredi* Jews or non-Jews, is still rare.

Other sexually defined *haredim* appear in the French film *L'homme est une femme comme les autres/Man is a Woman* and *When Do We Eat?* In the former film, the *haredi* is possibly gay but continues to wear traditional garb in order to mask his deviant, by Orthodox Jewish terms, sexuality and not to hurt his family. He morphs from a metaphorically 'queer' Jew to a literally queer yet tough Jew when he undresses to reveal a well-toned, fit, athletic body. The dress is a façade, including his glued-on *peyot*, which not only reveal that he is not a *haredi*, but also highlight the fact that he is an actor wearing a costume mirroring Simon's mimicry of straightness as he attempts to pass for heterosexual. In *When Do We Eat?* Ethan (Max Greenfield) is unable to resist the lure of his cousin, with whom he previously had an affair. Lusting and in a dramatic gesture, he clears the table clean and makes love to her during the Passover Seder, justifying it with the profanity, 'Fuck it, I'll atone on Yom Kippur.' In doing so, *haredim* are increasingly humanised and represented less as ciphers or symbols (explored further in Chapter 6). They are depicted as having the same sexual drives and needs as their more secular co-religionists. In this way, contemporary filmmakers are depicting their willingness to transgress previously held boundaries and to move into new territory that previously had not been extensively explored in such depth.

Conclusion: exposed erotic Jews

Increased exposure of Jewish body parts in sexual and erotic conditions, outside hardcore pornography, represents a significant departure from a mainstream cinematic tradition that tended to shy away from graphic displays of Jewish sexuality and nudity, preferring suggestiveness, innuendo, double entendre and outrageousness as typically represented by Woody Allen (Girgus 2002: 158). Thus, in this new guise, the Jewish body is presented as both spectacle and erotic. *Hitlerjunge Salomon/Europa Europa*, for example, fetishises the Jew's body by overt sexual engagement with it (Lungstrum 1998: 57). The sex in *Munich*, in Jewish cinematic terms at least, is fairly graphic. In *Seres Queridos/Only Human*, we are introduced to Tania (María Botto), a bellydancer, as she is topless in the bathroom. She holds her toothbrush between her breast and chestbone, drawing the viewer's attention to that area. As mentioned above, several topless shots of Rachel occur in *Zwartboek/Black Book*, including a close-up of her vagina. Nina Hartley is permanently naked in *Boogie Nights*. A close-up of Ben Stone's overweight buttocks appears in *Knocked Up*. And Marion in *Requiem for a Dream* is shown engaged in a very explicit sex act with another woman in front of a room of leering, cheering men. This cinematic display of sexual, eroticised Jewish bodies represents a clear cinematic shift. One of the reasons is surely propelled by the pornographisation of mainstream cinema in general. Indeed, a sexually explicitly Jewish porn film, *Nice Jewish Girls* (dir. Matthew Blade, 2009), was released, mocking the stereotype of JAP frigidity. The other reason is attributable to Jewish sexual confidence, extending to a spectrum of sexually defined and erotic Jews in terms of gender, sexual preference, age and religious identification.

Contemporary cinema, therefore, reverses many of the sexual stereotypes of the Jew/ess and begins to introduce a range of Jews engaged in *jouissance* (in its original French sense) that break down these constructions. The older anxieties, while not disappearing completely, are being coupled with a new confidence. Jewish neo-Nazi Danny Balint may ask his fellow antisemites in *The Believer*, 'Do we hate 'em [...] cos they have the most active sex lives?' but Jews are clearly taking pride in, as well as mocking, their hyper-sexual reputations. Jews' pride in their hyper-sexual relations also serves to overturn the countertrope, on the path towards normalisation.

CHAPTER 4

Passivity

Passive Jews

A classic Jewish adage states, 'Who is a hero? He who conquers his desire'. Since toughness was downgraded in normative rabbinic culture, physical, martial and bodily virtues, which flowered in natural surroundings, were rejected in favour of a scholarliness that thrived indoors. Denied the right to bear arms, ride horses, duel, joust or arch competitively, diaspora Jews, in return, rejected the competitive-drive ethos of what they disparagingly called *goyim naches*, 'those characteristics that in European culture have defined a man as manly: physical strength, martial activity and aggressiveness' (Boyarin 1997: 78). The word '*goy*' (Hebrew: lit. 'nation', but used to mean 'Gentile') is related to that of '*geviyah*' (Hebrew: 'body'), and the word '*goyim*' (plural of '*goy*') can also be interpreted to mean bodily. In this way, diaspora Jews rejected manly bodily pursuits, namely fighting, duelling, wrestling, hunting and sports.

As a consequence, for centuries Jewishness was intertwined with notions of weakness and timidity. Alain Finkelkraut characterised this as the 'tenacious [...] legend of Jewish passivity' (1994: 42). Freud summarised it thus:

> The preference which through two thousand years the Jews have given to spiritual endeavour has, of course, had its effect; it has helped to build a dike against brutality and the inclination to violence which are usually found

where athletic development becomes the ideal of the people. The harmonious development of spiritual and bodily activity, as achieved by the Greeks, was denied to the Jews [1967: 147].

Jean-Paul Sartre noted: 'The Jews are the mildest of men...passionately hostile to violence' (1965: 117). This was because 'Jews made a virtue, by constructing a remarkable culture of meekness, physical frailty, and gentleness, a pale, slouched identity nurtured in the stale air of their exclusion from the worlds of work and war' (Breines 1990: 45). As with representations of the Jew/ess, images of Jewish passivity fell into 'two longstanding, deeply ingrained stereotypes of the Jew': 'the Jewish weakling' and the gentle *schlemiel* (Breines 1990: 3). Overall, then, as Officer Michaels (Seth Rogen) in *Superbad* states about Jews, 'They're pretty docile.'

Contemporary cinema, however, complicates this historic picture of feminised and hysteric Jewish passivity. Not only is the queer–tough binary collapsed but also monolithic notions of undeserving victimhood are reversed. This is particularly evident in the Holocaust genre. Furthermore, portrayals that represent Jews as victims of antisemitic prejudice and discrimination are decreasing as Jews are seen to be deserving of their fates, some of which are also at the hands of their co-religionists. Indeed, intra-Jewish violence, that is Jews oppressing other Jews, is increasing as part of the shift towards normalisation. It is such representations that this chapter will explore.

A grey zone

In terms of Jewish passivity, the obvious place to begin is the Shoah. If, historically, the paradigmatic representation of Jews is as weak and passive, in film this was most evident in the Holocaust genre, in which Jews were nearly always portrayed as underserving victims. Taking *Schindler's List* as the benchmark, by choosing to focus on Schindler and Goeth, Spielberg marginalised key Jews to supporting roles (with the exception of Itzhak Stern [Ben Kingsley]), portraying them as an un-rounded, infantilised, monolithic and undifferentiated mass of weak feminised passivity, lacking in psychological depth, to be saved or killed at the whim of the Gentiles. Post-*Schindler's List*, however, contemporary cinema begins to present a new paradigm in Holocaust filmmaking in its refusal to present only this scenario, what Axel Bangert calls 'hagiographic transfigurations of Jews' (2008: 20).

As its very title indicates, *The Grey Zone* (dir. Tim Blake Nelson, 2001), which is based upon a true story, explores that ambiguous 'grey zone' in which the sharp distinctions between Nazi perpetrators and their victims are blurred. Indeed, by focusing on the role of the Sonderkommando (Special Commando), those camp inmates selected by the SS to assist with the killing process, in the mechanics of extermination, the film highlights the imbrication of the Holocaust's victims in the Final Solution, what Lawrence Baron called their 'moral debasement' (2005: 258). Thus, the film 'aims at revising the dominant image of Jewish victimhood' (Bangert 2008: 20). In *The Grey Zone*, the Sonderkommando do *not* look like victims. Since they are accorded special privileges, they eat, dress and sleep better than the other camp inmates. Bangert even suggested that 'the explicit language and aggressive bodily behaviour of the Sonderkommando members are reminiscent of the urban resistance film and indeed American gangster films of the '90s' (2008: 22).

Furthermore, the Sonderkommando is not presented as having a unifying sense of ethical/moral, national or religious values (even beyond mere survival). Differences are emphasised particularly in the literal clash between the Sonderkommando and the new arrivals. In a key scene, set in the anteroom of the gas chamber when the victims are asked to undress, a Jewish deportee (Lee Wilkof) accuses Hoffman (David Arquette) of complicity by insisting that Hoffman is lying when he reassures the new arrivals that they will be fine. 'Tell me, you fucking Nazi, tell me I am going to live.' Motivated by 'self-hatred resulting out of feelings of guilt and shame', Hoffman brutally beats the man into a bloody mess with his bare fists, resulting in the man's death (Bangert 2008: 22). As Hoffman crouches on the floor, ashamed and shocked by this act of violence, a Nazi guard observing the whole incident leers at him, a smirk playing across his face. His smile is presented in point-of-view close-up, suggesting that it is easy to kill Jews, and that Hoffman blurs the distinction between victim/Jew and perpetrator/Nazi.

Roman Polanski's historically based film *The Pianist* (2002) similarly refuses to idealise Jews as victims. Instead, Polanski's film depicts 'the whole spectrum of moral attitudes' of the population of the Warsaw Ghetto. 'While some Jews showed courage and altruism even when facing their own death, others were prepared to betray their compatriots to Germans to repossess their property and increase their power within the community' (Mazierska 2007: 18). In fact, as Mazierska points out, 'there are Jewish characters in *The Pianist* which conform to antisemitic stereotypes, such as the guests in the café where Szpilman (Adrien Brody) is playing the piano, checking whether their coins are made of real gold; however, they are minor characters, more than offset by the decent members of the Szpilman family' (2007: 158). Polanski also includes acts of Jewish resistance, including producing underground newspapers in the ghetto and the Warsaw Ghetto Uprising of 1943. Yet, unlike Nelson's film, *The Pianist* does not interrogate the 'grey zone' to any significant extent. While we see members of the Jewish police brutally herd fellow Jews onto the trains destined for Auschwitz, their motives are not explored, and the film still sets up a binary opposition between the 'grey zone' and the 'virtuous zone' of the fighters and the Szpilman family (Mazierska 2007: 160).

Two British films also ultimately refuse to distinguish sharply between Jew and German during the Holocaust. In *Bent* (dir. Sean Mathias, 1997) gay Max (Clive Owen) mimics Jewishness when he is sent to Dachau because he believes he will be better treated. It is a rare example of a Gentile seeking to pass as a Jew, particularly during the Holocaust. And in *The Boy in the Striped Pyjamas* (dir. Mark Herman, 2008) Bruno (Asa Butterfield) is the eight-year-old son of a concentration-camp commandment. Bored and lonely, he befriends a young Jewish camp inmate Shmuel (Jack Scanlon), the eponymous 'boy in the striped pyjamas'. The two boys, who are of equal age but vastly dissimilar backgrounds, develop an unlikely friendship. Failing fully to comprehend the gravity of Shmuel's situation, Bruno yearns to join his friend on the other side of the wire fence. One day, his wish is fulfilled, and he dons a set of striped pyjamas and wanders about the camp. However, during a round-up, both boys – since they are indistinguishable – are assembled and sent to the gas chambers, where as Gentile and Jew they both suffer the same death. Bruno's parents desperately search for him, grief-stricken and inconsolable when they realise his fate. In this way, the film suggests Bruno (and his parents) is as much a victim as Shmuel. It further resists and complicates essentialist and racialised constructions of Jews and Gentiles, suggesting that either can become a victim in the wrong clothing. In this instance, there is no binary of victimised–victimiser.

The Reader (dir. Stephen Daldry, 2008) also problematises victimhood. Jewish Holocaust survivor Ilana Mather (Lena Olin) is a middle-aged, well-to-do woman, living in New York in a large, tastefully decorated apartment, crammed with Judaica. She is portrayed as prudish and extremely wealthy, as if she cashed in on the Holocaust, having penned a successful autobiography. This is emphasised in comparison to her former SS guard, Hanna Schmitz (Kate Winslett), who is an aging woman on the verge of killing herself in prison. Abandoned, isolated and dirty, Hanna arouses empathy and pity. She dies alone and penniless. In her will, she donates the little money she has to Ilana, and this is delivered to her by Hanna's former lover Michael Berg (Ralph Fiennes). The contrast in wealth could not be clearer: the Jewish victim is rich while the Nazi perpetrator dies impoverished. Given that Ilana is a minor character in the drama, our sympathies as an audience are more with Hanna, not least because Ilana, who cannot show any forgiveness or magnanimity towards her former victimiser, refuses Hanna's charitable gesture. We are thus encouraged to view the perpetrator as the victim, a sense magnified by the audience's recognition of the well-known actress playing her and also because we view this unconventional female perpetrator through the lens of eroticism and sexuality (a significant portion of the film is devoted to Hanna and Michael's love affair); at least one critic commented on Kate Winslet's pale and creamy skin, as well as her 'taut belly and limbs gleaming under the caressing light' (Dargis 2008). Although Ilana exercises agency in this instance, and is not simply passive, it does not portray her in a sympathetic light, complicating the film's representation of the victim/perpetrator paradigm.

It is increasingly noticeable that the distinction between victim/Jew and Gentile/antisemite is becoming blurred. *Focus* (dir. Neal Slavin, 2001) similarly complicates the Jew-as-victim paradigm. Lawrence Newman (William H. Macy) is an antisemite forced by his boss to buy a new pair of glasses. Since glasses are both an in- and out-group signifier of Jewishness, Newman is mistaken for a Jew. Subsequently, he becomes the victim of antisemitism, culminating in violence whereby he is required to defend himself alongside Jewish shopkeeper Finkelstein (David Paymer). In *La fille du RER/The Girl on the Train*, Jeanne (Émilie Dequenne) mimics a victim of an antisemitic attack. Finally, *The Believer* complicates and destabilises these binaries in its representation of a self-hating Jew who externalises his internal self-hatred by becoming a neo-Nazi (explored below).

Queer/tough Jews

Walter Sobchak in *The Big Lebowski* collapses the queer/tough binary I mentioned at the outset of this chapter. Typically, as we have seen, diaspora-dwelling Jews were positioned as unmanly figures who are hysteric, effeminate and weak, therefore queer or sissy. But while Walter is not Israeli, he is represented as tough and Zionist. This is revealed when he arrives at a bowling alley, loudly quoting Herzl, and it is no coincidence that his weapon of choice is the Israeli-manufactured Uzi submachine gun, very much a symbol of the Israeli Defence Forces (IDF). In addition to his military bearing, dress, posture, attitudes and fetish for weaponry, Walter's character draws on the demobilised and 'war-traumatised men of the film noir as in the *Taxi Driver* [dir. Martin Scorsese, 1976)]/Vietnam movie types' (Körte, 1999: 201). Indeed, as a veteran of Vietnam, he constantly equates every situation with that conflict. He owns a security firm ('Sobchack Security'). He places his faith in physical force ('I grab one of them and beat it out of him') and is brutal in combat, biting off and spitting into the air the ear of a nihilist attacker. He 'also (literally) expresses the excessive rhetoric of the gun-toting individual frontiersman', contending that 'pacifism is not – look at our current situation with that camel-fucker in Iraq – pacifism is not something to hide behind', mimicking George H. W. Bush's belligerent rhetoric of 'unchecked aggression'. And he believes that violence is justified in 'seeking recompense for someone peeing on the Dude's rug!' (Martin-Jones 2006: 142). Finally, Walter is very competitive. The embodiment of *goyim naches*, he refuses to back down over a perceived infringement. He is a lone Jew in the *goyische* world of bowling competition.

Even as it may simultaneously reinforce his queerness, David Levinson's affiliation by placement next to such a strong black character as Steven Hiller in *Independence Day* signifies the construction of a more virile diaspora Jew (Brook 2006: 206). David's very name indicates that he will certainly defeat the Goliath in the form of the alien invaders. Like his biblical namesake, the Jewish geek is converted into a macho saviour as he enters the alien mother ship, uploads a computer virus, destroys it and returns home triumphantly to meet his admiring wife and smoke a large cigar, a clear signifier of his 'unironically hypermasculine' potency (Itzkovitz 2006: 234).[19] The symbolism of the cigar is far too pronounced to be coincidental. Phallic imagery aside, cigar smoking is used in film to portray a certain *ruggedness* and manliness, as it is associated with risk and a bad-boy image. Compare, for example, the contrast between the phallic cigar of General Jack D. Ripper (Sterling Hayden) (often shot in low angle to emphasise its size) in *Dr. Strangelove* (dir. Stanley Kubrick, 1964) and the rather pathetic cigarette of Dr. Strangelove (Peter Sellers). 'Cigar smoking provides a visual sign of masculinity that condense[s] images of virility, power, pleasure, social status with a narrative of initiation' (Root 2005: 41). Initially, David abhors smoking, admonishing his father for doing so. Yet, rejecting petty health worries, David is symbolically initiated into the fold of *goyim naches* through the sharing of tobacco. Coughing to begin with, he exits the spacecraft, smoking 'like a pro', after the destruction of the aliens. Through violence and smoking, the queer David becomes tough.

Unsympathetic losers

In *Quiz Show* (dir. Robert Redford, 1994), a film based on a true story, the character based on real-life Herb Stempel (John Turturro) is an unsympathetic loser. As a contestant on the game show *Twenty-One* (1956–58) he competes against Charles Van Doren (Ralph Fiennes), whose handsome, pedigreed and groomed Gentile body acutely emphasises Stempel's swarthy, 'unkempt, sweaty and ethnic' physiognomy, clothed in a borrowed, oversized coat (Taub 2005: 31). He is dismissed by one of the cunning Jews that run the show as 'an annoying Jewish guy with a sidewall haircut'. Herb is presented as the victim as he is forced to throw the final match at the request of the unscrupulous Jews who manage *Twenty-One* so Van Doren can win. Despite his intelligence and phenomenal memory, it is hard to feel empathy for Herb, as he lacks virtue, having, like Van Doren, cut a deal with the businessmen, revealing that he too was cheating.

Barton Fink features Turturro as another victimised Jewish brain. The film focuses on the eponymous young, idealistic, albeit self-deluded, Jewish writer who is making the transition from a celebrated New York playwright to an abject, angst-ridden, existentialist hack, churning out screenplays in the classical Hollywood studio system of the early 1940s. 'Principled and pretentious in equal measure, Fink sees himself as a pillar of literary purity. He is a quirky caricature of artistic self-involvement and intellectual pretension', as well as 'an incendiary study of intellect minus soul' (Russell 2001: 88). Fink is also victimised by fellow Jew Jack Lipnick (Michael Lerner), the Louis B. Mayer/Harry Cohn-inspired mogul of Capitol Pictures – the studio that has hired him – a fast-talking, loud-mouthed, burly man with a taste for expensive suits. He dwarfs, both literally and figuratively, the diminutive Fink, who shrivels in his domineering presence. Yet we fail to sympathise with the arrogant Fink, whose very name suggests an unpleasant or contemptible person, someone who informs on people to the authorities.

Jews in too deep or out of their depth

Many violent films depict Jews who are not only out of their depth, but also who, metaphorically speaking, cannot swim. Gangster films, in particular, present Jews as victims. Typically, the Jew attempts to pass as tough, posturing as a gangster, but is ultimately exposed as unable to cut the mustard criminally and ends up dead. At the same time, often little sympathy for their plight is demonstrated, as these Jews tend to be ugly, both morally/ethnically and physically. Morrie Kessler (Chuck Low) in *Goodfellas*, for example, is a Jew who fraternises with Italian and Irish gangsters but whose incessant nagging for money leads directly to his death when an ice pick is shoved into his neck.

With his skinhead haircut, Vinz in the French film *La Haine* aims to resist 'the very stereotype of the Jew' (Loshitzky 2005: 138). As Yosefa Loshitzky argues, Vinz seeks 'to construct a new image of the diasporic Jew which not only responds to traditional images of the Jew in western culture but also to the weakness and vulnerability associated with the Jew as a victim of the Holocaust' (2005: 138). However, despite Loshitzky's assertion that, 'it is the Jewish male who is assigned to revenge Jewish victimisation epitomised by the Holocaust' (2005: 138), Vinz is unable to enact revenge. From the moment we meet him, Vinz is obsessively fascinated with weaponry: he fantasises about killing, forming his fingers into a mimic gun that he fires into the bathroom mirror. He fetishises a gun he has stolen from a cop. But, as we shall see in Chapter 8, he can only exercise this power in private and in his imagination, emphasised by his inability to use the real gun. When he is confronted with a bleeding, powerless skinhead who has attacked his friends he is unable to shoot him, coding 'the larger Jewish [diasporic] struggle with the issue of power (or lack of power) and particularly post-Holocaust power' (Loshitzky 2005: 141). It is at this point that Vinz 'acknowledges his "weakness", his basic respect for human life and his fear of killing. Vinz confronts his "Jewish weakness" exactly at the moment when revenge and power can finally be obtained and even be morally justified' (Loshitzky 2005: 141). Vinz 'renounces hatred, revenge and violence' by handing the gun to his friend, but in a further irony the now-unarmed Vinz is shot and killed by an armed police detective. 'Renouncing violence by the Jew, Kassovitz implies, results in his liquidation' (Loshitzky 2005: 142). Thus, although Vinz is

> revengeful and obsessed with violence, at the moment of 'truth' he is discovered as 'weak'. Despite his fantasies of violence, real violence makes Vinz sick. The diasporic post-Holocaust Jew is unable to redeem the shame inflicted on the Holocaust Jew by the possessors of absolute power. It is not surprising therefore that in the final scene the Jew returns to his 'normal', 'natural' place: that of the victim [Loshitzky 2005: 142].

Vinz's weakness is emphasised in another sequence. He and the 'pure' French drug dealer, as implied by his Gallic name, Astérix (François Levantal), and Vinz compare guns hidden deep inside their trousers. Naturally, this is not merely a competition in gun size but a phallic game of power whereby the Jew's circumcised penis is measured against that of the Gentile (in his previous film, Métisse, Kassovitz similarly created a Jew worried about the size of his penis). Astérix then challenges Vinz to a game of Russian roulette, and the Jew is found wanting, losing his nerve. As Vinz leaves, Astérix demonstrates how he has surreptitiously neutered Vinz's weapon, publicly reinforcing Vinz's inferiority and feelings of humiliation and defeat, compounded by the waiting policemen on the street outside. Loshitzky describes the competition as 'a performance, a staging of symbolic penis envy of the French Jew towards the French non-Jew who demonstrates unquestionable superiority over the male Jew in mastering his pistol/penis' (2005: 142). That the flamboyant Astérix is able to best the Jew exposes how even the queer Gentile is tougher than the straight Jew.

American Buffalo portrays another post-Holocaust Jew. Teach is 'outraged equally by the Riverside's charging thirty-seven cents for coffee and by the inhumanity of the Holocaust' (Kane 1999: 51). Like Vinz, he is outwardly tough, a 'macho "super-Jew" who defends his right to carry a gun', presenting 'an image of the post-Holocaust Jew as "macho warrior"' (Kane 1999: 53). As Teach says, 'And take those fuckers that went into the concentration camps. You think they went in there by choice. They were dragged in there Don, kicking and screaming.' As well as foul-mouthed, he is prone to violence. He hits an innocent boy over the head with a telephone and threatens to 'go in there and gut this motherfucker'. The phrases 'It's kickass or kissass' and 'Action talks, bullshit walks' sum up his credo. Teach fancies himself as a businessman pursuing the legitimate concerns of free enterprise, and postures as tough as he plans the heist of a rare coin. In reality, however, he is merely a small-time crook whose plotting is futile, and who finally erupts in violence when his complete inadequacy and failure to carry out even a simple robbery becomes apparent and the frustration becomes unbearable.

In his *Assassin(s)*, Kassovitz again blurs the queer/tough divide. Kassovitz plays apprentice assassin Max Peloj, who is offered an apprenticeship in the world of assassins-for-hire, violence and murder when, by chance, he meets Wagner (Michel Serrault), an elderly contract killer. Wagner teaches Max to be a 'craftsman', to adhere to an ethical code, to complete the contract even if offered more money not to; as Wagner tells him, 'I have morals.' During the first half of the film, although an assassin, Max certainly does not project a tough image. He remains a queer/sissy, sensitive Jew. This is most clearly demonstrated when, as spectators, we are made to endure a 12-minute sequence that appears to unravel in real time as Max commits his first murder – that of a man named Vidal – under Wagner's tutelage. Higbee describes the sequence:

> Max does not simply appear, blow his elderly victim away and then move on to his next target [...] but rather suffers, and is forced to confront, along with the spectator, the 'reality' and consequences of the violent act for both victim and assassin. Vidal is viciously beaten, dragged and bound by his assailants, before Wagner bullies his young protégé into shooting the elderly man with his own hunting rifle. As Max weeps, struggling to keep the weapon trained on his victim, the camera cuts to Vidal's bloody face, filmed from the point of view of the young assassin [2006: 111].

'You're a nice kid,' Wagner tells him, after helping him to steady the gun during the killing. A teenager tells Max that he has no balls. Ultimately, Max becomes a victim at the hands of Wagner, who kills him. Our final glimpse of Max is a bird's-eye-view shot, focusing in on his face, his head framed by the pool of blood emanating from the back of his skull.

In *Miller's Crossing*, Bernie is a gay small-time criminal gangster. He is a loner whose 'friends didn't really like him'. As his sister puts it, 'he's different, people think he's a degenerate. People think he's scum.' This is because he is 'a cowardly, double-dealing, crooked weasel of a man' (Bergan 2001: 45) who has no 'ethics'. He is not a *mensch*. The film emphasises Bernie's isolation, homosexuality and Jewishness, triply queering him as the weak Jew of the diaspora. Bernie is referred to as the '*schmatte*' (Yiddish: a rag; a ragged or shabby garment), 'Sheeny' (a contemptuous term for a Jewish person), 'Hebrew' and 'Yid'. Thus Bernie embodies 'the Jewish villain' and the 'Jew-Sissy' marked by a high level of effeminacy (Friedman 2007: 36). He is the stereotypical hysterical and unnatural Jew. Turturro comments about his character, 'He's a guy who's trying to be a survivor. He's constantly on the move. Which is kind of Jewish history' (quoted in Horst 1999: 109).

Bernie is the venal main bookmaker of Italian boss Johnny Caspar (Jon Polito). He becomes dissatisfied with the honest money he makes from the '*vig*' (Yiddish: '*vigorish*', the amount charged by a bookmaker, or bookie, for his services or the interest on a loan), and is selling tips on how Caspar bets. Consequently, Caspar's anticipated profits suffer and he suspects that Bernie has been fiddling the odds on boxing matches, and so orders his death. Bernie is subsequently led to Miller's Crossing, 'a wooded area

Bernie Bernbaum in *Miller's Crossing*.

outside of town', by Tom Reagan, where he is to be shot. Throughout this sequence, Bernie is 'prostrate and humiliatingly weak' (Russell 2001: 61), emphasising his victim status. Bernie loses any semblance of dignity or pride, grovelling and pleading for his life, with abject fear and naked terror. He is the Jewish hysteric. 'Look into your heart,' he wails repeatedly. 'I'm praying to you.' More than one critic notes the deployment of archetypal Holocaust iconography in this sequence (Desalm 1999, Horst 1999, Russell 2001). At the determined moment of his death, however, Bernie's pleas for his life are answered. Tom takes pity on him, fires a shot into the air and tells him to disappear forever as payment for his compassion. By sparing his life and sending him into exile, as if doomed to be the Wandering Jew, Tom thus demonstrates a mercy that the Nazis never did. Yet Bernie double-crosses Tom, his saviour. He is a fink, sacrificing his lover Mink (Steve Buscemi) in order to save his own life, even laughing about his distasteful actions. Tom returns and shoots Bernie in the forehead.

Within the narrative economy of the film Bernie is seen as deserving of such punishment. Because he has no qualms about murdering his own lover, he cannot be trusted in a world that already doubts him because he is a Jew:

> Several elements encourage us to see his death as just reward for his own risky manoeuvrings – his switch from whining-pathetic victim to arrogant blackmailer [...] The film doesn't present Bernie as an innocent victim, and it doesn't allow the viewer to empathise with him, but rather demands that the victim be seen as someone who is only marginally more sympathetic and less corrupt than the men who are calling the shots [Horst 1999: 110].

Therefore, although Bernie ultimately becomes a victim, he is not a blameless sacrificial one.

In *Deep Cover* (dir. Bill Duke, 1992), David Jason (Jeff Goldblum) is 'the "outsider" Jew and insufficiently manly drug dealer' (Lubiano 1997: 142). He is the fast-talking (he is told, 'you talk too much'), wisecracking nervous Jew as brain, a combination of the two roles that he and Will Smith would play later in *Independence Day*. Despite his biblical and Greek names, which connote images of victory against superior forces, David is very much presented as the queer victimised diaspora Jew. He 'wears suits that are European cut – emphasising the Jewish lawyer as the European outsider in the American (albeit illegal drug) mise-en-scène' (Lubiano 1997: 142). He is well read, quoting Delmore Schwartz's 'In Dreams Begin

Responsibilities'. Furthermore, his queerness and Jewishness are both foregrounded as his arch-rival repeatedly questions David's heterosexual masculinity: 'bar mitzvah boy', '*shmuck*', 'nice Jewish boy', 'kike', 'pussy', 'faggot', 'it's a good thing he never went to jail, Gopher, because if he came out, he'd have an asshole big enough to swallow a watermelon' and 'are you growing balls?' David overcomes his queerness to become, albeit temporarily, a tough Jew. A black leather trenchcoat and sunglasses replace the European-cut suits, as he becomes more confident, less nervously talkative and colder. Sartorially resembling a Jewish Terminator towards the end of the film, he is able to kill his enemy, shooting him in the buttocks. Ultimately, however, David's partner (Laurence Fishburne), an undercover cop posing as a drug dealer, kills him, demonstrating that David was always in too deep (or, sexually, not deep enough).

Since Jews were historically involved in gangsterism, including Ace Rothstein, Meyer Lansky, Dutch Schultz and Bugsy Siegel, they have also long been represented in film, both in terms of historical and fictional creations. *Carlito's Way* presents a similar central Jewish character to both David and Bernie, in that he is seduced by venality but is out of his depth. David Kleinfeld (Sean Penn) is a corrupt, lowlife, coke-sniffing 'shyster' Mafia lawyer. He is described as 'filthy', 'a fucking cockroach'. One of his clients tells him, 'I never liked you, Kleinfeld. Not 'cause you're a Jew. I know plenty of Jews. It's 'cause you're a lyin' piece of shit.' He has a red Jewfro and wears sharp, flashy suits. At the same time, he identifies as a Jew: a *mezuzah* can be seen on the doorpost of his office. He is ambitious and deeply amoral, as well as spoiled, narcissistic, sneaky and smarmy. He is guilty of money-laundering, jury tampering and bribery. Like David in *Deep Cover* he is drawn to the glamour of crime, but without realising the consequences, and we watch as he steadily loses control to his cocaine habit and greed. Aptly, he owns a boat called the *Jezebel*. His Latina girlfriend describes him as a 'sexy animal' after he is shown having sex with her in the toilets of a nightclub. Yet later in the film this tough posturing is shown to be a mere façade – he takes so much cocaine that he cannot function fully sexually. Although he carries a gun, his friend and client Carlito Brigante (Al Pacino) tells him to hand over the weapon with the words, 'Since when are you a tough guy?' Kleinfeld replies, 'I'm not some law school *schmuck* who never saw a bad guy before.' But his pleas ring hollow until he murders a crime boss from whom he ripped off one million dollars, repeatedly smashing him over the head after having killed his son. Carlito warns him, 'You ain't a lawyer any more, Dave. You're a gangster now. You're on the other side.' Ultimately, Kleinfeld does not last long on 'the other side', as he is hospitalised with knife wounds before, in an echo of *Miller's Crossing* and foreshadowing Penn's role in *Milk*, being shot in the forehead, his blood splattering against the wall of his hospital room.

Where such films differ from other genres in offering up the Jew as victim is in their refusal to do so simply because of the Jew's religion and/or ethnicity, as, say, compared to Holocaust films. While the Jewish characters' humiliations still tend to mark their difference, within the conventions and ethical codes of the gangster film these Jews deserve to die for they either kill and/or cross their friends. Their executions, then, are normalised, because they are in accordance with the demands of the gangster code and not necessarily the result of their ethnic/religious identities.

Jews oppressing Jews

Typically, Jews are victims of non-Jews in cinema and rarely, were they victims of each other before 1990. But in contemporary cinema images of Jews oppressing, hurting or killing Jews are multiplying. In part it is a reflection of the historical Jewish involvement in gangsterism. It is also part of the growing normalisation of Jews in cinema, in contrast to a previous tendency towards hagiography. Another possible cause of the onset of Jew/ ess-on-Jew/ess violence in film was the assassination of Israeli Prime Minister Yitzhak Rabin by Yigal Amir, a radical right-wing Orthodox Jew who opposed the signing of the Oslo Accords, in 1995, which dramatically illustrated the issue of Jew/ess killing Jew/ess (Barr 1996). In *Bugsy* (dir. Barry Levinson, 1991) Benjamin 'Bugsy' Siegel (Warren Beatty) murders Harry Greenberg (Elliott Gould). *We Own the Night* (dir. James Gray, 2007) features Jews on both sides of the law, as US police and Russian gangsters, who kill each other regardless of their shared ethnicity. In both *Defiance* (dir. Edward Zwick, 2008) and *The Grey Zone*, Jews are shown killing other Jews during the Holocaust. *A Stranger Among Us* features a Jewess who murders her husband. *The Believer* has a Jewish neo-Nazi attack and abuse his fellow Jews. *A Price Above Rubies* and *Kadosh/Sacred* both depict *haredi* misogyny in the form of domestic violence and rape.

In *Lucky Number Slevin,* Jewish gambler Max (Scott Gibson) bets borrowed money on a fixed horse race. The mobsters financing the fix discover others betting on it, leading them to murder Max, his wife and his son. One of the mobsters is Jewish gangster Shlomo the Rabbi (Ben Kingsley), thus in *Slevin* Jew kills Jew. Twenty years later, Max's son Slevin Kelevra (Josh Hartnett) is still alive and seeking to avenge his family. *Haredi* bodyguards surround Shlomo, and two ex-Mossad agents protect his son. Slevin, however, kills all of them and there is a body count of at least eleven Jews during the course of the film. Many shots depict them either dead or dying, but in general deserving of their fates.[20] It is a clear reversal of the past that many of these Jews were killed by a co-religionist. Furthermore, they deserve to die because they have not only participated in the murder of his parents, but also paid to have him killed as a young boy. Since many of those Slevin shoots are *haredim*, the film also clearly takes sides in which representation it prefers, as the secular tough Jew kills the transgressive, tough and queer *haredim*.

Israeli incompetence

Even the reputation of the Israeli soldier or Mossad secret agent, typically represented as tough, is reversed in contemporary cinema. This is attributable to a number of factors. Decreasing identification with Israel coincided with deep divisions among diaspora Jews and Israelis, characterised by 'the growing political polarisation between religious and secular visions of Israel's future' (Aviv and Shneer 2005: xvi). Israel's invasion of Lebanon in 1982, the First (1987–93) and Second *Intifadas* (2000–5) in the occupied territories, Rabin's assassination, the Second Lebanon War of 2006, Operation Cast Lead of 2008, and the perception of the continuing intransigence of right-wing Israeli governments backed by zealous settlers and religious fanatics, led many diaspora Jews to question their ties to the state. Many publicly refused to support uncritically the actions and policies of the Israeli government, creating deep and vocal rifts within diaspora Jewry. This became particularly evident in the United States, where Steven M. Cohen and Ari Kelman (2007) found that 'non-Orthodox younger Jews, on the whole, feel much less attached to Israel than their elders', with many professing 'a near-total absence of positive feelings'. Peter Beinart controversially wrote in 2010, 'Particularly in the younger generations, fewer and fewer American Jewish liberals are Zionists; fewer and fewer American Jewish Zionists are liberal.'

The fallout of these trends is increasingly negative portrayals of the tough Israeli. As early as 1981 portraits of Israelis as suave assassins, villainous diplomats and manipulative undercover agents appeared in *Eyewitness* (dir. Peter Yates, 1981) and *The Little Drummer Girl* (dir. George Roy Hill, 1984), but these have increased in number in the post-1990 period. In *Homicide*, (dir. David Mamet, 1991) Israeli secret agents blackmail and double-cross a Jewish cop despite his assistance. Two ex-Mossad bodyguards assigned to protect Yitzchok in *Lucky Number Slevin* fail in their duty and are outwitted and shot dead by a supposedly weak diaspora Jew. *You Don't Mess with the Zohan* pokes fun at the image of the Israeli super-agent who ultimately fulfils his dream by cutting and styling hair, as well as the ex-pat and ex-military Israelis who populate New York City. And *Nick and Norah's Infinite Playlist* lampoons a wannabe Israeli band 'Oz-rael' ('We bring the Jew fire […] it's like anarchy meets Zionism, you know. It's ironic'), whose sleazy singer is using his Jewish-American girlfriend in hopes her famous dad will produce his 'Jew-power' album.

The Sum of All Fears (dir. Phil Alden Robinson, 2002) opens with an image of Israeli military might, as a nuclear missile is loaded onto a tactical Israeli Air Force fighter aircraft. However, it morphs into one of weakness and victimisation when its incompetent pilot stoops down to retrieve a fallen photograph of his wife and child, distracting him from an oncoming missile that hits his aircraft. Shot down over the Golan Heights, the sequence

Yitzchok the Fairy in *Lucky Number Slevin*.

ends with a portrayal of the jet's smouldering remains. The nuclear missile is recovered and sold to neo-Nazis, who smuggle it out from under the Israelis' noses at Haifa port no less. Several close-ups of the packing crate, inscribed with the words 'Haifa' in both English and Hebrew, serve to reinforce this image of Israeli incompetence. The bomb is eventually detonated in the United States, bringing the world to the brink of all-out nuclear war.

Munich begins and ends with images of the capture and killing of the eleven Israeli athletes at the 1972 Olympic Games, illustrating Israel's failure to protect its citizens abroad. The counter-assassination team assigned to kill the leaders of Black September responsible for the massacre, together with the larger organisation of which it was a part, are not represented as being as efficient as Mossad's global reputation suggests. Mistakes, blunders and errors occur throughout the film. The team are unduly reliant on a shadowy French outfit for their logistics, weapons, intelligence and safe houses, and this leads to one mix-up when both Israelis and Palestinians share a room for the night. Three of the original five members are killed, one at the hands of a female mercenary, which not only problematises his masculine identity, but also in death his body is represented as passive and hence feminine, submissive and impotent. Another, Belgian bomb specialist Robert (Mathieu Kassovitz), reprising his role in *Assassin(s)*, is recruited without anyone realising that his actual skill was in *dismantling* such devices. One bomb he makes is so large that an Israeli woman, honeymooning with her Lebanese husband in the room next to the target, is blinded in the explosion. Robert later dies when a bomb he is creating (accidentally?) explodes. Ultimately, the team are ineffectual against the hydra-like rise of terror and, by the end of the film, its leader Avner becomes an obsessive paranoid. Convinced that Mossad wants him dead, he rejects Israel, abandons his homeland for the United States, permanently relocating his family to Brooklyn, suggesting that this part of the diaspora is the safest haven for Jews.

Given that they are at the forefront of the conflict, Israeli films are even harsher in their depictions. In *Walk on Water*, Mossad operative Eyal (Lior Ashkenazi) moves from tough to impotent during the course of the film. In the opening sequences we witness him effortlessly assassinate a Hamas leader by injecting him with poison. By the end of the film, however, literally paralysed by doubt, he is unable to kill an elderly Nazi war criminal. Indeed, compounding his humiliation, the killing is carried out by the Nazi's gay grandson. In this way, Eyal 'comes to opt out of the killing machine, revealing the "feminine" side of the macho Israeli' (Shohat 2010: 265). *Beaufort, Waltz with Bashir* and *Lebanon* all depict the Israeli military during the 1982 invasion and subsequent occupation of Lebanon in a less than flattering light. Finally, in the Israeli film *Ha-Hov* (dir. Assaf Bernstein, 2007), remade in Britain as *The Debt* (dir. John Madden, 2010), three young Mossad agents are sent on a secret mission to capture and kill a notorious Nazi war criminal. When, thirty years later, a man claiming to be that Nazi surfaces in the Ukraine, it is revealed that not only did they fail in their original mission (the Nazi escapes and permanently scars the heroine) but also they have covered up their failure for three decades. Overall, therefore, these images impugn the once-sacrosanct notion of Israeli efficiency, and suggest that the Mossad agent/IDF soldier is not as one-dimensionally tough as presented in the past.

Conclusion

Increasingly, contemporary cinema complicates the picture of the Jew/ess as victim. Films in the post-1990 period no longer present images of Jewish victimisation as simply monolithic and undeserving. This representation of the Jewish victim not only complicates the queer/tough divide, but also includes those Jews who, within the codes and conventions of their respective genres, deserve to die or lose. In addition, these Jews are often victimised and/or killed by other Jews, further blurring the picture. The most conclusive proof of a paradigm shift, however, is that this picture widens to include the previously untouchable tough Israeli Jew/ess. The polarities of Jewish imagery, then, are being normalised.

CHAPTER 5

Agency

Jewish James and Jane Bonds

In response to the nationalistic antisemitism of the late nineteenth and early twentieth centuries there emerged an emphasis on Jewish 'toughness, courage and physicality [...] loyalty, self-discipline, readiness for self-sacrifice, robustness, manliness,' that is the inversion of the weak, victimised Jew (Breines 1990: 126–27). Initially, this was encoded in the body of the 'Muscle-Jew'. As Zionism developed, he was replaced by 'the hardy, bronzed kibbutznik' (Breines 1990: 3), followed in the mid-twentieth century in Israel by the IDF paratrooper and the Mossad agent and in the United States by the Jewish boxer and gangster. In the late 1960s and early 1970s, US culture and literature saw the emergence of 'more manly and muscular types, sometimes referred to as Jewish James Bonds' who 'kill their enemies, and take their women to bed with neurosis-free, seemingly un-Jewish alacrity, as if to avenge all the helpless Jewish victims of history' (Breines 1990: 3–4).

In contemporary cinema, representations of tough, Jewish agency have proliferated. They reject the centuries-old stereotype of the Jew as unfit for or unwilling to perform military service, and have widened to embrace the Jewess. This is even the case in regard to the Holocaust, typically an arena for emphasising Jewish passivity. In doing so, however, these Jews are not one-dimensionally tough, adhering to *goyim naches*, as they often exhibit ethical values, that is *Yiddishkeit* and *menschlikayt*.

'Don't fuck with the Jews': Jews as (ethical) Jaws

If earlier I offered up the idea of Jews who, metaphorically, cannot swim, here I shall talk about their converse: Jews as Jaws, or Jewish hunters and killers. *Munich* reverses the traditional paradigm of the Jew-as-victim. At least one reviewer described the team as handsome, scrupulous, exceptionally well-mannered Jewish agents. Their leader, Avner, is the son of a Holocaust survivor, thus transforming the victimised into the victimiser. Played by Eric Bana, a non-Jewish hunk, his casting draws upon his previous incarnations as psychos and killers in *Chopper* (dir. Andrew Dominik, 2000), *Black Hawk Down* (dir. Ridley Scott, 2001) and *The Hulk* (dir. Ang Lee, 2003). As played by Bana, Avner is certainly a handsome and loving husband (even if he does abandon his family and home for the greater cause of his homeland). As the only member of the team depicted naked, he is the fulfilment of the Zionist project of a 'Jewry of muscles'. He is virile and shown having loving sex with his beautiful, flushed and pregnant wife. The subsequent birth of their child proves his potency, and ultimately Avner is presented as a good father when he takes his family to the relative safety of pre-9/11 Brooklyn. Indeed, Bana's performance is inter-textually and inter-referentially celebrated by young American Jews for its reversal of the typical cinematic queer Jew-as-victim paradigm. In *Knocked Up*, Jew Tang Clan members Ben, Jay (Jay Baruchel) and Jonah (Jonah Hill) discuss the sexually alluring power of *Munich*'s protagonist:

> Ben: You know what movie I just saw again the other day which is fucking, like, mind-blowing, and I haven't seen it since it came out? *Munich*.
> Jay: *Munich!*
> Jonah: Dude, *Munich* fuckin' rules.
> Jay: *Munich* is awesome!
> Ben: That movie was Eric Bana kicking fuckin' ass! [They all agree.]
> Ben (cont'd): Dude, every movie with Jews, we're the ones getting killed. *Munich* flips it on its ear. We cappin' motherfuckers.
> Jonah: Not only killing, but fuckin', like, takin' names.
> Ben: If any of us get laid tonight, it's because of Eric Bana in *Munich*.
> Jonah: I agree with that.
> Jay: I agree.

Their admiration for Avner, as a major ego boost to the contemporary Jew, says much about the changing cultural representations and cinematic stereotypes of Jews.

These Jews are, on the surface, assassins driven by bloodlust as well as vengeance. Jewish officials are shown to be zealous, chilly and clearly using the team. Their handler Ephraim (Geoffrey Rush) instructs them, 'You'll do what the terrorists do. Do you think they report back to home base?' The team is seen killing in cold blood and sometimes taking cavalier, intemperate and undisciplined revenge. Steve (Daniel Craig), the South African driver, articulates these sentiments unambiguously: 'the only blood that matters to me is Jewish blood' and 'Don't fuck with the Jews.' Jewish violence is therefore initially presented as 'brutal, heartless and methodical, not the expression of individuals willingly sacrificing themselves for a just cause but the coldly mechanical and calculated product of the intelligence apparatus of an aggressive state' (Schoenfeld 2006).

Yet these agents are not monochromatically tough. With the exceptions of the non-Jewish Eric Bana and Daniel Craig, announced as the next James Bond while filming *Munich*, they are in the main presented as *ordinary* and normal. Unlike their superiors, they have moral qualms about their task, and as their collective mood sinks the film gets darker in both tone and lighting. With the exception of Steve, they struggle with the assignment, disagreeing with it, yet unable to refuse it at the same time. The team grapples with the 'core problem of the tough Jew': 'that to enter the world of bodies politically speaking and to be normal there *means* to kill' (Breines 1990: 48). Reversing enduring antisemitic slurs concerning the Jew's relationship to money, in which the Jew is stereotyped as caring more for the financial than the human costs of their actions, *Munich* articulates 'a deep, historically formed Jewish need: the need to be ethical' through financial metaphors (Breines 1990: 73). Avner is admonished to obtain receipts for all expenditure, no matter how trivial, and his fellow team members fret over such things as the price per kill. It is clear that their *menschlikayt* is affecting them, as they consider the moral/ethical *costs* of their actions. Their first kill, Carl (Ciarán Hinds) notes ruefully, 'cost us, by my calculations, $352,000.' Similarly, Robert wonders, 'we're supposed to be righteous. It's a beautiful thing, that's Jewish. That's what I knew, that's what I was taught. And now I'm losing it and, I lose that, that's everything, that's my soul.' He tells us that his civilian occupation is a toy-maker, and we see him begin to revert to his toy-making role, constructing small wire figurines after a botched, hand-grenade assassination. This attempted return to his former life signifies a desire and longing to regain the *menschlikayt* that he feels he is 'losing'. Thus *Munich* contrasts the conflicting concepts of *goyim naches* and *Yiddishkeit*, that is the 'muscular defense of state power against its enemies' versus 'a loquacious, *heimisch*-folksy moralism' (Levine 2006).

Indeed, echoing the film's theme of the futility of meeting violence with violence, the characters' *menschlikayt* is in conflict with their Mossad duties. This conflict is signified by the duality of the assassins' lifestyles and occupations. Avner is a cook, and is often depicted wearing an apron, frantically, almost compulsively, chopping and preparing food, as if he is desperately trying to retain his true identity. The scene that follows Avner's meeting with Papa (Michael Lonsdale), during which he is told that his hands are too big to be those of a cook ('I'd have been a master but I have thick stupid butcher's hands, like yours. We are tragic men'), shows Avner quite literally 'cooking up a storm', manically chopping vegetables, as if protesting Papa's insinuation that he has the hands of a butcher and is therefore a murderer.

Furthermore, Avner's role as the father/provider figure, signified by his flying home illicitly, endangering himself and potentially jeopardising the mission, to witness the birth of his daughter, is in direct conflict with his Mossad duties, and symbolised by Papa's suggestion of 'butcher's hands, gentle souls'. Avner wrestles with his actions as a soldier, father, husband, son and lover, resulting in 'a male anxiety that balances macho aggressiveness' with 'awkward uncertainty' (Friedman 2006: 7–8). He never fully knows how to relate to his family and 'fumbles around his emotions' (Friedman 2006: 7–8). This is highlighted at the end of the film when scenes of Avner making love to his wife are intercut with those of the last minutes of the 1972 hostage crisis. Avner reaches a hard, sad climax in time with the soundtrack, just as the terrorists open fire on the Israeli athletes and coach, entwining love and death. While sex provides both catharsis and redemption, allowing Avner 'to regain his humanity and cleanse himself, through an act of lovemaking, of the arguably immoral deeds which he committed' (Friedman 2007: 184), 'lovemaking' might be the incorrect term here because Avner does not appear to be engaged in pleasuring his wife but rather in working out his own ethical issues over what he did in the name of his homeland.

You Don't Mess with the Zohan, more satirically, mocks one-dimensional Israeli toughness. Zohan is the IDF's finest counter-terrorist agent, a 'Rembrandt with a grenade'. A skilled fighting machine, he is fit, muscled, complete with beard and large Jewfro, and able to take on cohorts of terrorists single-handedly. He does not make mistakes. Zohan is not only physically and sexually imposing, but also a superhero with quasi-supernatural powers (similar to several other Sandler characters). At the same time, he is a *mensch*, a caring and decent individual who aims to minimise 'collateral damage' (civilian casualties). Yet, Zohan has always dreamed of being a hairdresser. When he tells his parents of his dream they laugh and mock him as a *'faygeleh'*, prompting him to sob uncontrollably in bed that night. Sick and tired of killing, and in pursuit of his goal, Zohan fakes his own death during a game of hand-grenade tennis against his arch-enemy the Phantom (John Turturro). He stows away to New York City, trims his beard and restyles his 'fro into the 'Avalon', a Paul Mitchell haircut popular in the 1980s, in order to pass unrecognised as 'Scrappy Coco', a super-stylist and hairdresser, a combination that has a hint of Sacha Baron-Cohen's creations Borat and Brüno (indeed sections of the film are very reminiscent of the former). In a mockery of his tough Israeli origins, Zohan must be 'the best' by excelling at cutting and styling, a refrain he constantly reiterates throughout the film. Indeed, Zohan's hairdressing

Zohan Dvir in *You Don't Mess with the Zohan*.

prowess is comparable to that of Edward Scissorhands (Johnny Depp) in Tim Burton's 1990 film of the same name. Oori (Ido Mosseri), another ex-pat Israeli, recognises Zohan and they become friends. Oori calls the Zohan 'a hair homo', a suggestion reinforced by his cut-off shorts and Mariah Carey T-shirt. While this is undoubtedly a sly dig at Israeli machismo (and homophobia), it serves to collapse the previously rigid boundaries between the queer and tough Jew that are increasingly being reversed by contemporary cinematic representations.

Effortlessly violent, the Zohan is also a master of beauty and adornment. And although not gay – having already demonstrated his extraordinary cock(manship) in Israel with a bevy of Israeli beauties, Zohan repeatedly reemphasises his physical prowess in the film by having sex with a succession of middle-aged and elderly women, before eventually obtaining his prize: his Palestinian employer Dalia (Emmanuelle Chriqui) – his combination of queer and toughness would not necessarily be out of place in such a film as *Yossi & Jagger* or *Walk on Water*, two Israeli films featuring a love affair between two soldiers stationed in Lebanon and a tough Mossad agent who eventually overcomes his anti-German, anti-Arab and homophobic prejudices respectively. Eventually, the Zohan sheds his toughness forever: he refuses to fight the Phantom, forms an alliance with him to fight against a band of racists sent to provoke an Israeli–Palestinian conflict in New York, marries the Phantom's sister and opens a hair salon with her. (The Phantom opens a shoe store in the same shopping mall.) Ultimately, therefore, the film emphasises the Semitic bond between the Israelis and Palestinians in terms of looks, food, behaviour and even language, reinforced by the casting of Turturro who, as we have seen, has played a succession of Jews. In doing so, *You Don't Mess with the Zohan* is a vindication of the so-called queer values of *menschlikyat* over the tough ones of *goyim naches*.

Victims-cum-victimisers

The role of Jews in the invention and development of the superhero genre, in particular the X-Men, Superman, Batman, Spiderman, Iron Man, the Fantastic Four, inter alia, is well known. Here, the representation of Erik Magnus Lehnsherr (Ian McKellen) in the *X-Men* films (dirs Bryan Singer, 2000, 2003, Brett Ratner, 2006, Matthew Vaughn, 2011), as both victim and victimiser simultaneously, stands out. The opening sequence of *X-Men* (reprised in *X-Men: First Class*) depicts Erik (Brett Morris), a young Jewish boy, being forcibly separated from his parents at the gates of a Nazi death camp in Poland in 1944. Erik is a Jewish (he is wearing a yellow badge) genetic mutant who possesses special mind-based powers. As his family is led away, he demonstrates a telepathic ability to generate a magnetic field with which he can manipulate, bend or deflect metal objects, here the camp gates. In this way, his representation invokes antisemitic discourses that constructed Jews as 'super intelligent' and 'freakish', especially given that his mutant power derives from his mind – Jew as brain/*Yiddische kopf* – rather than his body, which, in contrast, is much weaker. At the same time, however, his mutant powers are a reversal of the traditional superhero representation in that Erik is openly Jewish and not *hyper*-masculine, unlike both Superman and Spiderman, who were only conceptually/symbolically Jewish.

Erik is thus triply marked, as a Jew, a Holocaust victim/survivor and a mutant. Erik's status as survivor is reinforced in narrative terms. Scarred, this traumatic moment is seared forever on his body, memory and consciousness: 'I have heard these arguments before. It was a long time ago' and 'Women and children. Whole families destroyed, simply because they were born different.' We see a close-up shot of the tattooed number on his arm. We learn that he is also a victim of Nazi medical experimentation. Despite his genetic powers, he is powerless to prevent the murder of his parents and the wider genocide, and is thus seemingly no different from other Jews. Yet, once liberated and grown up, Erik (Michael Fassbender) uses his powers to track down and kill Nazis. He is transformed into a muscular and militant, angry and avenging tough Jew. In reference to his mutancy, Erik adopts the name 'Magneto' as an adult.

Magneto is superficially represented as an evil Jew. He fits Russell's comment on Barton Fink: 'an incendiary study of intellect minus soul' (2001: 88). Magneto grows up with an obsession to supplant humankind with mutants like himself. In the film's diegesis, as the leader of 'the Brotherhood of Evil Mutants', whose aim it is to overthrow humanity, he is the villain, juxtaposed to the 'hero', Dr Charles Xavier (James McAvoy/Patrick Stewart), who, in contrast, founds a school to teach mutant teenagers 'to learn to use our powers for the benefit of mankind'. As Baron points out, in its representation of Xavier as a man confined to a wheelchair whose special power is mind-reading, the films reverse 'the traditional stereotype of Jewish males as intellectuals with weak bodies' and apply it to the Gentile (2003: 47). Furthermore, it is Xavier, and not Magneto, who is the *mensch*, pursuing the traditional Jewish social justice agenda of *Tikkun Olam* (Hebrew: 'Fixing/healing the world'). As Norah in *Nick and Norah's Infinite Playlist* explains, 'There's this part of Judaism that I like. *Tikkun Olam*. It said that the world is broken into pieces and everyone has to find them and put them back together.'

A further reading of the film suggests that both are heroes who, like contemporary American Jewish Democrats and Republicans (mainly the former), use *Yiddishkeit* to achieve their different political objectives. While Xavier is the *mensch*, unequivocally decent, using his powers for the benefit of humanity, Magneto embodies *goyim naches*, but is not Xavier's binary opposite nor represented as unequivocally 'evil'. Magneto's behaviour and beliefs are given a convincing ideological foundation. In their insistence on depicting events from his childhood and constantly reminding us of his survivor status, as well as the Holocaust, through a series of visual and aural

signifiers, the films give Magneto genuinely understandable motives, summed up by his words 'Never again.' Indeed, a bigoted senator (Bruce Davison) proposes a bill to register and number all mutants, transforming them into symbolic Jews, persecuted in a similar fashion to the Nazi racial laws. Magneto wants to prevent another Holocaust, albeit this time against mutants. In this light, then, it is the non-mutants who are evil in their desire to locate, categorise and demonise others simply because they are different. Furthermore, perhaps it is Xavier and his optimistic Panglossian naiveté (for which he pays the ultimate price) who

Magneto in *X-Men*.   is the real, albeit unwitting, villain of the films, for he seeks to protect the very humans who seek to kill him and his kind. Overall, then, Magneto presents an unusual combination: the intellectual Jew defined by his mind, but with tough *goyische* values.

Jews who fight back

In his survey of Holocaust films in the last two decades, Baron observed how 'not all Jews accept their fate as victims' (2005: 105). Indeed, films in which Jews fight back during the Shoah, setting out to reverse the representation of European Jews as simply helpless passive victims of the Nazis, proliferate in contemporary cinema. In *Defiance*, a film based on actual historical events, a band of rural Jews, led by a trio of brothers, the Bielskis, wage war against the Nazis and their collaborators from their stronghold in the woods in German-occupied Byelorussia. In the wake of the invading German army, local fascists kill the Bielskis' parents. Hiding in the forest, the brothers resolve to resist the invaders and their allies, and to avenge their parents' deaths. On learning which pro-Nazi militiaman murdered his parents, the leader of the partisans, Tuvia Bielski (Daniel Craig), kills him and his sons. Dubbing themselves the Bielski Otriad (Brigade), and based behind German lines in the forests, the brothers attack German convoys, acquire arms and attract Jewish refugees from the ghettoes. Other Jews join the brothers, becoming the largest Jewish partisan band of the war, killing more Germans and saving more Jews than any other. As their leader, Craig revisits his role in *Munich* as well as James Bond, riding a white horse (that he later nobly shoots to feed the hungry), clearly signifying that these Jews are tough. Indeed, the brothers are brought before a Soviet army officer, who looks them scornfully up and down. 'Jews don't fight,' he scoffs. 'These Jews do,' growls Tuvia.

At the same time, like their counterparts in *Munich*, these Jews do not want to become like their enemies. The Jews in *Defiance* kill Nazis and their collaborators, but they periodically stop to debate the merits and drawbacks of killing, expressing their *menschlikayt*. 'We may be hunted like animals – but we will not become animals,' Tuvia exhorts his followers, reflecting the aphorism 'he is a *mensch* – not an animal' (Rosten 1969: 240). *Defiance* therefore is 'something of a corrective' to narratives of Gentile redemption and Jewish passivity, as well as to the more sentimentalised Holocaust films such as *Jakob the Liar* and *La vita è bella/ Life is Beautiful* (Goldberg 2009).

Inglourious Basterds is a Jewish revenge fantasy. The eponymous Basterds are a sadistic 'Hebraic Dirty Dozen' (Stone 2009: B3), an elite guerrilla commando squadron of American-Jewish GI Nazi-hunters who parachute into occupied France. Their mission is to kill, scalp, maim and torture as many Germans and Nazis as possible. Their leader, Lieutenant Aldo Raine (Brad Pitt), instructs his men, 'We will be cruel to the German, and through our cruelty they will know who we are. They will find the evidence of our cruelty in the disembowelled, dismembered, and disfigured bodies of their brothers we leave behind us.' In its fairy-tale ending the entire Nazi leadership, including Hitler, Goering, Bormann and Goebbels, is burned alive and/or shot.

Unlike *Defiance* and *Munich*, these Jews have no qualms about their actions. Tarantino produced 'a story of emotionally uncomplicated, physically threatening, non-morally-anguished Jews dealing out spaghetti-Western justice to their would-be exterminators' (Goldberg 2009).[21] Indeed, each soldier's task is to collect 100 scalps. The Basterds make no distinction between Nazis and Germans: all Germans in uniform are Nazis. They take no prisoners, instead gunning down disarmed captives, except when they want to send a message by mutilation and torture. Thus several graphic sequences show Jewish soldiers scalping, disembowelling, maiming, crushing skulls and killing enemy soldiers. In one particularly graphic sequence, Donnie 'The Bear Jew' Donowitz (Eli Roth) beats a Wehrmacht officer to death with a baseball bat, to the amusement of his fellow soldiers. Later he completely shreds Hitler's body with a machine gun. The final scene of the film depicts a swastika being carved onto the forehead of an SS officer. *Inglourious Basterds* thus extends the revenge category of the Holocaust genre. As Tarantino put it, 'Holocaust movies always have Jews as victims. We've seen that story before. I want to see something different. Let's see Germans that are scared of Jews' (quoted in Goldberg 2009).

Other Holocaust films also focus on Jewish resistance, reversing the stereotype of Jewish passivity. In *The Grey Zone*, the Jewish Sonderkommando clandestinely stockpile weapons for a revolt in which one crematorium is blown up and a number of concentration-camp guards are shot. As Baron points out, the film's publicity emphasised the 'brave defiance of the Twelfth Sonderkommando' (2005: 258). Another type of Holocaust revenge is extracted in Spike Lee's *Inside Man* (2006). Chaim (Bernie Rachelle), an Orthodox Jew, is part of a team of robbers that deliberately targets a bank founded on profits directly accrued from victims of the Nazis. The Manhattan Trust Bank has been established by Arthur Case (Christopher Plummer), an American banker who, during the Holocaust, willingly accepted Nazi blandishments and stolen Jewish goods, even betraying his Jewish friends whom he could have helped. By not only robbing the bank but also leaving a clue for a cop to uncover the trail of Case's wealth back to the Nazis, the group exact revenge.

Overall, then, these films suggest that 'a generational shift may be underway in how Jewish-American men (and women) approach the topic of historic Jewish victimisation: by constructing and nourishing a counternarrative of violent Jewish resistance to Gentile (including Arab and Muslim) violence' (Katz 2010: 71).

Shtarkers and villains

In the previous chapter, we encountered many Jewish gangsters and criminals who end up dead. In contrast, there have been many such characters who, like their real-life counterparts, mock and reverse the canard of Jewish weakness and passivity, particularly in the post-Holocaust era. In addition to those mentioned earlier, we can add Marty Augustine (Mark Rydell) in *The Long Goodbye* (dir. Robert Altman, 1973), crime czar Hyman Roth (Lee Strasberg) in *The Godfather: Part II* (dir. Francis Ford Coppola, 1974) – a fictional character, based heavily on real-life gangster Meyer Lansky – the eponymous *Lepke*, Dutch Schultz (James Remar) in *The Cotton Club* (dir. Francis Ford Coppola, 1984), Sergio Leone's Jewish gangsters in his *Once Upon a Time in America* (1984) and, more recently, Abraham 'Cousin Avi' Denovitz (Dennis Farina) in the British film *Snatch* (dir. Guy Ritchie, 2000). Such gangsters and villains are not queer; they are not mere mimics, they fight back. They make 'victims instead of just being victims' (Rubin 2002: 8–9). In Yiddish such Jews are known as *shtarkers* (lit. 'strong ones', toughs, enforcers).

Although there were extremely violent Jewish gangsters, criminals, killers and corrupt bookmakers before 1990, their numbers have multiplied in contemporary cinema. Jewish villains appear with increasing regularity, many of which are superfluous and/or gratuitous. Throughout *Criminal* (dir. Gregory Jacobs, 2004), we hear about but never meet 'the Jew', the partner to a con man. Sandler (Oscar Nuñez) is a secondary character in an Argentinian con-within-a-con film *Nueve reinas/Nine Queens* (Dir. Fabián Bielinsky, 2000). Salomon Sorowitsch (Karl Markovics) in the German film *The Counterfeiters* (dir. Stefan Ruzowitzky, 2007) is a professional currency forger. Reuben Tishkoff (Elliot Gould) and Saul Bloom (Carl Reiner) play supporting con men in Steven Soderbergh's *Ocean's Eleven* (2001), *Ocean's Twelve* (2004) and *Ocean's Thirteen* (2007). Ben Kingsley's portrayal of Fagin in Roman Polanski's *Oliver Twist* (2005) restores 'the dark and problematic complexity of his character' (*Heeb* 2009). A visually similar character, the hook-nosed, greedy slave owner Watto (Andrew Secombe), is found in *Star Wars: Episode I – The Phantom Menace* (dir. George Lucas, 1999) and Mickey Bergman (Danny DeVito) is a vicious Yiddish-speaking, money-obsessed ('Everyone needs money – that's why they *call* it money') fence of ambiguous ethnicity in *Heist* (dir. David Mamet, 2001). His dwarfish, short and fat stature is another 'Jewish moment'. The grotesque identification of Jews with dwarfish freaks is longstanding in Western European antisemitism. George Mosse described the antisemitic stereotype of the Jew as 'a contorted figure resting on short legs, a greedy and sensual corpulence' (1964: 140). Mickey's antagonist calls him 'Rumpelstiltskin', clearly referring to his diminutive stature, but a name rich in antisemitic allusion. As Leon Botstein comments, 'The dwarf has always been the emblem of the Jew since Rumpelstiltskin, who wove gold from straw, had an unpronounceable name and charged a price that was a kind of ritual murder of the gentile baby. The Jew-as-dwarf metaphor was a particularly nasty one' (quoted in Bombaci 2002: 167). These numerous characterisations cement the notion of the Jew as villain.

Clearly influenced by Francis Ford Coppola's *Godfather* trilogy, for example, *Le Grand Pardon II/Day of Atonement* (dir. Alexandre Arcady, 1992) depicts the life of France's leading crime organisation, a French-Algerian Jewish family, which made a fortune money-laundering and participating in the booming cocaine trade. Sammy 'Ace' Rothstein (Robert de Niro) in *Casino* (dir. Martin Scorsese, 1995) is a professional gambler hired by the mob to look after their casino *The Tangiers* in Las Vegas. Ace does not belong among the city's good-old-boy network and refuses to adhere to its code of *goyim naches*, revealing just how the cowboy-hat-wearing establishment feel about an East-Coast Jewish bookie they do not accept among their ranks. He is subject to a host of antisemitic insults: 'crazy Jew fuck' and 'We may have to kick a kike's ass out of town.' Although the Mafia employs Sammy, he is never outwardly tough. He does not personally commit any violence, although he certainly authorises its use. Instead, he walks around in a variety of flamboyant pastel-coloured suits, directing the casino's activities. At home he wears a pink robe and uses a cigarette holder, leading his Italian friend Nicky Santoro (Joe Pesci) to question his masculinity: 'Where's your fucking balls? You're walking around like John Barrymore.' Despite his queer appearance, however, unlike the Gentile Nicky, who is undeniably tough, Sammy survives the film, even emerging from a car bombing largely unscathed except for a pair of symbolically Jewish, oversized glasses.

Bugsy, as played by non-Jewish hunk Warren Beatty, similarly merges the images of the tough gangster Jew and the smart Jew. The film shows how Bugsy helped to set up the West Coast headquarters of the New York City Mafia before building the first luxury hotel-casino in Las Vegas, the Flamingo, in the 1930s and 1940s. Bugsy is a ruthless borderline psychotic who also exudes charisma, style, success, eroticism and general bad-guy status. He is not a victim. This is emphasised in a sequence depicting Bugsy towering over mob boss Jack Dragna (Richard C. Sarafian), an Italian associate who, in the preceding scene, has referred to Bugsy as a 'Jew prick'. Knowing that he has stolen money from him, Bugsy lambasts Jack, screaming inches from his face. He then forces Jack to walk on all fours and imitate a dog.

Oligarch Platon Makovskii in the Russian film *Oligarkh/Tycoon* (dir. Pavel Lungin, 2002) is another complex gangster. Like Shlomo the Rabbi in *Lucky Number Slevin*, Platon is a 'Jewish scholar-criminal' (Pozefsky 2008: 310). He is a hard-working, talented optimistic idealist who is the victim of antisemitic abuse. His enemies 'regard him as a stereotypically avaricious Jew, who used his cunning to steal the hard-earned wealth of the simple Russians whose interests they claim to represent [...] exploit[ing] resonant anti-Semitic myths to mobilise public opinion against him' (Pozefsky 2008: 306). For example, he is described by his nemesis as a *polukrovka* (Russian: 'half-breed'). Platon has *Yiddische kopf*. He is clever, outwitting his enemies. For most of the film, we are led to believe that Platon is in fact dead, having been killed by assassins linked to the Kremlin. However, his funeral reveals an empty coffin and, shortly thereafter, he emerges from hiding to avenge his simulated death. Platon becomes a tough and ruthless Jew. Although untrained as a hit man, he executes a traitorous lieutenant. Platon pursues the wife of his superior and later kills his best and oldest friend. Following these bloody killings, he is toughened: his hollow gaze is framed by congealed blood, externally indicating his internal moral transformation (Pozefsky 2008: 317–18). In the final scene, having successfully eradicated his enemies, as well as the friend who has betrayed him, he heads towards Moscow in a gold-coloured Rolls Royce, leading a caravan of cars and an army of bodyguards.

Similarly, *Analyze This* (dir. Harold Ramis, 1999) features a Jewish shrink who mimics and ultimately passes as an Italian gangster. Ben Sobel (Billy Crystal) is hired to help an Italian mobster, Paul Vitti (Robert De Niro), to recover from depression. Eventually, his professional role moves beyond simply providing psychoanalysis, as Sobel's failure to assist Vitti's recovery culminates in him being asked to represent his client at a syndicate meeting that Vitti is unable to attend as the result of a depressive episode. Sobel pretends to be Vitti's new advisor, Ben Sobeleone, aka 'the fuckin' doctor'. In doing so, Sobel, like *Goodfellas*'s Karen Hill, provides an interesting reversal of the attempts of the Jew to pass as either white and/or black by having him pose as an Italian-American. Ironically, Jews have often played Italians and vice versa, most notably John Turturro, as we have seen. Sobel's shape-shifting propensity here recalls Woody Allen's *Zelig*, yet at the same time it is not his physical characteristics that enable him to pull off this act of mimicry, but rather his performative abilities and his *Yiddische kopf*. Sobel has watched *The Godfather* films so many times that he is able to mimic them perfectly. Furthermore, he is quick-thinking and sharp-witted, able to reinvent himself, at the drop of a hat, as Sobeleone. As Rubin puts it, 'the Jew saves the day because of his ability to use his naturalised Jewish intellect to *seem* tough' (2002: 13). Crystal reprises the role in *Analyze That* (dir. Harold Ramis, 2002) and, rising to the occasion, does indeed become tough. After some initial performance anxiety that involves putting a gun down his trousers and fumbling around with it until it falls down his leg, Sobel not only punches out a rival gangster but also participates in an armed heist, earning the following praise: 'You hung in there. It took a lot of balls. I saw the monster in you. The beast.' He emerges with the moniker 'one tough shrink'.

Jewish cops and dicks

Stereotypically, the world of the police is seen as one that excludes the Jew. Hannah Arendt described 'the traditional Jewish fear of the "cop" – that seeming incarnation of a hostile world' (1944: 111). Unfortunately, as a result, since policing embodies *goyim naches*, self-hatred becomes 'the price of acceptance into the police "family"' for Jews who have to pose as non-Jewish in order to pass (L. Roth 2004: 182). Consequently, the idea of the Jewish cop is considered an oxymoron, and often treated as a fertile subject for humour. In *North by Northwest* (dir. Alfred Hitchcock, 1959), for example, Roger Thornhill (Cary Grant), after being hauled into a police station for drunk driving, makes a call to his mother. She asks what the cop's name is and he replies 'Seargent Emil Klinger.' After a double-take, he says with a chuckle, 'No. I didn't believe it either.' Such films as *Last Action Hero* (dir. John McTiernan, 1993) and *Superbad* still mock the odd fit between Jew and cop. An early serious exception to this rule, however, occurs in *The Killers* (dir. Robert Siodmak, 1946), in which Sam Levene plays police lieutenant Sam Lubinsky.

Contemporary cinema is widening its spectrum to embrace more Jewish cops. The satirical *The Hebrew Hammer*, which bills itself as the first 'Jewsxploitation' film, does this through mimicry, mockery and reversal. While not strictly a police officer, the eponymous Brooklyn-based *haredi* crimefighter Carver is not so much a Jewish James Bond as a Semitic Shaft, 'the kike who won't cop out when Gentiles are all about'. *The Hebrew Hammer* is 'dedicated to all the Jewish brothers and sisters who've had enough of the Gentile'. Carver is a tough Yiddish-speaking action hero modelled on the Black Panthers. He is also a (bizarrely) tattooed muscle-Jew. As 'the baddest Heeb this side of Tel Aviv', he is recruited by the Jewish Justice League (whose emblem parodies that of the Jewish Defense League and which is housed in a building resembling the Pentagon but in a star of David shape), an umbrella organisation for such groups as 'The Anti-Denigration League', 'The Worldwide Jewish Media Conspiracy' and 'the Coalition of Jewish Athletes' (whose delegate is, predictably, absent) to prevent an antisemitic psycho-Santa from destroying Chanukah.

The Hebrew Hammer self-consciously and ironically mocks and reverses a whole range of Jewish stereotypes. On the one hand we have his overbearing Jewish mother, his JAP girlfriend and her Moshe Dayan look-a-like father. Carver himself manifests every Jewish neurosis: he is allergic to dust, he has a taste for Manischewitz (Black Label) and he cannot handle too much pressure and expectation. When his enemies seek to distract him they do so by throwing money on the ground. On the other hand, *The Hebrew Hammer* reverses the antisemitic canard that Jews are physically weak and cowardly. 'We're often depicted as intellectual, but weak and uncool,' says director Jonathan Kessleman. 'It's important to take back these stereotypes and own them.' (Smith 2003) Carver is a powerful Jewish action hero. He exhorts a young Jew who is being bullied by his Gentile schoolmates to 'stay Jewish'. In one of the film's best sequences, he enters a neo-Nazi dive bar (named 'Duke's'), orders a Manischewitz ('straight up') and pays with a 'fistful of shekels', before pulling out two shotguns from underneath his trenchcoat and greeting the other drinkers with the words, 'Shabbat Shalom, muthafuckers.' He then shoots up the bar, and a cut to an exterior shot shows the neo-Nazis spilling out of the bar, afraid and wounded. The sequence ends with Carver, Ku Klux Klan-style, burning a star of David into the grass outside.

If *The Hebrew Hammer* uses mockery to eke out a place for the Jew in the Gentile world of crimefighting, in the post-1990 period less comic cop films have emerged. The number of serious (and not necessarily self-hating) Jewish policemen is proliferating as a result, as a series of films suggest a reversal of the past to embrace the notion of the Jewish cop. Examples include the father and son policemen in *We Own the Night* or Levine, the secular, non-religious and self-hating cop in *A Stranger Among Us* who does not even merit a first name, simply going by the ethnic surname 'Levine', which both clearly codes him as a Jew and hence excludes him.

A similar character is found in *Homicide*. Robert 'Bobby' Gold (Joe Mantegna) is a highly decorated (22 citations for valour) homicide police detective in New York City. Although a tough cop, he is an expert in the art of hostage negotiation, earning him the label 'the orator', emphasising his intellectual and verbal qualities. Although Gold desires to fit in with his fellow cops, he is constantly reminded of his Jewishness. Mamet describes Gold thus: 'To the non-cops he's a cop, but to the cops he's a Jew' (quoted in Kane 1999: 279). Early in the film a black superior officer calls him a 'kike'. And no matter how hard he tries, he cannot escape queer ethnic identification. As Gold admits, 'They said ... I was a *pussy* all my life. They said I was a pussy, because I was a Jew. Onna' [sic: honour] cops, they'd say, send a Jew, mizewell send a *broad* on the job, send a *broad* through the door...all my goddamned life, and I listened to it...uh-huh...? I was the donkey...I was the clown.' The equation of 'pussy' and 'broad' feminises and queers Gold as a sissy Jew.

Gold, however, desires to outperform, to become tougher in the eyes of his fellow cops. But as he is gradually 'drawn into a mysterious, covert conflict between neo-Nazis and Israeli secret agents' (L. Roth 2004: 187), the tough Israelis only serve to underscore Gold's weakness. Their leader, Benjamin (Adolph Mall), challenges him: 'Are you a Jew, Mr Gold?...Then be a Jew!' Gold eventually mimics toughness, rejecting the attire of his colleagues that he is wearing at the beginning of the film, increasingly resembling the Israelis: leather jacket and dark shirt (Roth 2004: 194). At their prompting, he blows up a print shop that appears to be a neo-Nazi front. But Gold is not able to pass as tough. His refusal to pass the Israelis confidential police information, as it conflicts with his ethical duties as a cop, means he does not belong with them either, and hence retains his marginalised, liminal and queer diaspora status. As a result, the Israelis blackmail Gold, double-crossing him, despite his compliance. By the end of the film, Gold is neither clothed in the garb of a cop nor that of a Jew/Israeli. He is dressed in jeans and a letterman's jacket, thus marking him as both 'juvenile' and 'civilian' (Roth 2004: 194). He is also injured, having been shot twice, and shedding his tough uniform he reverts to a sissy Jew. But, although he has failed in his confrontation with his quarry, he survives, unlike his Gentile partner, thus not simply ending as the queer victim.

Similarly, the Jewish cop of *American Gangster* (dir. Ridley Scott, 2007), which is based on a true story, is alone and isolated. New Jersey cop detective Richie Roberts (Russell Crowe) is the head of a narcotics squad entrusted with the task of discovering the identity of the kingpin – Frank Lucas (Denzel Washington) – behind the flood of 'blue magic' heroin onto New York's streets in the late 1960s. Roberts is presented as a model of professionalism and integrity, adhering to a rigorous ethical professional code. These qualities make him appear a self-righteous outcast among his more corrupt Gentile peers. Roberts is very explicit in distinguishing himself from the bent cops, even though it almost endangers his life: 'They ain't my kind.' In an early sequence he discovers $987,000 in unmarked cash in the boot of a car, but turns it in even when his partner admonishes him to keep it because, in his own words, 'It was the right thing to do.' The subsequent sequence of shots within the police station establishes his distance from the other, less clean, cops, one of whom calls him a 'fucking boy scout.' Later, they refuse to provide him with back-up assistance in a potentially dangerous situation.

Roberts is both tough and vulnerable. Like most other cinematic Jewish cops, Roberts contends with police prejudice and antisemitism, at one point grovelling to his New York counterparts when they inadvertently rip off the cash he is using for a drugs buy. The language throughout the film reflects the rampant racism of the 1970s, with characters calling him a 'kike'. Not only do his corrupt colleagues dislike him for being honest, but also he is estranged from his wife and son, coding him as one of those policemen commonly shown as deserted and abandoned by their families. A divorced parent, he is alone. His drab life, which is contrasted constantly with Lucas's life of luxury surrounded by his large family (brothers, mothers and extended family), is full of marital spats and custody hearings. Where the Jew is typically defined by family, Roberts is not. The occasion of Thanksgiving is used to emphasise this: as Lucas dines with his family in opulence, Roberts eats a tuna and potato-chip sandwich on his own.

Roberts, though, is not a victim. Indeed Roberts is played by Russell Crowe, who not only is not Jewish but also has generally been cast as a hyper-macho, non-Jewish type. He works out, lifting weights, sporting a star of David. He beats up a suspect, repeatedly kicking him. At the same time, he uses his *Yiddische kopf* and ingenuity to get out of potentially fatal situations. Although an outcast, or perhaps because of it, Roberts's maverick status enables him to rise through the ranks. He is hard-working and intelligent but close to the action on the streets at the same time, allowing him to detect a tectonic shift in the illegal drugs world, realising that a black gangster has outmanoeuvred the Mafia. He is also represented as charismatic, charming and sexually desirable: a blonde eyes him up as he strolls through the park; his ex-wife is very attractive; and following one hearing he is shown screwing his (blonde, naturally) lawyer ('Fuck me like a cop, Richie. Not a lawyer,' she urges him). That the Jewish cop is appearing with increasing regularity is yet another sign of Jewish cinematic normalisation.

Tough Jewesses who sweat; or the Jewess under duress

Historically, the trope of the tough Jew has not been applied to the Jewess. Where such an option was available, it was only in the antisemitic imagination, which often paired the 'womanly male Jew' with the 'manly Jewess'. In contemporary cinema, however, we have witnessed the advent of the tough Jewess, reflecting the recent explosion of tough women in popular media in general and film in particular. This in turn is based on changes in US society, from the workplace to the sports field, which has produced 'a new vision of womanhood, one tougher than before', whereby women adopted more aggressive, active and independent roles than were hitherto available to them (Inness 2004: 6). Cinema in particular saw the emergence of 'a new breed of arse-kicking female protagonists in action genre films' (Hills 1999: 38).

Towards the end of *Mr & Mrs Smith* (dir. Doug Liman, 2005), Jane Smith (Angelina Jolie), who spins a web of lies to hide her secret life as a professional killer from her husband John (Brad Pitt), admits to him, along with many other revelations, 'I'm Jewish.' While it is no doubt played for laughs, and a gratuitous or superfluous throwaway line – a sign of the increased cultural confidence of the post-1990 New Jews – in these two simple words, representations of the Jewess in US cinema are reversed. Jane tangos, climbs mountains and runs her own professional-gun-for-hire business. She is a lithe and attractive assassin. She is played by the non-Jewish super-sex symbol *par excellence*, Jolie. She cannot cook (she has

Mrs Jane Smith in *Mr & Mrs Smith*.

never made a meal), but she is very proficient with kitchen cutlery, guns and other implements of death. In one sequence, dressed as a dominatrix and mimicking a high-class call girl, she handcuffs, whips and then breaks the neck of her target. She is the antithesis of the Mother and the Princess. Jane works for a living. She sweats. She makes men sweat. Her body is not for mere passive adornment. Thus, when she confesses her Jewishness, we witness a new phenomenon in contemporary cinema: the tough, sexy, highly erotic, female Jewish assassin. Jane Smith is a tough Jewess.

And this is not the only example. In *Munich*, Golda Meir approves a secret counter-assassination mission. She may be visually portrayed as a mother to the nation, personally serving coffee to Avner, but her nerves are steely: 'Forget peace for now, we have to show them we're strong.' In *Enemy at the Gates* (dir. Jean-Jacques Annaud, 2001) Tania Chernova (Rachel Weisz) is a tough Jewess with Attitude. She is intelligent and 'highly educated', having studied German at Moscow University, as signified by her book-lined room (containing Goethe, Schiller and Marx among others). But her Zionist father also taught her to shoot. When she learns that the Nazis have murdered her parents she chooses to fight rather than to work back at the Soviet HQ in the battle for Stalingrad during the Second World War. As a solder in the Red Army, she is shown in uniform and with a gun, in stark contrast to Commissar Danilov (Joseph Fiennes), a young bespectacled and idealistic Jewish Red Army political officer, who does not fight. He does not even know how to shoot a gun. His weapon is the typewriter. *Homicide* offers up more images of the tough Jewess. Chava (Natalia Nogulich) is an undercover Israeli agent. An elderly, apparently helpless Jewess is murdered in what appears to be a hate crime but is not entirely what she seems. A delayed montage edit depicts in close-up that she has hidden a gun in a cigar box. Later on, documentation relating to rifles is discovered in her cellar, as is an old photograph portraying her as a gun-toting fighter. 'Here then is encoded a cinematic archetype of the woman with a gun' (Borden 2001: 248).

Verna in *Miller's Crossing* is another tough Jewess. As we have seen, she is sexually attractive, drinks, smokes, swears and even throws the occasional punch. As Tom describes her, 'she can look after herself,' and he certainly thinks that she is capable of murder in the pursuit of her aims. Verna's toughness ensures her survival in the male domain of the underworld. She seduces Tom while simultaneously sleeping with his Irish crime boss

Leo, coldly and unemotionally manipulating them both into protecting her brother Bernie. Mara (Tracy Pollan) in *A Stranger Among Us* poses as a *haredi baalat teshuvah* (Hebrew: lit. 'she who has returned', but referring to a formerly non-religious Jewess who adopts more orthodox ways) who kills her husband.

In *Hostel II*, Beth Salinger presents the arresting image of a tough Jewess with Attitude. As we have seen, Beth is defined by her *Yiddische kopf*, but she is not simply a talker. She is physically tough, prone to violence. This is augured early in the film when some Italian men on their train call her a 'fucking cunt'. Beth refuses to take the insult passively. 'What the fuck did you call me?' she responds angrily as her friend Whitney drags her away. She is prepared for the fight. Similarly, in the torture cell, having talked herself into being unshackled, Stuart attempts to rape her. As he prepares to penetrate her, she overcomes him by head-butting him, before hitting him twice with an iron bar. Twisting a metal chain around his neck, Beth orders Stuart to 'get in the chair. Get in the *fucking* chair. *Fucker*.'

Manacling Stuart to the chair transforms Beth from victim to victimiser, reversing the power dynamic, and Beth is now in command. Her face is tense and determined. This is emphasised as she grills Stuart for the code to exit the cell. When he refuses to tell her, she stabs an ice pick in his ear. Inadvertently, however, Beth summons the guards to the cell. But again she refuses to be passive, and actively takes control of the situation. As they enter, she has a gun in one hand and holds a pair of scissors to Stuart's genitalia with the other. She negotiates her release with her captors, but in order to leave the factory alive, she is told, she must kill. 'They're still gonna kill you, you fucking stupid cunt,' Stuart hisses. 'What did you say to me?' Beth replies in disbelief. Stuart repeats, 'You're a stupid fucking cunt!' In response Beth literally emasculates him by cutting off his penis and throwing it to the guard-dogs with the remark, 'Let him bleed to death'. Beth's blood-lust, though, is not sated, as she seeks out the woman who lured her in the first place and, dressed as the grim reaper or angel of death, she avenges her friends by decapitating her with an axe, ironically repeating her victim's earlier words, 'Nastrovia' ('To your health').

As we have seen, Beth is tattooed. The trope of the tattoo is an ironic reversal of the Holocaust, for here it is a sign of survival, empowerment and a badge of honour even, rather than simple passive victimisation, providing a reversed mirror-image of the victimised queer Jew, Josh (Derek

Richardson), graphically tortured to death in a sequence lasting five minutes during the first instalment of *Hostel*. Schubart (2010) describes Beth as the victim turned avenger 'who is captured, tortured, rises to the occasion and beats her opponent. She is not nice. Not sweet. And certainly not politically correct. She is ready to play ball with the bad guys to survive in a capitalist world driven by desire, greed, and money.' Beth thus refuses to become a helpless, abject, and passive victim, turning from victim to killer, and emerges alive and victorious from her ordeal, as the tough Jewess with Attitude.

Finally, *Predators* (dir. Nimród Antal, 2010) features Isabelle (Alice Braga) as a beautiful, gritty and badass IDF sniper captured in an operation after her spotter is killed, and transported to an alien planet, where she and her male companions are hunted like prey by an alien species. Isabelle is another superfluous and gratuitous Jewess, for we are given no moments or codes to read her as Jewish and/or Israeli (she is clearly Latina, played by a non-Jewish Brazilian actress) other than another character asking her if she is IDF. As a tough Jewess with Attitude she is constantly armed with a precision sniper rifle mounted with a scope and a sidearm and who, by the end of the film, has survived the ordeal. Although murderers and mercenaries surround her, she is shown to be unlike them, adhering to a code of *menschlikayt*, even when it endangers her own life. Isabelle may well be the first serious Jewess in cinematic outer space!

Avenging Jewesses

Even Holocaust films, an arena for emphasising Jewish passivity in general and Jewish female passivity[22] in particular are showing Jewish female resistance, reversing Dines's claim in 2006 that cinema excludes the authentic stories of Jewish women during the Shoah ('we fought together with Jewish men in the resistance and died alongside them'). I have already discussed Felice in *Aimée & Jaguar* and *Zwartboek/Black Book*'s Rachel. As mentioned above, *The Grey Zone* depicts the involvement of female inmates in a Sonderkommando plot to blow up the Birkenau crematoria and gas chambers. Three Jewesses within the camp serve a key role for the rebellious Sonderkommando's plan. Their part is one of supply and concealment. Anja (Lisa Benavides), Dina (Mira Sorvino) and Rosa (Natasha Lyonne) smuggle explosive powder from the UNIO munitions factory at Auschwitz to the Sonderkommando, hiding it on the bodies of dead Jews for the Sonderkommando to find and store. Although they realise that such conspiratorial activity endangers the lives of their fellow inmates, their leader comments, 'What's the fucking difference when you're dead anyway?' When their activity is discovered, they are rounded up for brutal interrogation. Dina exhorts Anja to 'Say nothing.' Rosa is beaten to death by the guards, Dina is tortured with electric shocks. Despite the savagery and intimidation, all three women maintain their silence, even when Anja and Dina are made to watch as the other female inmates, ignorant of the conspiracy, are executed one by one. Rather than submit, the women exercise agency by opting to kill themselves (Dina chooses her own death by suicidal electrification), thus defying the Nazis and sealing their own fates. Throughout these scenes, not one word is said, emphasising the women's toughness and attitude, as well as their selfless acts in maintaining silence, thus allowing the plot to continue undetected.

Defiance depicts other fighting Jewesses. Women were a core part of the Bielski Otriad, and while they are depicted as fulfilling the 'traditional' gendered roles of cooking, cleaning, washing clothes and caring for the children within the encampment, some are inducted into the armed community and trained to use weapons. When a German soldier is captured, along with their male counterparts they beat him to death, as an act of revenge for their murdered relatives and friends.

Shoshanna in *Inglourious Basterds* is the epitome of this new tough Jewess with Attitude in the Holocaust genre.[23] With the entire Nazi hierarchy, including Hitler, gathered in her cinema for a film premier, Shoshanna plans her own spectacular form of resistance – the mass incineration of the Nazi high command and their wives during the screening – by locking the doors of the auditorium and setting fire to the theatre's highly flammable collection of nitrate prints. In this way, Shoshanna uses cinema – earlier in the film identified as a 'degenerate' and 'Jewish' medium – to exact her revenge. As a prelude, she films a scene which she forces a collaborator to print and develop for her by threatening to kill him and his family. Clutching an axe, she warns him, 'Bring that fucker over here! Put his head down on that table. You either do what the fuck we tell you or I'll bury this axe in your collaborating skull. Marcel [Jacky Ido], do his wife and children know you? [...] Then after we kill this dog for the Germans we'll go and silence them.'

In the chapter of the film entitled 'Revenge of the giant face', Shoshanna carries out her plan almost single-handedly. She splices a close-up shot of her own face in the midst of the propaganda film. Looking down upon the audience of captive Nazis, she tells them, 'I have a message for Germany: that you are all going to die. And I want you all to look deep into the face of the Jew who is going to do it.' Meanwhile, she instructs her lover to burn the degenerate and 'Jewish' celluloid stockpiled in her cinema, which causes the cinema to catch fire. The screen erupts into flames, consuming Shoshanna's laughing image, taunting its audience with the words, 'This is the face of Jewish vengeance.' Projected onto the billows of smoke pouring forth from the proscenium, Shoshanna 'hovers over the doomed audience like an avenging wraith' (Taylor 2010: 105). A 'holocaust' or charnel house is created as Shoshanna ironically appropriates her own cinema, as well as the 'Jewish' medium of film, used by the Nazis to demonise the Jew, transforming both literally into instruments of death. Just as the Nazis cremated Jewish bodies, Shoshanna uses her cinema to burn alive the Nazi high command, thus avenging not just her family but all the other murdered Jews. Rachel Abramowitz (n.d.) thus concludes that Shoshanna is one 'of the toughest Jewesses on screen'.

Those films that focus on female participation in violent resistance are a significant development in cinematic depictions of the Holocaust, showing the signs of reversing the Jewess from the passive, brutalised and raped stereotype of *la belle juive* into the tough Jewess with Attitude. This Jewess is assigned the righteous position of avenger as audiences recall the violence enacted against her and her family, whether seen or not, justifying the vengeful reaction on her part. As Breines explains, 'the image of Jewish victimisation vindicates the image of the Jewish victimiser' (1990: 50).

A new character-type has emerged in contemporary cinema, one reversing previous notions of the Jewess. While this new image stems from and is rooted in previous stereotypes, it simultaneously reverses them. In disrupting entrenched binaries, the tough Jewess with Attitude upsets the implicit hierarchies created by those binary structures. In line with her tough Gentile counterparts, the tough Jewess with Attitude not only rebels against stereo(typical) gender roles, demonstrating that she can perform the same roles and tasks as the Jew, but also questions the duality of gender in the first place, confounding both general and Jewish binary logic. As mentioned previously, film stereotypes change as real women's lives change and women cannot be represented in the same old stereotypical ways as previously. The rise of the tough female action heroine in general and the tough Jewess in particular, therefore, is a sign of the different roles available to women in real life. It also mirrors the toughening of the Jew.

Conclusion: Jewish 'musculinity'

The relative absence of muscular Jewish bodies in cinema before 1990 is reversed to include a diaspora 'musculinity' (Tasker 1993) that is no longer just confined to the tough Israeli. The representation of the diaspora Jew as powerful and tough may not be an entirely new development, but in terms of the Jew, such films present contradictory sentiments, blending strong physicality with queer ethical/moral values. Whether a cop, gangster, assassin or killer, this Jew adheres to some sort of rigorous ethical code, mentioned earlier as 'a deep, historically formed Jewish need: the need to be ethical' (Breines 1990: 73). Even those Jews who do not possess this impulse have motives that are explained by their desire to avenge wrongs committed against them. While the protagonist of *Lucky Number Slevin* is a cold, calculating and ruthless Jewish killer, symbolised by his surname *kelev ra* (Hebrew: 'bad dog'), his revenge is justified. Thus, despite their toughness, and whether they fall on the right side of the law or not, tough Jews are rarely unequivocally and one-dimensionally 'evil'. Furthermore, tough Jewesses with Attitude now accompany tough Jews. Thus, contemporary cinema produces a new breed of Jew/ess who falls between or merges the dichotomy of tough and queer, what Breines calls 'the schlemiel as terminator' (1990: 11). It is a sign of the cinematic Jew/ess's increasing normalisation.

CHAPTER 6

Religion

Jewishness vs Judaism

Given the volume of research dedicated to analysing the Jewish contribution to film, both in front of and behind the camera, it is surprising to note that to date not much work has been done on *Judaism*, overshadowed by a tendency to focus either on the *image* of the Jew/ess or on the Holocaust on film. As a consequence, it is possible to read entire books on these subjects with almost no references to Judaism. This is because, in the past, film studies scholarship largely focused on ethnicity (*Jewishness*) as an analytic category for the study of Jewish representations and industry participation. As Robyn Wiegman notes, 'This is the case even though early cinematic representations of Jews were predicated on nineteenth-century *racialised* notions of Jewish identity' (1998: 159, my emphasis). Religion is typically ignored because, as Carolina Rocha notes, 'Jewish traditions and rites are absent in the many Eastern European and American films analysed' (2010: 47). In contrast, this chapter explores the religious factor (*Judaism*) in contemporary cinema. It starts from the premise that there is a clear distinction between Jewishness as racial, ethnic, political and cultural identities, and Judaism as a religion and set of beliefs, behaviours and values. Where Gertel (2003) began to map these representations, his desire to criticise what he sees as their distortions of Judaism clouds what is an otherwise useful survey. In this chapter, then, I propose a corrective to these studies to explore the specifically religious aspects of Judaism in contemporary cinema in order to show how it has introduced a normalising spectrum moving beyond the binaries of the past.

Judaism on film: a brief history

Cinema's engagement with Judaism stretches back to the early twentieth century, including such films as *His People*, *The Jazz Singer* and *A Passover Miracle* (dir. Anon., 1914), all of which depicted a range of Jewish practices, including the Sabbath, the kissing of the *mezuzah*, synagogue services and the Passover Seder. Yet, the first thing to note is that given the volume of Jews who have appeared on film since its very inception, the absence of explicit depictions of Judaism, as a religion, is conspicuous and notable. This is because, as mentioned above, cinema tended to define Jewishness in secular ethnic rather than religious terms. However, this did not preclude the inclusion of Jewish ritual, practices and beliefs, although these have tended to be used as backdrops to the main action, and are often not the focus or reason of the representation itself.

Certainly, during the heyday of the Hollywood studio system from the 1930s until the mid-1950s, Judaism rarely, if ever, appeared onscreen, as the Jewish moguls preferred to hide their ethnic and religious heritage in attempting to widen the appeal of their products. What Popkin referred to as 'the great retreat' was prompted by a rise in antisemitism and the moguls' understandable defensiveness, given the perception of Jewish 'control' of the film industry, about foregrounding Jewishness onscreen. Perhaps the most notable exceptions were *Tevye* (dir. Maurice Schwartz, 1939), the remake of *The Jazz Singer* (dir. Michael Curtiz, 1952) and *The Diary of Anne Frank*, in which, intriguingly, the significance of the festival of Chanukah was greatly exaggerated in comparison to the original book. The typical trend was, however, as Popkin points out, 'the absence of recognisable Jews in films that *require* their presence' (1952: 52). Thus, even in a film about the formative moment of Israelite nationalism and the birth of Judaism such as *The Ten Commandments*, the specifically Jewish elements were removed in order to broaden the story for audiences. Thus, something as Jewish as the giving of the Ten Commandments became de-Semitised, de-Judainised and Americanised. Not only did the Gentile Charlton Heston play Moses, but also when he descends Sinai with the two tablets, his very pose resembles that of the Statue of Liberty. Likewise in other biblical epics, 'Jews generally appear as mere historical necessities and filmmakers Henry King, Cecil B. DeMille, and King Vidor make no attempt to understand the Jews' religious and cultural heritage' (Friedman 1982: 146).

Then, in the 1960s and 1970s, Jewish-American filmmakers began making movies that explored Jewish self-definition after years of ignoring such issues. Yet, their films did not attempt to explore Judaism in any depth. The trend during this period is summed up in the words of Colonel David 'Mickey' Marcus (Kirk Douglas) in *Cast A Giant Shadow* (dir. Melville Shavelson, 1966): 'My religion is American. I went to Temple at thirteen for my Bar-Mitzvah, and once it was over, I was done with the Jews.' If Jews on film practised anything beyond that, it is encapsulated in the film *It's My Turn* (dir. Claudia Weill, 1980), in which despite holding an endogamous and traditional Jewish wedding ceremony – complete with *chuppah, yarmulke,* the bride and groom drinking from the traditional single cup of wine and the concluding ritual of the smashing of the glass – neither of the Jewish characters 'display any outward signs of their Judaism or any attachment to Jewish culture other than their participation in this wedding ceremony' (Friedman 1982: 294). It was also a field of representation particularly prone to caricature, as in the films of Mel Brooks and Woody Allen.

There have been exceptions to the above, but these remain oddities. Earlier I mentioned *His People, The Jazz Singer, A Passover Miracle* and *The Diary of Anne Frank*, to which can be added the 1980 version of *The Jazz Singer* (dir. Richard Fleischer), which, like its predecessors, deals, respectfully, with Orthodox (not *haredi*) Judaism. The period film *The Chosen* (dir. Jeremy Kagan, 1981) is a rare example of a film that not only accurately and faithfully treats Judaism as a set of religious practices but also pays attention to intra-Jewish philosophic and religious differences, rather than assuming a unified community. Similarly *Yentl*, released the following year, shows 'genuine respect for the Jewish tradition', as demonstrated by 'the loving camera attention on the artefacts of Jewish domestic and religious life' (Rosenberg 1996: 33). Finally, *Driving Miss Daisy* (dir. Bruce Beresford, 1989), another period piece, offers an unusual view of 'a southern Judaism that differed greatly from Northern versions', as well as a disdain for Jews who celebrate Christmas (Rowe 2004: 233). While these films signal a welcome development from previous representations of Judaism, the general trend, however, was to render Judaism invisible, or where represented, de-Semitised, de-Judainised, de-contextualised, universalised, caricatured and only very occasionally realistic.

The *Halacha* of representing Judaism on film, pre-1990

Surveying Judaism on film from the origins of cinema until 1990, the following general rules can be discerned. First, films about Jews were often meticulously non-specific in religious terms. Many Jewish directors perceived themselves in secular, ethnic terms, and religion played little part in their personal lives. Few practised Judaism in any form, and hence their work was 'clearly uninformed by the practice or study of Judaism' (Rosenberg 2006: 43). Consequently, as Taub states, 'practically nothing ethnic/religious is passed on, neither in the form of education, nor in shared traditions' (2005: 18).

Many Jews on film, as we have seen, were only conceptually Jewish. As a result, individuals who are neither ethnically nor religiously Jewish become *Jewish* onscreen but with the result of a complete emptying out of any religious content. Thus, Jewishness as opposed to Judaism becomes a mere simulacrum, as these protagonists 'exhibit identifiably Jewish cultural and ethnic (although not usually religious) characteristics and were created by Jewish writers and producers, but their Judaism almost never is discussed or problematised' (Rockler 2006: 456). They are distinguishable – for those that can read the signs – by a series of *ethnic* markers such as physical appearance, names, profession and locality. Many characters are so assimilated that we get no sign of their Jewishness other than easily-recognisable family names such as Levy and Cohen. And given that so many non-Jews often play Jews, characters do not even conform to preconceived and stereotypical notions of a 'Jewish look' (even if such a thing does not exist in reality, as Jewishness is not essentialist or racial). Despite the appearance of a myriad of Jews onscreen, therefore, 'viewers can attune to or disregard' their Jewishness (Rockler 2006: 456). A clear example of this is *When Harry Met Sally*, in which nowhere is there any explicit mention of anybody's ethnicity or religion. Yet we can read Harry (Billy Crystal) as Jewish and (Sally) Meg Ryan as Gentile based on those 'Jewish moments' I referred to in my introduction in which the viewer is given the possibility of 'reading Jewish', albeit not with certainty, by employing that largely unconscious complex of codes that cross-check each other, of which the Jewish identities of actors/ actresses is a key, but by no means the only, part.

Jews (and hence Judaism) are presented as being little different from Gentiles. This was part of an assimilatory drive that also emphasised such holidays as Chanukah and Passover as being almost the same as Christmas and Easter, but not quite, or focused on Jews celebrating Thanksgiving and other non-Jewish and/or civic holidays. *The Diary of Anne Frank*, for example, transformed Chanukah from a specific Jewish festival to a signifier of US religion in general, amounting to a domestication of the Other. Prayers and songs were conducted in English rather than Hebrew. As the non-Jewish president of Twentieth Century Fox (the studio responsible for producing the film), Spyrous Skouras, declared, 'This isn't a Jewish picture. This is a picture for the world' (quoted in Whitfield 1999: 182). As a result, the specifically Jewish Chanukah was universalised for its American audiences. Consequently, 'Jews are portrayed as participants in an American civil religion, whose members attend either the church or synagogue of their choice but are not otherwise marked by great differences of appearance, speech, custom, or behavior' (Rosenberg 1996: 22). Furthermore, '[R]epresentations of the Jews historically have downplayed significant Jewish holidays, the issue of interfaith marriage, and other important Jewish issues' that might mark Jews as different (Rockler 2006: 465). Indeed, despite the prevalence of exogamous relationships, the problems surrounding such unions are rarely discussed in any depth. Instead, a cross-cultural love affair is the standard in which the moral of the story is 'love conquers all'. Films of the 1970s such as *Portnoy's Complaint* and *The Heartbreak Kid* are particularly notable in this respect.

Film did not, nor did it often aim to, convey any sophisticated or subtle understanding of Judaism, its beliefs, rituals and practices. Secular symbols of Jewishness are ubiquitous. Film therefore failed, in general, to contextualise Judaism in any way that provided historical, cultural or religious meaning. Thus de-contextualised, Judaism became superficial, empty almost, when conveyed. Often Judaism was viewed from the outside so that the focus was on the subjective experiences of the Gentile rather than the Jews themselves. Indeed, US film has shied away from realistically or effectively portraying any non-Christian religion in general.

Where Judaism was represented onscreen, in the main Jews tended to be non-Orthodox. They were either assimilated, deracinated, or members of various non-Orthodox denominations such as Reform, Liberal and Conservative, although these are never explicitly described or delineated. It is implicitly inferable by the lack of outward markers that would identify an Orthodox Jew, such as a *yarmulke, tzitzit* (fringes), dress and clothing. Furthermore, Reform Jews are, to all intents and purposes, 'white', represented as no different from the vast majority of Americans. Indeed, some of them are downright ignorant about their Judaism. When, in *A Stranger Among Us* Levine proposes to the non-Jewish Emily, she rejects him with the words that she is waiting for her *bashert* (Yiddish: destiny or a divinely inspired match); he asks her what that means, to which she ripostes, 'Ask your rabbi'.

Judaism is most often deployed as a means to inject humour into film. In *Airplane!* (dirs Jim Abrahams and David Zucker, 1980), a *tallit*-clad Jewish airliner is taking its time to clear the landing strip until a rather annoyed command is issued from the control tower: 'Air Israel, please clear the runway.' Prince John (Richard Lewis) in *Robin Hood: Men in Tights* (dir. Mel Brooks, 1993) worries that a roast boar is *treyf*. In *Love at First Bite* (dir. Stan Dragoti, 1979), Dr Jeffrey Rosenberg (Richard Benjamin), who plays the nemesis of Count Dracula (George Hamilton), holds up a star of David rather than a crucifix, causing Dracula to double-take. And knowledge of ancient Hebrew in *The Mummy* (dir. Stephen Sommers, 1999) saves the life of Beni Gabor (Kevin J. O'Connor).

When Orthodoxy is represented, it is usually solely in terms of *haredism*, since it is 'the most obviously distinctive and colorful' branch of Judaism (Elber 1997). *Haredism* works as a shorthand for an instantly recognisable Jewish religious status. Indeed *haredism* tends to stand as a metonym for *all* Orthodoxy. Often the image of the *haredi* is used in several further respects. It acts 'strictly as a sight gag' (Miles 1996: 217 n.40), which is particularly evident in the films of Allen and Brooks (in which *haredim* appear anachronistically in medieval England and during the Spanish Inquisition), but also in other films, such as *Last Action Hero* and *Orgazmo*. In *Welcome to Collinwood* (dirs Anthony Russo and Joe Russo, 2002), George Clooney cameos as a tattooed safecracker mimicking a *haredi*. Finally, it stands as 'a familiar cultural icon of a multi-ethnic urbanised America, one that could serve equally well an ideology of tolerance (as a sign of the thriving cultural vitality of American urban life) or intolerance (as part of the cultural detritus of a "mongrelised" America, of an imperial nation in decline', such as the blink-and-you'll-miss-it *haredi* in Ridley Scott's 1982 dystopic futurist sci-fi *Blade Runner* (Rosenberg 1996: 31).

The representation of *haredism* is conversely prone to nostalgia, romanticisation, sentimentalisation and idealisation, such as in *Fiddler on the Roof* and *Yentl*, and it is nearly always represented from the *outside*, rarely from the perspective of the insider. Thus, the *haredi* becomes a symbol of the exotic Other, of 'mystique, power, and purity' (L. Roth 2004: 185). As mentioned in Chapter 1, there was a tendency to subsume all *haredim* into the category of 'black hat/s', that is the full male *haredi* garb of black coat, suit, hat and *yarmulke*, as well as a beard and *peyot*. This uniform representation elides and ignores the marked differences and multifaceted nature of *haredi* society, in which there is 'a range of hats, clothes, haircuts, beard styles and even sidelock curls. Each *haredi* group has a singular fashion which allows it to be identified from afar according to the length of beard, broadness of the hat's brim, trouser length, and so on' (Aran 2006: 85–86).

Because such films were shot from the outside and not from the perspective of or within the *haredi* communities themselves, the sense of variation within *haredism* itself is absent. Inaccurate one-dimensional portraits of *haredism* as monolithic and uniformly pathological, sadistic, oppressive, constricted and misogynistic result, and non-*haredi* Jews, as well as non-Jews, might therefore fall into the trap of believing such films as representative of all *haredim*. Indeed, that there is very little input from the *haredim* themselves reminds us that such films constitute a form of internal Jewish mimicry – with actors literally 'blacking up' by donning *haredi* garb – deployed to mock and critique *haredi* values from a secular or non-*haredi* viewpoint. The gay lapsed Jew mimicking an observant *haredi* in the French film *L'homme est une femme comme les autres/Man is a Woman* is a rare example of a film self-reflexively drawing attention to this process, which arguably occurs in all mainstream fiction films depicting *haredim*.

As a result, there was thus no sense of the variety and complexity of Judaism. Intra-religious differences were downplayed, and even when they were highlighted, the underlying message was that everyone is basically the same underneath despite any outwardly different religious observances. There is thus no sense of the sectarian, and often minute visual, divisions within these two binary opposites – from Liberal, Reform, Conservative and Reconstructionist to modern Orthodox, Lubavitch, Litvish, Yeshivish, Gur, Neturei Karta and Satmar – as they are all represented as being on the same continuum. Only a keen eye would be able to spot those differences, even if and when they were represented on film. Certainly Liberal or modern Orthodoxy is 'rarely, if ever, portrayed on film' (Rosenberg 1996: 33), nor is there any sense of difference or distinction between Sephardi (North African, Southern European, Asian subcontinent), Mizrahi (Middle Eastern), Ashkenazi (Eastern and Central European) and Beta Israel (Ethiopian) traditions. Indeed, film often 'ethnocentrically projects an Ashkenzi culture onto a Sephardic history' (Shohat 1991: 250 n.44), as in Mel Brooks's Spanish Inquisition sequence in his *History of the World, Part 1*, featuring singing and dancing Yiddish-accented *haredim*. Again, Jewry is presented as not only ritually and theologically monolithic but as geographically homogeneous, with almost no sense of national, regional or coastal distinctions. In its place is a simplistic cinematic division between Reform and *haredism*. This is denoted by the prevalence of the use of the word 'Temple' by Reform Jews to describe their synagogues, and by the absence of the word '*shul*' (Yiddish: 'synagogue'), used by the Orthodox and *haredim* to refer to theirs.

In addition, when Judaism does appear, it is usually in terms of the Jewish character's flight from a repressive and restrictive culture that limits his/her social mobility or marriage prospects. For example, in *Next Stop, Greenwich Village*, Judaism codes a suffocating Jewish home life. When Larry Lapinsky (Lenny Baker) moves out of his parents' house, he takes his *yarmulke* – a clear sign of Judaism – out of the drawer, contemplates it for a moment, and then throws it back. This abandonment of his parents' religion is completed when, on his subway ride to Greenwich Village, he places a beret on his head, a symbol of cosmopolitan intellectualism. *Haredism* is represented as particularly oppressive and rigid, embodied by the stern, tyrannical but pious patriarch who rejects rather than embraces American ways, such as the father in *Left Luggage* (dir. Jeroen Krabbé, 1998) and *Kadosh/Sacred*, two films that deal very specifically with the traditions and rigorously conservative ways of *haredism*. Such themes are even more evident when looking at the various ways that *kashrut* has been deployed in film, which will be explored in more detail in the following chapter.

Yet, plotlines rarely comment on Judaism directly, preferring to use it as a means to make other comments about Jews and their relationships with and to Gentiles. Typically, in Allen's oeuvre and elsewhere, Jewish *kashrut* practices are used to code the differences between Jews and Gentiles, even if the former are not particularly observant, such as the lobster sequence in *Annie Hall*, in which Alvy is afraid of them. Although many of these films rarely comment on US Judaism, they certainly do provide commentary on its adherents.

The post-denominational era

In contrast, contemporary cinema has revised the '*Halacha*' outlined above. It defines Jewish identity both ethnically *and/or* religiously. In doing so, it mocks normative Judaism (in its various incarnations) on a fairly consistent basis, featuring many attacks on observant Jews. Contemporary cinema's comfort with an increasing range of Jewish religious identification beyond the secular/*haredi* binary was the product of the factors outlined in my introduction, most prominently the revitalisation of Jewish religious beliefs, practices and literature in the United States (and beyond) during the 1980s and 1990s. This occurred as a result of greater enrolment in Jewish day schools, improvements in Jewish education at all levels, the expansion of Jewish studies on the university campus, the publication of Jewish literature, the number of secular Jewish organisations that observe Jewish holidays, and in the Jewish programming offered in Jewish community centres. It was also a reflection of an era of growing post-denominationalism. Twenty- to forty-year-olds in the United States (and Europe) were increasingly indicating a sense of alienation from Jewish communal organisations and experiences that were perceived as boring and uninviting. The result was a general decline in synagogue membership, financial contributions and denominational affiliation, as greater numbers of younger Jews began to identify as 'just Jewish' rather than Reform, Conservative or Reconstructionist than in the past. Rather than following their parents into the halls of synagogues and Jewish federations, a significant segment of younger Jews sought to create new avenues of, and opportunities for, Jewish involvement that did not replicate older patterns of Jewish communal participation. Instead, they began exploring their own opportunities for Jewish experiences outside and independent of the existing communal infrastructure.

Commentators defined this experience as that of the 'post-denominational' Jew/ess, refusing to be labelled by existing religious institutions and rejecting existing branches of Judaism, creating something more fluid. The post-denominational Jew/ess 'refuses to be labelled or categorised in a religion that thrives on stereotypes. He [sic] has seen what the institutional branches of Judaism have to offer and believes that a better Judaism can be created' (Rosenthal 2006: 20). Rather than reject Judaism wholesale, or 'engage in community structures they find alienating or bland' (Kelman and Schonberg 2008: 12), the post-denominational Jew/ess uses his/her creativity and commitment to organise independently, to build meaningful Jewish experiences and to create ritual on her/his own terms outside community institutions but within her/his own organic community of friends and family. It is possible now to lead a full and fulfilling post-denominational Jewish existence outside, and unrelated to, mainstream organisations and institutions. One does not need to go to a synagogue to be Jewish anymore. Known as '*Do-it-Yourself (DIY) Judaism*' (Kelman and Schonberg 2008: 12), it emerged from a postmodern mix-and-match tendency in general, what David Graham called 'Pick 'n' mix Judaism', reflecting an environment that is 'open and welcoming and encourages choice and personal preference above rules and dictates' (2004: 22).

As a consequence, contemporary cinema reverses the previous binary model of Judaism on film outlined above to produce a multiplication of religiously defined Jews onscreen. Not only have these representations increased, they have also taken on different forms, marking a departure from the past towards more unselfconscious, self-critical, deeper, subtle, nuanced, playful and even outrageous representations of Judaism. There is even some extensive attempt to understand and explore religious beliefs and the ideas and philosophy behind these rituals, as well as to mock, mimic and reverse them. Film now represents not only subjective Judaic (I use this term to distinguish it from ethnic Jewishness) experiences, but also to no overt educational purpose. Jews are increasingly being identified through religious rather than simply ethnic (names, physical looks, professions, locations) markers. Key points in the Jewish religious calendar, other than just Chanukah and Passover, are depicted. In this way, contemporary cinema moves towards a more sophisticated understanding of Judaism, its beliefs, rituals and practices, portraying the range of Jewish denominational affiliation (rather than just secular and *haredi*) such that 'multiple cultures are shown to thrive *within* Jewish life itself' (Rosenberg 1996: 44). Judaism on film is normalising.

Heterogeneous *haredim*

Contemporary cinema is moving beyond using *haredim* as a mere cipher, instead presenting its adherents in a proliferating variety of unusual settings. *A Stranger Among Us* provides many explanations about *haredi* lifestyle, beliefs and customs. Where it is different, however, as we have seen, is in making the murderer a *haredi* Jewess and in the character Ariel, who serves to simultaneously 'represent and to undermine the image of the Hasid – he is both an *ilui*, a scholarly prodigy, and a real man capable of shooting a gun (though not without fainting)' (L. Roth 2004: 180).

In the British film *Snatch*, a gang of thieves mimicking *haredim* pull off a jewel heist. One of them, 'Franky Four Fingers' (Benicio Del Toro) turns out to be an actual *haredi* in the film. *Lucky Number Slevin* features a *haredi* criminal gang who wear the distinctive long black coats, hats, *yarmulkes* and side curls. Reversing traditional characterisations, these *haredi* Jews are violent. Thus, the queer *haredi* scholar paradoxically becomes tough and, within the film's narrative, brutal and cruel.

Lapsed *haredim* also appear with increasing regularity. *Mendy* (dir. Adam Vardy, 2003) and *Holy Rollers* (dir. Kevin Asch, 2010), which is based on a true story, both feature *haredi* drug smugglers (on the flight home one of them is given a mysterious bag and instructed to 'act Jewish' when passing through customs). *Kadosh/Sacred* includes a lapsed, but still Orthodox, *haredi* rock singer named Yaakov (Sami Huri) whose lyrics celebrate the Torah. Another lapsed *haredi* appears in the film *Down in the Valley* (dir. David Jacobson, 2005). Modern-day urban cowboy Harlan (Edward Norton) is revealed to be Jewish when he returns to his childhood neighbourhood and is shown sitting in synagogue while *haredim*, wearing *tefillin* (phylacteries) and *tallitim*, pray in Hebrew. His white Stetson stands out in stark contrast among the black hats. Although this initially resembles a visual joke, this film is unquestionably serious (in fact, the first serious film featuring a Jewish cowboy since 1912), especially as Harlan is a deluded ex-*haredi*, defined by his now-lapsed religious practice rather than any other visible ethnic or cultural markers, of which there are none, especially as he is played by the non-Jewish Edward Norton.

Other films, while continuing the trend of mimicking and mocking *haredim*, also introduce a hitherto absent spectrum. The eponymous Hebrew Hammer is depicted as a *haredi* in his dress and observance, clearly deploying religious Jewish symbolism. He wears a black trenchcoat, cowboy boots, star of David-shaped spurs and belt buckle, two exaggeratedly large gold *chai* (Hebrew: the number eighteen or 'life') neckchains and a *tallit* as a scarf. He drives a white Cadillac with star of David ornamentation and two furry *dreidels* (Yiddish: spinning tops used during the festival of Purim) hanging from his rear-view mirror. His registration plate reads 'L'Chaim' (Hebrew: lit. 'To Life'/'Cheers'). Using his *tefillin* he climbs a building like a superhero. The film thus rejects the depiction of *haredim* as intellectual, weak and scholarly but reverses such stereotypes in an act of appropriation. The farcical *Walk Hard: The Dewey Cox Story* (dir. Jake Kasdan, 2007) features two *haredi* music-industry executives who are seen dancing the *hora*. In a similar vein, Mel Brooks introduced a *haredi* Rabbi Tuckman, a travelling clergyman and *mohel* (Hebrew: person trained to carry out circumcision), into his *Robin Hood: Men in Tights*, a parody of medieval England from which in reality the Jews had been expelled.

Mordechai Jefferson Carver in *The Hebrew Hammer*.

Rabbi Tuckman in *Robin Hood: Men in Tights*.

Haredism is increasingly being explored 'as a total lived culture' (Wright 2009: 103). Two Israeli films, *Kadosh/Sacred* and *Ushpizin/Guests* (dir. Giddi Dar, 2004), both investigate aspects of this world. Similarly, the drama *A Price Above Rubies* is set within the *haredi* community of Boro Park, Brooklyn, and moves beyond obvious stereotype and caricature in its characterisations. Sonia is an attractive young *haredi* wife and mother married to a pious, gentle, asexual but unloving and sexually undemanding husband (Glenn Fitzgerald) who is too busy praying and studying to satisfy her physical and emotional needs. Her judgemental sister-in-law (Julianna Margulies) kidnaps her baby; her brother-in-law Sender is a 'deeply unpleasant' *haredi* Jew, a 'snake', an adulterer who rapes Sonia in return for a job in his untaxed jewellery business (Caplan 1999). Sender is a villain. He is not a *mensch*. He clearly has no qualms about using his power to gain sex from his own brother's wife. He is an unreligious, worldly, brash, aggressive, sexual and assertive man in pious garb, his mimicry of which masks his inner desires behind outward respectability (Rubel 2010: 84–85). The second time they have sex, Sender sings the 'Woman of Worth' love poem from which the title of the film is derived ('Who can find a virtuous woman?/For her price is far above rubies'). Sender's abuse of the poem, which is traditionally sung on the Friday night when welcoming the Sabbath, provides an ironic and critical commentary on his outward Judaism but inner lack of *menschlikayt*.

Sonia, however, is an atypical *haredi* Jewess. Her desires are active and her viewpoint (or gaze) is privileged. Sonia 'accepts' being raped by Sender because she is desperate for the physical contact her husband cannot offer her and because she knows it is also an escape route out of the suffocating confines of Boro Park (in contrast, the raped wife in *Kadosh/Sacred* has no agency or choice, and she reacts to her loneliness through masturbation). Sonia's new employment in downtown New York City is also a radical departure in a community in which the women rarely work outside the home, let alone beyond Boro Park. Eventually, Sonia leaves Boro Park and her family (including her baby) completely, finding solace, love and even passion in the arms of the binary opposite of the *haredi*: a sensitive Catholic Puerto Rican sculptor Ramon (Alan Payne). Since Ramon works with his hands he is dextrous, but he is also tough, muscular, shirtless and hence 'overtly sexualised' as the 'nonwhite "Other"' in contrast to the modestly attired and frail *haredi* (Rubel 2010: 88). Her choice of Ramon is an explicit rejection of the societal values and norms of her community, and thus the film sticks to the paradigm of representing *haredim* as oppressive and restrictive (valuing children over wives and mothers, who are deemed replaceable and hence dispensable). And even though the director insisted that the film's main concern is societal repression, the film ends up resembling an outside critique of the *haredi* way of life. Nonetheless, while it is impossible to ascertain the accuracy of such a representation, not least since the community on which it is based is close-knit and closed to outsiders – and objected to the film on the basis of seeing the sets and wardrobe alone (Elber 1997) – it certainly marks a departure from the pre-1990 era not only in its lack of cardboard characterisations, but also in its depiction of *haredim* as normal, thinking, feeling people in a variety of everyday settings.

Contemporary cinema also explores *haredi* concepts. Kabbalah (Jewish mysticism) is cited in *A Stranger Among Us* when Ariel teaches Emily that 'God counts the tears of women'. It is also at the heart of *Bee Season* (dirs Scott McGehee and David Siegel, 2005). Saul Naumann (Richard Gere) is a professor of religious studies at the University of California, Berkeley, having written his graduate thesis on the Kabbalist Abraham Abulafia. When his daughter Eliza (Flora Cross) wins her class spelling bee, Saul coaches her in Kabbalah to help her keep winning. 'There are people who believe that letters are an expression of a very special primal energy and when they combine to make words they hold all the secrets of the universe,' he tells her. Eliza continues to do well at spelling bees because of a higher spiritual connection; visions appear to her and help her spell the word, no matter how difficult. Kane (1999) demonstrates how Mamet's work (explored above) is rich in biblical allusion and scriptural exegesis, including Kabbalah and *gematria* (a Kabbalistic method of interpreting the Bible by calculating the numerical value of words, based on the values of their constituent letters), and it is argued that Kabbalistic ideas, symbols and numerological references informed Guy Ritchie's *Revolver* (2005), including the naming a trio of characters after the biblical patriarchs. The use of Kabbalah is taken even further in *Pi* (dir. Darren Aronofsky, 1998). A group of *haredim* are engaged in mathematical Torah research, deriving from the belief that the Torah is really a string of numbers that form a code sent by God. They are thus searching the text for the 216-digit number they believe is the true name of God.

Indeed, *Pi*'s representation of religion stands out in several respects. It attempts to engage with, in a serious fashion, *haredi* beliefs, rather than simply presenting them as oddities, curiosities ripe for visual humour, or as foils for secular liberalism; indeed, the *haredi* worldview is explained in some detail with little or no gloss and simplifications. The film is rich in religious Jewish imagery: *haredi* dress, synagogue interiors and other Jewish items figure frequently. There are even quite detailed discussions about the nature of the name of God, Jewish history and belief, and the messianic age. The protagonist, a tortured mathematics genius, Max Cohen (Sean Gullette), meets the *haredi* group's leader, Lenny Meyer (Ben Shenkman), who explains to him the significance of a daily Jewish practice that is rarely depicted on film: the wearing of *teffilin*. Lenny takes Max to a synagogue, where he teaches him to put on the *tefillin* and to recite the correct blessing in Hebrew. At the same time, there is no sentimentalisation. These *haredim* are determined, aggressive even, in their desire to obtain the true name of God. As Aronofsky put it, 'I wanted to make a movie about God, math and badass Jews.' They are ruthless, dangerous and threatening. At one point, they rough up and kidnap Max, and their leader Rabbi Cohen (Stephen Pearlman) emotionally harasses him when he refuses to reveal the number. Since the film refuses to distinguish between capitalistic and religious motivations, the *haredim* are presented as no different to their Wall Street counterparts, who also seek the number, if only for financial rather than mystical gain. Neither group is interested in

Max, nor do they offer him support or comfort. In this sense *Pi's haredim* resemble those of *Lucky Number Slevin*. Finally, the *haredim* are not simply represented as the exotic 'Other'. They are not entirely other-worldly. They are shown using the most modern methods available to them to achieve their aims. They drive cars, use computers, and generally engage with technology. Most importantly, as *Heeb* magazine pointed out in 2009, they speak English like they 'came from a crappy Brooklyn yeshiva,'[24] instead of a casting call from *Witness* (dir. Peter Weir, 1985)'. Overall, then, 'bearded Jews are no longer comical and marginal figures, but three-dimensional characters who command the audience's attention and, occasionally, even its sympathy' (Taub 2005: 36). *Haredim* have been normalised.

Beyond the fringes

Alongside more subtle and diverse representations of *haredim* are those of other denominations of Judaism, as contemporary cinema increasingly begins to explore intra-religious differences, those *between* Jews. *Novia que te vea/Like a Bride* illustrates how Sephardi and Ashkenazi Jews locate themselves in Mexico after the Second World War while collectively struggling against being targeted as 'Christ killers'. While the film reflects on what it means to be Jewish amidst Mexican Catholicism, it also explores the complexities of Jewish identity in Mexico, as well as the cleavages and differences within the Jewish community itself. When an aunt marries, for instance, her new husband boasts that his Judaism is 'superior' because they 'don't practice the religion the way we are supposed to,' reflecting the internal divisions among the Jewish community in Mexico. *The Grey Zone* makes constant reference, and ascribes value, to national origin (most notably Poland and Hungary), something that is typically elided in cinema, and this is repeated in *Munich*, which constantly plays on the differences between 'Polack' (Polish), 'yekke' (German) and 'Galitzianer' (southern Polish) Jews, reflecting the diverse origins of European and Israeli Jews. *Kadosh/Sacred*, however, is more troubling in its representation of Jewish difference in that it casts Sephardic or Mizrahi actors (those considered 'black' in Israel) in all of the villainous and 'evil' male roles, and Ashkenazi actors with European roots in the more heroic but oppressed female roles (Biale 2000: 69, Rubel 2010: 36).

Non-*haredi* Judaism is explored in a more complex fashion. In *School Ties* (dir. Robert Mandel, 1992) David Greene (Brendan Fraser) is identified as a practising Jew. On Rosh Hashanah, he recites the prayer 'Avinu Malkenu' ('Our Father Our King'). Since this is a Hebrew prayer and David can read it from the prayer book, this marks him out as a traditional Jew. But as he does not wear a *yarmulke*, plays football on a Jewish holiday, against his father's wishes, and does not have any 'particular eating habits' he is certainly not Orthodox. Thus, in addition to various ethnic markers such as his name and his wearing of a star of David, David is defined through a religious practice pronounced enough to be envisaged negatively as a barrier to passing, that is social mobility and advancement, as well as a distancing device from his peers, most of whom are bigoted if not outright antisemites. David's willingness to mimic Gentility allows him to assimilate into the school's *goyische* culture and pass as white. At the same time, however, David is not represented as simplistically and fully abandoning his Judaism. He is also shown adhering to the values of *menschlikayt*, in contrast to the school's competitive and racist *goyim naches*.

Judaism rather than Jewish ethnicity defines Walter Sobchak in *The Big Lebowski*. Walter is doubly unusual in that he is a convert and, for a non-*haredi* Jew, maintains a level of Jewish Orthodox practice. Walter appreciates, understands and takes his adopted faith very seriously, perhaps more so than many other non-*haredi* Jews on film, and certainly more so than any of the Coens' other Jewish characters: Larry Gopnik in *A Serious Man* does not know what a *get* (religious divorce) is, the eponymous Barton Fink resents his upbringing, and Verna and Bernie in *Miller's Crossing* have little regard for the teachings of the Torah. Throughout *The Big Lebowski*, Walter reaffirms his identity as a Jew. He continually reminds his bowling peers of the sanctity of the Sabbath, and is extremely angered when the Dude's emergency turns out not to be sufficiently critical to warrant Walter operating a car on a Saturday. As we have seen in Chapter 1, Walter is proud of the 'beautiful' Jewish tradition and hence is more happy to 'live in the past'.

Walter (again demonstrating his fondness for rules and regulations) demands that the bowling league fixtures are changed from Saturday to Wednesday, to accommodate the Jewish day of rest. In an expletive-ridden speech (containing nine 'fucks' and three other racial, sexual and other epithets), he explains that he can't bowl ('roll') or drive on Saturdays because he is 'shomer shabbes', and absolutely refuses to do so unless it is an emergency. His language here is multiply coded, using the correct insider terminology, which will be understood by Jews familiar with Hebrew and bowling aficionados respectively. At the same time, Walter's interpolation of the word 'fucking' between those of 'shomer' and 'shabbes' is a shocking juxtaposition of the holy and profane, and a homage to the Jewish gangster in *The Long Goodbye* who is upset at having to work on the Sabbath. It begs the question, however: would the sort of person that observed the Sabbath say s/he was 'shomer fucking shabbes'? Nevertheless, *Heeb* magazine (2009) crowned Walter's outburst as its number one 'greatest Jewish movie moment'. In a passage worth quoting at length, it stated,

> That Woody Allen marathon on Christmas Day might leave you with the feeling that Judaism is just a culture and not a religion, but along come the Coen Brothers with Walter Sobchak's […] most powerful expression of Jewish identity in cinema history – framed explicitly in religious terms. However comic the scene may be, if you had told the Hollywood moguls of yesteryear that in just a couple of generations, a major character in a major film would proclaim his refusal to 'roll on Shabbos', they would have thought you were dreaming.

Although Walter's religion is portrayed as comically obsessive, the fact that his Jewishness is a source of such pride cannot be disregarded.

At the same time, the Coens use Walter to mock the de-Semitising and de-Judainising strategies of the past. One cannot help reading him as nothing less than a deliberate parody of those Jewish directors who denuded their films of Jews and Judaism and/or who produced crass, sentimentalised caricatures for Gentile consumption. Furthermore, Walter's passionate, even fanatical, adherence to the rules of bowling can be read as a critique of the increasing stringency among Orthodox and *haredi* Jews who, it is argued, prioritise obedience over spirituality. Walter thus becomes a satirical representation of a particularly dogmatic and buffoonish rabbi. And, when Smokey's team-mate, Jesus Quintana (John Turturro), later confronts Walter over this incident, it is transformed into 'an obscene parody of the New Testament' (Tyree and Walters 2007: 80). When Jesus asks Walter, 'What's this "day of rest" shit? I don't fucking care! It don't matter to Jesus!' Walter becomes 'a comic Pharisee' as *Lebowksi*'s Jesus 'echoes Jesus's argument against the Pharisees for their over-scrupulous observance of religious boundaries, as in the Gospel of Luke when they accuse Jesus of healing the sick on the Sabbath' (Tyree and Walters 2007: 80). Walter thus introduces a *spectrum* into cinematic Judaism, being neither the conceptual secularised ethnic Jew nor the *haredi*, both so beloved in Jewish cinema of the past, falling between these two dichotomous poles.

A critique of Conservative Judaism is at the heart of the Coens' *A Serious Man*, a film that contains an abundance of unexplained religious references. The film disingenuously opens with an epigraph from the medieval Jewish sage and commentator Rashi: 'Receive with simplicity everything that happens to you.' It then launches into a subtitled Yiddish-language prologue set in a Polish *shtetl* concerning a *dybbuk* (Yiddish: a spirit of a dead person). Fast-forwarding into the 1960s, the next language heard is Hebrew, and while English dominates the dialogue thereafter it is punctuated with un-translated Hebrew and Yiddish idioms. On one level a reworking of the Book of Job, the film follows its *schlemiel* protagonist, Larry, whose wife has requested a *get*, as he shuffles from rabbi to rabbi in an attempt to make sense of what is happening to him. The rabbis look perplexed when told about the *get*. The first rabbi (Simon Helberg) is too young and callow to offer any decent advice, being too preoccupied with perspectives and parking lots to remember Larry's concerns about his wife, but significantly using the oblique and respectful Hebraic designation 'Hashem' to refer to God. 'Hashem doesn't owe us the answer, Larry. Hashem doesn't owe us anything. The obligation runs the other way.' The second middle-aged and more senior Rabbi Nachtner (George Wyner) garrulously recounts an elaborate tale of a Jewish dentist who finds Hebrew letters spelling out the words 'Help me' on the reverse of a *goy*'s teeth, but is unable to provide any interpretation or answers. As Larry is still unsatisfied with all the unanswered questions about Hashem, Rabbi Nachtner explains that 'we can't know everything', to which Larry exclaims 'It sounds like you don't know anything!' Finally, in his desperation to learn the answers to God's intentions, Larry heads towards Rabbi Marshak (Alan Mandell), the wisest and most influential of the three clergymen, who refuses to even see him ('The rabbi is busy. He's thinking'). Broken, Larry returns to the Jolly Roger Motel, none the wiser. In contrast, Larry's son Danny gains an unsolicited audience with Marshak, who provides him wise (and hip) counsel, albeit derived not from the Torah or Talmud, but from Jefferson Airplane's 'Somebody to Love'.

Building upon *The Big Lebowski*, *A Serious Man* is the epitome of the contemporary cinematic trend of rejecting previous assimilatory attempts at universalisation of Jewishness – that is of attempting to remake Judaism as a civil American religion – in favour of an ethnic specificity that is untranslatable into American analogues. At the same time, it is steeped in the Coen brothers' autobiographical experience and recollections of their own childhoods. 'We're not trying to help anyone understand the Jewish experience,' Joel Coen explains. 'It's just a story about community and family [...] and we're trying to be specific in the telling of that story. Specificity is important' (quoted in Hiller 2009). The Coens reject convention in terms of the representation of Judaism onscreen, preferring to reuse their own Jewish characteristics found in their earlier works. Thus these are not Jews for the Gentile world, that is stereotypically exaggerated versions of reality familiar to a non-Jewish society, explaining why the film attracted so much criticism from the more public-relations-minded professionals in the American Jewish community. Orthodox Rabbi Benjamin Blech (2009) wrote, for example, that *A Serious Man* 'lampooned, satirised and stereotyped to anti-Semitic perfection'. But as representatives of the younger generation of filmmakers, the Coens are not concerned to reach out in an inter-faith fashion, or with what their co-religionists might think. Indeed, the film mocks 1960s Conservative Judaism and its communal leaders. As Sofie Roberts (2010) put it so well, 'Walter won't roll on *Shabbos*; the Coens won't roll with convention.'

In a similar fashion to *A Serious Man*, *The Believer* is very scathing of contemporary Judaism and its dogmas. Based on a true story, it is even more unusual in its representation of Judaism. The film similarly presents non-*haredi* Orthodox Judaism. As the script states, 'These are not Hasidim, but Orthodox Jews: normal American kids in yarmulkes.' The synagogue scenes depict the more egalitarian, in gender terms at least, Conservative variety of modern Judaism. There is mixed seating, and women are shown wearing both *yarmulkes* and prayer shawls. The community represented is shown as such by a variety of factors: dress (white shirts, *tzitzit*, *yarmulkes*); the educational environment shown in the flashback scenes of the protagonist's early life; and the use of Hebrew liturgy and terminology, such as '*daven*' ('to pray').

It contains fairly accurate critiques of Judaism's belief system. Danny Balint rejects his upbringing and background and, in externalising his internal self-hatred, transforms himself into a mimic neo-Nazi. Yet, he still retains a reverence for Jewish learning and texts. Indeed, the film is perhaps an attempt to understand the inner workings of Judaism and how one individual can turn its injunctions into a form of self-hatred. Flashback sequences recall the 12-year-old Danny confronting his *yeshiva* teacher. Danny's childhood rants contain incisive questions about the nature of Judaism, faith and God. He even quotes an obscure *midrash* (Hebrew: lit. 'commentary'), which not even many Jews know, that Abraham actually sacrificed his son Isaac. These sequences clearly highlight the inability of the rabbi to answer or counterbalance Danny's arguments beyond banal platitudes which Danny easily rebuts. In critiquing Judaism (as well as antisemitism, for it becomes abundantly clear that Danny knows far more than his ignorant fellow neo-Nazis), *The Believer* offers uncomfortable and highly unconventional images. A skinhead wearing a *tallit* and leading the *shul* service on Rosh Hashanah; a neo-Nazi, in a 'Sieg heil' salute, chanting Hebrew words. The images of Danny, standing before a mirror, performing the Hitler salute while singing '*va'zot ha-torah...*' are potentially shocking and subversive, mirroring two similar sequences in *Hitlerjunge Salomon/Europa Europa* in which Solly, dressed in the uniform of the Hitler Youth, practices his salute, and also holds his hands up in imitation of the priestly sign.

Other films are unafraid to mock openly the assimilatory and universalising strategies Hollywood adopted in previous decades. The mockumentary *For Your Consideration* (dir. Christopher Guest, 2006) parodies studio executive Martin Gibb (Ricky Gervais), who considers the project *Coming Home for Purim* to be 'too Jewish' and insists it is changed to *Coming Home for Thanksgiving*. 'All I'm saying is, have it there, have it there, don't shove it down people's throat. I don't run around going, "I'm a Gentile, look at my foreskin!" I don't shove it down your throat, because I don't care.' Gibb's fear that the film is too specific mocks and reverses the Hollywood Jewish moguls who, as we have seen, from the 1930s until the early 1960s, divested films such as *The Ten Commandments* of their ethnic origins, de-Semitising, de-Judainising and Americanising them as a universal message. At the same time, a *Wedding Daze* (dir. Michael Ian Black, 2006) includes an Orthodox Jewish character who invents toys targeted at Jewish children. His 'jewnicorn' is a unicorn bedecked in stars of David, which, when squeezed, recites the Hebrew blessing for lighting the Chanukah candles, the 'jewla hoop' is a hula hoop in the shape of a star of David which, owing to its shape, doesn't work. They are, in the words of the lead character, who cannot think of anything better or complimentary to say, very 'specific'.

In addition, Judaism *qua* Judaism itself is critiqued. Arguably, this is at the heart of *The Believer*, and the cause of Danny's self-hatred. He loves Judaism, but despites what Jews have done with it. I have already referred to *A Serious Man* in detail above, and Harry in *Deconstructing Harry* calls Jewish tradition 'the illusion of permanence' and divisive. 'They're clubs, they're exclusionary, all of them. They foster the concept of the other so you know clearly who you should hate.' A particularly stringent Orthodox rabbi (Matt Lucas) is punched in British film *The Infidel* (dir. Josh Appignanesi, 2010) because of his intransigence and insensitivity. The Jewish writer (David Baddiel) and director (Appignanesi) of the film unapologetically explained the scene by describing the rabbi as a deserving 'villain'. *Keeping the Faith* mimics, mocks and critiques the introduction into Jewish worship of such non-normative methods of worship as meditation circles, a Black gospel choir, rabbinic stand-up comedy, karaoke and pop quizzes that characterise some forms of contemporary non-Orthodox Judaism. In this way, contemporary cinema disconnects itself from the past to reject institutional Jewish life of many varieties in the new post-denominational context.

Contemporary cinema is also manifesting greater inclusivity, increasingly embracing converts to Judaism, as compared to the pre-1990 period, when they were rare commodities in film. In addition to Walter in *The Big Lebowski*, Gentile Anna (Jenna Elfman) in *Keeping the Faith* secretly attends conversion classes so she can marry Rabbi Jake (Ben Stiller). *Lord of War* (dir. Andrew Niccol, 2005) takes the concept one step further. The Orlov family pretends to be Jewish in order to escape the Soviet Union in the 1970s. As Yuri Orlov (Nicholas Cage) recounts, 'There have been few occasions in the twentieth century when it's been an advantage to be a Jew.' While the Orlov family is composed of Russian Gentiles only mimicking Jewishness in order to pass in the United States, Yuri's father, Anatoly (Jean-Pierre Nshanian) 'took his assumed identity to heart'. He refuses to eat shellfish because it is *treyf*. He owns a kosher restaurant in Little Odessa and likes wearing his hat because 'it reminds us there's something above us'. His mimicry is excessive; he is like other Jews, only more so. As his son dryly comments, 'He was more Jewish than most Jews', and going to Temple 'more than the rabbi', complains his wife (Shake Tukhmanyan). Indeed,

Independence Day even hints at the conversion of the entire United States to Judaism, reversing the past universalising of Judaism. While David is in space, at the peak of the human fight-back against the aliens, Julius forms a prayer circle to recite the *Shema*. When the former secretary of state Albert Nimzicki (James Rebhorn) is invited to join in, he responds that he is not Jewish. Julius, in a reprise of the final line of *Some Like It Hot* (dir. Billy Wilder, 1959), quips, 'Nobody's perfect.' Whether genuine or mere mimics, these cinematic converts point to a greater acceptance within contemporary Judaism itself, at least among the younger generation of filmmakers, writers and actors/actresses.

Finally, contemporary cinema is also including more obscure Judaism, in mainstream terms at least. This is part of the 'process of de-hiding' I mentioned in my introduction which, in religious terms, 'takes the form of illustrating certain rituals of [...] Jewish culture that have previously scarcely been touched upon in cinematic representations' (Rocha 2010: 39). Where Jews were once gathered around the Thanksgiving table, film increasingly deploys the Passover Seder instead, suggesting a post-assimilatory shift from the all-American day to ethnically specific festivals. Films as diverse as *When Do We Eat?*, *Judíos en el espacio/Jews in Space* and *Schindler's List* all feature the Seder table as the device for concentrating diverse and often conflicting family members (and their partners and offspring) into one place. *A Family Affair* even reinvents Passover as a 'festival freedom for all our GLBT loved ones'. *The Prince of Egypt* (dirs Brenda Chapman, Steve Hickner and Simon Wells), an animated version of the Exodus, was released in 1998. And where the Seder

Judaism in *Independence Day*.

is not explicit, it is alluded to, as in *Munich* when the discussion of the morality of the first assassination is conducted via an explicit reference to a *midrash* that is connected to the Exodus from Egypt.

Other religious festivals are being increasingly referenced. As we have seen, key scenes in *School Ties* and *The Believer* are staged on Rosh Hashanah, as is a debate on issues of survivor-guilt and theodicy between two Holocaust survivors, one Orthodox, the other secular, in Eli Cohen's 1991 film *The Quarrel*. In 2002, the first US Chanukah film (*Eight Crazy Nights*, dir. Seth Kearsley, 2002) to compare to the classical Hollywood Christmas films was released, and the festival also appeared in *The Holiday* (dir. Nancy Meyers, 2006). The narrative of *The Hebrew Hammer* is not only focused around Chanukah, but its protagonist is named after the hero of the ancient story: Judah HaMaccabbee (Judah the Hammer). In *Harold & Kumar Get the Munchies*, we see a broken menorah in Goldstein and Rosenberg's apartment, and in *X-Men: First Class*, we glimpse a childhood memory of Chanukah candles.

Purim (in the past explained away and divorced of its ethnic specificity as either 'Jewish mardi gras' or compared to Halloween) pops up in several films. A full photocopied page from the Book of Esther fills the screen in extreme close-up in *Homicide*, developing the themes of being a Jew in a Gentile culture, as well as those of mimicry/hiding/deception and revelation that are key to understanding both the Purim story and the film. Rosina performs as Queen Esther for her Gentile lover in *The Governess*. *The Hebrew Hammer*'s main characters are called Mordechai and Esther respectively, referencing the two key Jewish characters in the Purim story. And *For Your Consideration* features a film within a film entitled *Coming Home for Purim*.

A series of widely contrasting films foreground key Jewish religious rituals and beliefs. Funerals that follow the Jewish tradition appear in a range of films, including such practices as sitting *shiva* and the recital of the *Kaddish* (the memorial prayer for the dead). *Deconstructing Harry* features a *Star Wars*-themed bar mitzvah. The rite of passage is included in two films in 2006 alone, *Sixty Six* and *Keeping Up with the Steins* (dir. Scott Marshall, 2006), followed by *Hey Hey It's Esther Blueburger* in 2008 (in which the bar mitzvah is not the focus but merely another passing event) and *A Serious Man* in 2009. *Mezuzot* (Hebrew: plural of *mezuzah*) are proliferating onscreen. They have long appeared in films featuring Orthodox and *haredi*

Jews, but we are also seeing them in films with less observant Jews such as *Lucky Number Slevin*, *Carlito's Way*, the *Harold & Kumar* films, *A Serious Man* and *The Infidel*. In the latter three films, they are incorrectly placed on the left- instead of the right-hand lintel, possibly as a nod and a wink, an in-joke to those who can read the codes. A *mezuzah* is written in the opening scene of *Esther Kahn* (dir. Arnaud Desplechin, 2000). A Jewish exorcism is carried out in *The Unborn* (dir. David S. Goyer, 2009), albeit preceded by the blowing of a somewhat enlarged and therefore highly unrealistic *shofar*. Another more accurate *shofar* is used as a bong in *Harold & Kumar Go to White Castle/Get the Munchies*.

Conclusion: religious freedoms

In 2003, Malina Sarah Saval lamented the dearth of mainstream Jewish films. She wrote, 'Perhaps the most noticeable absence in recent years occurred during the 1990s, in which period not one American movie featured a rabbi' (16). Saval must have been watching with her eyes closed because, as we have seen, a plethora of films have depicted rabbis of all stripes. This desire for more rabbis onscreen 'suggests that Jewish identity has moved toward a more conventionally recognisable and stable identification with religiosity at its foundation' (Itzkovitz 2006: 243). Judaism on film is being normalised. Furthermore, given the new liberties taken with Judaism on film since 1990, it strikes me that Jews have become not only very comfortable with their religion but also extraordinarily self-confident about it. Judaism is no longer shown as exclusively repressive and controlling or standing in the way of assimilation. It is not simplistically divided into secularised ethnics versus exotic, othered *haredim*. Cinema does not require 'the abandonment of Judaism, or its thoroughgoing accommodation to non-Jewish norms' (Wright 2009: 99) in its search to embrace Judaism and the non-Jewish world simultaneously.

At the same time, increasingly multicultural and postethnic societies are far more receptive and tolerant of religious imagery, particularly in what many feel to be the more openly religious society that has emerged in the United States and Europe since 2001. As befitting an increasingly post-denominational context among the younger generation of Jews, especially twenty- to forty-year-olds, the range of religious identities which do not simply conform to the established sectarian lines within Judaism has multiplied.

And if I only focus on mainstream fiction films for the purposes of this book, then it is possible to argue that documentaries push the boundaries even further. In *Capturing the Friedmans* (dir. Andrew Jarecki, 2003), a documentary charting the decline of a Jewish family when the father, Arnold, and youngest son, Jesse, are accused of sexually abusing dozens of young boys who came to the Friedman home for computer classes, traditional Jewish family scenes, in particular the Passover Seder, serve as the backdrop to the crumbling family's last weeks together, as captured on 8mm videotape. *Trembling Before G-d* is another documentary charting the experiences of gay and lesbian *haredi* and Orthodox Jews and the problems they face.

In this chapter, I have tried to bring together a small selection of films as a step towards beefing up the study of cinematic Judaism, giving some illustrative examples of the rich selection of films to be productively researched further. I have only scratched the surface here, but as Pearl and Pearl (1999) and Gertel (2003) have shown, there is clearly plenty of material for further exploration, and I hope that, in the future, the links between film studies, and Jewishness as Judaism, will be confronted in more depth.

CHAPTER 7

Food

Introduction

There is a deliciously long list of films in which foods – marked as Jewish and kosher, Jewish but not kosher, or *goyish* and *treyf* – are not simply glimpsed as part of a film's setting, but are also employed as important plot devices that explore cultural, ethnic and religious issues. Woody Allen, for example, makes much use of the nature and function of food and dining in his films. His movies abound with memorable moments and food allusions: the Chinese food scene in *Manhattan* (1979), the crazy Seder in *Sleeper* (1973), the split-screen families and their foods in *Annie Hall* (1977), the serious discussion at the Seder in *Crimes and Misdemeanors* (1989), the jokes about kosher food and fasting during Yom Kippur in *Radio Days* (1987), Carnegie Deli and the plates of kosher meat in *Broadway Danny Rose* (1994), and so on. Certainly, Allen's use of food in his films intrinsically connects that food to Jewish culture.

Surprisingly, however, given the Jewish religious and cultural interest in food, there is very little scholarship about the topic of Jewish cultural representation through food in films. Building on my own work (Abrams 2004) I will continue filling this gap here, by exploring the ways in which 'Jewish', kosher and *treyf* foods are represented in film. My discussion will include observations on the ways in which Jews have been represented and stereotyped in film through food. Specifically, in this chapter I will explore the connections between food and Jewish cultural traditions, history, identity, sex and nostalgia. Finally, I will also examine cinematic representations of the Jewish family meal as the primary site of philosophical debate about the Jewish condition and Jewish identity.

Reubens, bagels, brisket and balls

Foodstuffs are intimately related to Jewish identity and culture in film. Although many of these products have long been assimilated into mainstream US and other cultures, on film a corned beef or pastrami sandwich on rye bread, bagels and lox, gefilte fish, chicken soup or matzo typically code the Jewish world semiotically. Referring back to the notions of 'reading Jewish' and 'double coding' I outlined in my introduction, there is, I suggest, a Jewish audience that may glean Jewish specificity from such products that a general audience may decode as universal (Bial 2005: 152). Bagels, being a Jewish tradition imported into the United States and other Western countries, stand as an obvious signifier of Jewishness. In *Amy's O* we understand the protagonist's Jewishness because, over a breakfast of bagels, her parents express their concern over her lack of dating. At the beginning of *The Hebrew Hammer* the eponymous hero is teased by his Gentile counterparts, 'Hey Mordechai, want a bagel?' while a non-Jewish boy feigns choking. Here, the bagel not only identifies Mordechai but also marks him as a subject of difference. Another breadstuff, *challah*, is particularly important in Jewish practice as it is eaten on the Sabbath and holy days and so it is seen in the *haredi* milieu of *A Price Above Rubies* – once at a circumcision and another at the Shabbat meal – as well as in *You Don't Mess with the Zohan* and *Seres Queridos/Only Human*. In *Saving Private Ryan* (dir. Steven Spielberg, 1998), a Jewish GI, private Stanley Mellish, is handed a Hitler Youth knife from the remains of a dead German soldier. He flips it and, in an act of reversal, responds in a sardonic tone, 'And now it's a Shabbat *challah* cutter, right?' And in the Russian film, *Lyubov/Love*, for example, the family's Jewishness and hence religious observance is marked by their serving matzo with tea, instead of biscuits, rather than as a part of Passover celebrations (Gershenson 2008: 183).

Chicken soup with dumplings or balls made from matzo-meal might now be considered a universal panacea, popularised even further by the bestselling series *Chicken Soup for the Soul*, but it has also been identified as quintessentially Jewish. David in *Prime* (dir. Ben Younger, 2005) and Jessica in *Kissing Jessica Stein* both make chicken soup for their sick partners, and the latter calls it 'Jewish penicillin'. At the bar mitzvah party in *Keeping Up with the Steins*, 'Mom's Matzo Ball Soup' is one of the delicious homemade dishes on display. Similarly, the Jewishness of a family in *You Don't Mess with the Zohan* is established when the mother serves matzo ball soup for dinner.

Brisket is another food associated with Jews, since it is the primary component of the traditional Jewish dish *cholent* (a slowly simmered stew of beans, potatoes, beef and other ingredients) that Jews the world over eat on Shabbat. Brisket has further specifically Jewish connotations, hence why in *Annie Hall*, for example, Woody Allen depicts the oh-so-Jewish Singer family arguing over a brisket. A joke even connects the cut of meat with the cut of circumcision: 'If a doctor carries a black bag and a plumber carries a toolbox, what does a *mohel* carry? A Bris-kit!' (Silverman 2006: 125). Brisket is particularly popular among Jews in the United States, and hence 'Grandma's brisket' is served at the bar mitzvah in *Keeping Up with the Steins*. It is no coincidence, therefore, that the first act Avner performs once his counter-assassination team is assembled in *Munich* is to prepare a plate of hot brisket for them. The choice of brisket as the main dish is significant, for it hints at Avner's Jewish heritage and hence places him in his milieu.

Brisket in *Munich* was probably also chosen for other reasons. Brisket fits into the film's economy, literally, for early on in the narrative, as mentioned in Chapter 5, a Mossad accountant quite forcefully explains to Avner the need to obtain expenses receipts. This becomes a repeated refrain during the film, as his fellow agents fret over such things as the price per kill. 'Brisket,' Ruth Reichl notes, 'a large, flat, fatty cut of meat from the front of the steer, was long a favorite of peasant cooks because it was considered rather undesirable and was therefore inexpensive' (2004: 423). 'Because a brisket stretched into many meals,' Joan Nathan points out further, 'it was an economical cut for large families in Europe' (1995: 175). The brisket is thus not only economical but also becomes a visual reinforcement of the film's theme concerning the true costs of killing. Ultimately, the film concludes, no amount of expenditure can produce the required results – peace and security for one's home (land).

The brisket may suggest yet further meanings. To prepare brisket requires care and long, slow cooking. Any good cook knows that brisket, being a cheap cut, needs 'to be simmered slowly to transform it' (Nathan 1995: 175). Reichl adds, 'Over the centuries, a panoply of excellent brisket dishes developed, all based on the simple fact that long, slow cooking renders this cut superlatively tender' (2004: 423). The brisket, therefore, enjoys further double coding: on the one hand, as a testament to Avner's skills as a chef, and hence killer, as *Munich*'s culinary motif serves to equate killing with cooking and eating. An example of this is the use of the term 'butcher', which can refer to a person who cuts up and sells meat as a trade, someone who slaughters animals for food, or a person who kills brutally or indiscriminately. In this way, Avner's ability to cook is closely aligned with his ability to kill. And, on the other hand, the brisket serves as a symbol for the peace process – it is something that cannot be rushed, cannot be produced overnight, but takes time, care, love and attention.

Although *treyf*, the Reuben sandwich – a grilled combination of corned beef, Swiss cheese and sauerkraut (or coleslaw) on sourdough pumpernickel bread – is a clear signifier of ethnicity. Its specific origins may be unclear, but it is associated inextricably with New York Jewish delicatessens (and its name implies Jewishness, too).[25] Jewish comedian Lenny Bruce once quipped, 'Pumpernickel is Jewish' (quoted in Novak and Waldoks 1981: 60). In *Quiz Show* the Reuben sandwich is semiotically deployed to code Jewishness and difference. Social-climbing Jewish lawyer Dick Goodwin (Rob Morrow) orders the sandwich as the special of the day at the Atheneum, an elitist Manhattan club to which he is invited for lunch. Aware of his ethnic interloper and parvenu status and the unwillingness of the patrician elite to allow him to pass, Goodwin remarks that the sandwich was named after Reuben Kay of Nebraska, before dryly observing about the club, 'Unfortunately, they have the sandwich here, but they don't seem to have any Reubens.' In this way, Goodwin uses the Reuben sandwich to accuse the WASP establishment of the *Gentleman's Agreement* type of genteel antisemitism, just as it codes his sense of out-of-placeness.

Later, when Goodwin is invited to the Van Dorens' rural estate in Connecticut, food emphasises the distance between them. While Goodwin is slowly seduced by, aspires to and envies their wealthy *goyische* lifestyle, he also clearly feels out of place and uncomfortable in such surroundings. He is served distinctly WASP and genteel *goyische* foods such as fresh and homegrown corn on the cob and tomato salad, which he awkwardly picks at, as they are seemingly unfamiliar to him, unlike the recognisable, ethnic and hence comforting Reuben sandwich he eats at the Atheneum. This conflict between the WASP world he aspires to join and his own ethnic/religious background is highlighted in another key food sequence when Goodwin visits Herb Stempel's apartment to interview him about his allegations that the quiz shows are rigged. Stempel does not initially recognise Goodwin as Jewish, as Goodwin carries all the signifiers of the successful and accepted Gentile WASP. He is a smooth, well-mannered, groomed and manicured (his teeth are perfectly straight and white) government-employed Harvard graduate, dressed in well-tailored suits and carrying a briefcase. Stempel offers Goodwin some *ruggelach* (an Eastern European Jewish pastry), which he, as a working-class Jew, clearly feels he must explain to Goodwin, somewhat exaggeratedly, as 'a Jewish delicacy'. When Goodwin declines, Stempel encourages him ('C'mon, you don't know what you're missing'). Goodwin replies that he is 'quite familiar with *ruggelach*'. Genuinely surprised, Stempel asks him, alluding to the anti-Jewish quotas that existed there, 'How did a guy like you get into Harvard?' Goodwin accepts and eats the *ruggelach*, coding simultaneously how he has not forgotten his ethnic origins, and thus feels trapped between the overtly Jewish Stempel who embodies his past and the urbane Van Doren clan that represents his aspirational future. His is the dilemma of the transitional Jewish figure in US culture, suspended between the WASP dream and his ethnic origins, here coded through food.[26]

Sweet kosher wine is another signifier of Jewishness, as it is drunk on the Sabbath and festivals and at any time that a celebration or other occasion requires a blessing over grapes. The brand Manischewitz, in particular, is synonymous with kosher wine and is the Jewish brand of choice in the United States; in 1953, for example, more than ten million gallons were imbibed, nearly one-tenth of the total American wine production. Jack Benny taught Bing Crosby the word, and Bob Hope introduced an Irish quartet on St Patrick's Day as sponsored by Manischewitz. Consequently, Manischewitz is identified in the American public mind with Jewishness. A clear cinematic example of this is deployed in *The Hebrew Hammer*, in which the wine is used at several points in the script in order to reinforce Carver's Jewishness. Mordechai has a taste for Manischewitz (Black Label), which he drinks neat like the variety of Johnny Walker it is clearly mocking. The joke here is that Jews typically drink Manischewitz solely for sacramental use rather than for reasons of taste. Miles (Jack Black) in *The Holiday* points out that because 'he's had too much of the Manischewitz' he is going 'to have to be cut off' (obliquely suggesting circumcision and/or excision). David in *Prime* mentions how Jews drink it every Friday night. In *Lucky Number Slevin*, during his introductory voiceover narrative, Mr Goodkat (Bruce Willis) describes the gossip among Jews as 'that Manischewitz grapevine'. As we have seen in *Harold & Kumar Go to White Castle/Get the Munchies*, playing on the brand name, the two Jewish characters are referred to as 'Manny' and 'Shevitz', a clear reference to their Jewishness. Finally, in *Goodfellas* the Italian-American gangster Tommy (Joe Pesci) goes out on a date with a 'Jew broad' during which he quips to her, 'You might prefer Manischewitz, but it'd look funny on my table.' Here the use of the wine manifestly not only codes her Jewishness, but also serves to distance the two characters culturally.

Genteel foods

In contrast to such Jewish foods stand those that code gentility. Nora Ephron commented on the socio-ethnic construction of mayonnaise, in particular Hellmann's, as 'Gentile' (Tannen 1989: 156). White bread also signifies the competitive world of *goyim naches*. In *Glengarry Glen Ross*, a Jew insults a Gentile colleague with the words, 'You're *scum*, you're fucking white-bread.' In particular, it codes class divisions, distinguishing 'those who ate white bread', symbolising an 'unattainable style of life', from those who did not (Heinze 1990: 34–35). White bread stands for whiteness due to its white appearance but even more so in relation to its blandness, tastelessness and lack of nutritional value. As Lenny Bruce observed, 'White bread is very *goyish*' (quoted in Novak and Waldoks 1981: 60). Although not about Jewishness (but similarly positing a distinct ethnicity – Greek in this case – as against 'American-ness'), *My Big Fat Greek Wedding* (dir. Joel Zwick, 2002) perpetuates this linkage between white bread and assimilation into whiteness. As its Greek protagonist moves into the American mainstream, she swaps moussaka for white-bread sandwiches, and is hence accepted by her white peers, whereas hitherto her consumption of ethnic foods symbolised her distance from the American mainstream. Similarly, in *A Walk on the Moon* (dir. Tony Goldwyn, 1999) we clearly see a loaf of white bread in the background as Pearl Kantrowitz (Diane Lane) is preparing dinner. Here the loaf stands for her acculturation, even while she is holidaying in the Jewish Catskills resort.

Liberty Heights makes a particular play on these food items, using them to code how out of place Ben feels when he lunches at a Gentile classmate's house. A bird's-eye-view shot of a white-bread sandwich and glass of milk is accompanied by Ben's voiceover narration: 'I began to sense that there was a world beyond what I knew when I had lunch at Butch Johnson's house.' He tells Mrs Johnson (Katie Finneran) 'There's too much white here. The milk's white. The bread's white. It's all white stuff.' When Ben returns home to tell his mother (Bebe Neuwirth) that 'Everything was white,' she concludes sagely, 'Well, they must not be Jewish,' before adding, 'They're the other kind.'

'Spam is *goyish* and rye bread is Jewish'

In addition to serving as cultural identifiers of Jewishness and gentility, food stands as a trope for the clash between the Jewish and *goyish* worlds. Pig, since the *kashrut* laws proscribe it, thus frequently occurs as a symbol of the cultural gulf between Jews and Gentiles. Bruce's kosher/*treyf* taxonomy articulates this culinary side of Jewish self-definition: 'Spam is *goyish* and rye bread is Jewish.' Spam is quintessentially *goyish*, in Bruce's formulation, not only because it is a pork product, but also because, like white bread, it implies a manufactured, artificial, *processed* blandness. Pig and spam, therefore, stand as tropes for all that is *goyish* and *treyf*. This connection is explicitly made in *Pulp Fiction* (dir. Quentin Tarantino, 1994):

> Vincent (John Travolta): Want a sausage?
> Jules (Samuel L. Jackson): Naw, I don't eat pork.
> Vincent: Are you Jewish?
> Jules: I ain't Jewish man, I just don't dig on swine.

Although neither character is Jewish, and it is possible that Jules is Muslim, the ensuing discussion as to why Jules does not eat pork has a decidedly Talmudic flavour to it nevertheless, as they bat back and forth Jules's reasoning for not consuming pig. In this way it takes the form of a *pilpul*, that rabbinical method of careful and subtle Talmudic disputation.

Often the consumption of forbidden foods symbolises rebellion and/or the rejection of traditional ethnic roots. In *Mr Saturday Night* (dir. Billy Crystal, 1992), Buddy Young, Jr. (Billy Crystal) lures a beautiful Jewess in the audience away from her parents and invites her to dinner, where roast pork is consumed. She later becomes his wife. Sonia Horowitz in *A Price Above Rubies* uses food to demonstrate her rebellion from *haredi* tradition, by eating a *treyf* egg roll in Chinatown, and loving it. The shot of her biting into the roll and the exaggerated sound effect of the resulting crunch only serve to reinforce its tastiness. 'Mmm, it's delicious!' she declares with no sense of remorse or shame, even when she learns it contains pig. The effect is later compounded when her husband and their Rabbi/therapist are shocked to learn that she keeps kosher 'at home' only. Here, the food codes Sonia's desire to escape the confines of her community, which is emphasised by her geographical status – she is sitting in Chinatown, Lower Manhattan, some distance from her home in Boro Park, Brooklyn.

Kashrut also can be seen as a barrier to social advancement. Normative Judaism's food restrictions limit gastronomic exploration, but more importantly they can curtail social and geographic mobility, which has led many Jews in real life to break away from such religious sanctions as they sought their 'place at the table'. Therefore it is not surprising to find that, in order to achieve higher social identification, Jews in film have eaten forbidden foods, as the conspicuous consumption of such food is an important indicator of status. Consequently, the consumption of such products becomes emblematic of attempts to assimilate, to move away from Jewish origins. In *School Ties*, David is advised by the football coach not to make a fuss about any 'particular eating habits'. Thus kosher food serves as a potential obstacle to his athletic/academic career, but David's flexibility on this issue allows him to assimilate into the school culture (even if not entirely, as we have seen) but only at the expense of his ethnic/religious identity. In *Hitlerjunge Salomon/Europa Europa*, Solly, posing as a Hitler Youth, is served ham at his German girlfriend's house, coding the dilemmas in that period between *kashrut* and survival. Here his consumption of ham is used as part of his mimicry, used to disguise his Jewishness.

As shellfish is forbidden by *kashrut*, it is deployed to assert non-Jewishness. In *Focus*, Gentile antisemite Lawrence Newman is repeatedly mistaken for a Jew because of his glasses. After being denied a room in a 'restricted' hotel that clearly has vacancies, Newman and his wife Gertrude (Laura Dern) go to lunch, during which he uses food to emphasise his Gentile identity:

Lawrence: Do Jews eat clams?
Gertrude: No shellfish.
Waitress: Have you decided?
Lawrence. Yes. Clams. My wife will have clams, and I'll have clams, too.
Waitress: That's a large order of clams for two, sir. Okay. Anything else?

Newman's request of a *treyf* dish to emphasise his gentility in this instance ironically only serves to make him *seem* more Jewish. His excessive portion suggests the Jewish saying that 'Jews are like everyone else, only more so,' that the visibility of their efforts, their excess, marks them as different, 'almost the same, but not quite'.

Along with assimilation, certain other *treyf* foods also signal sophistication and the desire to gentrify. In *Commentary* magazine, for example, a full-page colour advert for Bolla Italian wine during the 1970s depicts lobster, clearly encoding it (along with other *treyf* foodstuffs, including various shellfish) as the epitome of worldliness and cosmopolitanism. But even as a food like lobster signals acculturation and sophistication, it can become emblematic of the cultural gap between Jews and Gentiles that is predicated on dietary difference. Woody Allen uses lobster to such effect in *Annie Hall*. Similarly, in the British film *Leon the Pig Farmer*, lobster symbolises the inherent and insurmountable distance between the Jewish protagonist and the *shiksa* of his erotic infatuation. On their first date at a restaurant, a neurotic and nervous Leon (Mark Frankel) accidentally orders lobster. Not only does Leon keep kosher, but also his date does not know he is Jewish because he fears that she will be put off. The waiter brings the lobster to the table, but before we can glimpse it the magnified shadow of its pincers is projected onto the restaurant's wall, an ominous foreshadowing of Leon's anxiety. Coupled with the lobster's loud cries of pain, the snipping pincers hint at Leon's own circumcision, as if revealing his deception (Aaron 2010: 177–78).

Forbidden fruits

The link between dietary and sexual prohibition in Judaism is oft repeated in *Yiddishkeit*, and interpretations linking sex and *kashrut* food regulations have long been made. Indeed, since Adam and Eve ate the apple in the Garden of Eden, food and sex have been inextricably linked, hence the term 'forbidden fruit'. Isaac Rosenfeld explained the link:

When the Lord forbade Adam and Eve to eat of the Tree, He started something which has persisted throughout our history: the attachment of all sorts of forbidden meanings to food, and the use of food in a system of taboos which, though meant to regulate diet, have also had as their function – perhaps the primary one – the regulation of sexual conduct [1949: 385–86].

Furthermore, Rosenfeld points out, 'Pork means the uncircumcised' (1949: 387). The eating of pork also suggests sexual deviancy and perversion. As Stacy S. Mulder observes, 'eating forbidden foods' is analogous to 'engaging in prohibited sexual liaisons' (2002: 268).

Meat and milk in Jewish law cannot be mixed and/or eaten together, for example, a prohibition deriving from the enigmatic biblical injunction against 'seething a kid in its mother's milk'. Jean Soler (1979) argues that this biblical ban on cooking a kid in its mother's milk was linked to an incest taboo, wittily observing, 'You shall not put a mother and her son into the same pot, any more than into the same bed.' Fish is only kosher if it has fins and scales. Furthermore, the symbolic or allegorical interpretation of the *kashrut* laws suggests that fins and scales on a fish are signs of endurance and self-control; the lack of them can be construed to mean wild, impetuous abandon. *Treyf* seafoods like lobster thus signify 'the whole world of forbidden sexuality, the sexuality of the *goyim*, and there all the delights are imagined to lie, with the *shiksas* and *shkotzim* [Yiddish: offensive term for non-Jew, plural of *shaygetz*] who are unrestrained and not made kosher' (Rosenfeld 1949: 387).

Many films have connected food and *kashrut* with sexuality. It is no coincidence, for example, that Alisa Lebow and Cynthia Madansky named their 1998 documentary about Jewish lesbians *Treyf*. Similarly, growing sexual awareness is signalled in *A Walk on the Moon*, when two teenage Jewesses, one of whom is Orthodox, are shown swapping information about sex while the other fries bacon in a pan. The latter asks the Orthodox girl, 'Are you allowed to kiss guys?' to which she replies, 'Guys I can kiss. Bacon is a different story.' A close-up of the bacon in the frying pan segues into an exchange about tongue-kissing. While we do not see either girl consume the bacon, its very presence equates to the gradual loss of their adolescent sexual innocence. In *A Price Above Rubies*, Sonia connects her pork egg roll with sex when her brother Yossi (Shelton Dane) warns her that because she is eating *treyf* she is 'going to hell.' 'Really?' she replies. 'And yesterday ... when I was lying on a desk getting *schtupped* by my brother-in-law ... yesterday I wasn't going to hell?' Throughout the entire conversation Sonia continues to consume her egg roll, speaking with her mouth full, emphasising her enjoyment of the *treyf*. Her consumption of the pig sets her on a path by which she not only gains her freedom from the oppressive *haredi* community to which she never truly belongs, but also by which she ultimately finds solace in the arms and bed of a sensitive Catholic Puerto Rican.

The Governess connects sex to a Gentile dessert. Rosina compares the texture and taste of semen to semolina: 'You know Gentiles eat a dessert that looks like semen. It's called semolina. I've seen it,' even though she has neither seen nor tasted either semen or semolina. The connection here between semen and semolina suggests that it is a Gentile practice to eat both, and thus beyond the boundaries prohibited by Jewish sexual law. Indeed, for Rosina and her sister Rosa, 'drinking semen' and eating semolina are something only prostitutes and Gentiles do. As Judith Lewin points out, 'Semen itself becomes an emblem of mature sexuality and is viewed as a curiosity – Gentile and *treyf* – Rosina would like to observe but not commit to' (2008a: 94): 'I would like to see it but not to drink it.' Rosina later unwittingly eats semolina during her first meal as a governess at the Cavendish household on Skye, thus suggesting that she has crossed – or is about to – the boundary marker between Jewish and Gentile sexuality. Like Sonia's eating the egg roll, Rosina's consumption of semolina sets her on a

Jim in *American Pie*.

path that leads to her sleeping with her Gentile employer. It also suggests that she will be 'drinking' other things.

American Pie connects another Gentile dessert with sex. Having been informed by one of his friends that 'second base' feels like 'warm apple pie', Jim sexually abuses the wholesome American product – the apple pie suggested in the title – in his quest for greater sexual knowledge. It recalls the earlier *Portnoy's Complaint*, in which the eponymous 'hero', Alexander Portnoy (Richard Benjamin) masturbates with a piece of raw liver that is subsequently eaten for the family supper. The shift from sexually abusing the ethnically coded liver – liver, in particular chopped liver, is widely considered to be a Jewish food – to superfluously and gratuitously *schtupping* a key symbol of Americanness suggests a move from ethnic specificity (here Jewishness) to assimilation, Americanisation and the absorption of Jews into the US mainstream. It is also a sign of confidence that the film's heavily coded Jewish protagonist is the one with the pie.

The link between food and sex in film is further explored through the use of certain settings as part of a film's *mise-en-scène*. The prominence of Jewish summer resorts in the Catskills – otherwise known as the 'borscht belt' – continues the connection between kosher food and kosher dating, since such places consciously linked Jewish traditions of matchmaking with kosher cuisine. The advertising for the most famous of them, Grossinger's, suggested that under this hotel's guidance food was an opportunity for sociability as well as the means to endogamous marriage and reproduction. Indeed, Grossinger's enjoyed a high reputation as an ideal place to look for a mate. Building on the earlier *Dirty Dancing* (dir. Emile Ardolino, 1987), *A Walk on the Moon* is deliberately situated at a kosher resort hotel in which a protagonist is seeking love or eligible marriage material.

Nostalgic nosh

Yet another function of Jewish foods in cinema involves the expression of nostalgia for a somehow happier past. The knishes and jars of kosher chocolate syrup in *A Walk on the Moon* all address concerns about holding onto lost traditions. Indeed, set as it is in the heyday of the Catskills as a Jewish holiday resort during the televised moon landings, the film is all about nostalgia, actively inviting its viewers to recall their own memories of watching it, if they are old enough, or to identify with such memories if they are not (Furnish 2005: 18). Food in contemporary film, therefore, sometimes focuses on the issue of continuing or losing or changing Jewish cultural traditions and thus expresses a desire to preserve the past, as if in a sterilised jar.

Many films look back to remember the past nostalgically as a golden age, depicting family life with dashes of sentimentality, bitterness, longing and mockery. Since *Yiddishkeit* focuses on the importance of family, the eating and partaking of food together, particularly on ritual occasions, is a cherished cinematic ritual, especially in contemporary cinema, where the connection has been enhanced since 1990. The Sabbath and Passover meals show up, in particular, as obvious cultural expressions. *Schindler's List* opens and (almost) closes with the inauguration of the Shabbat, marked by the lighting of candles and the *kiddush* (blessing of the wine). In *A Stranger Among Us* many explanations about food and other customs are given, including a detailed sequence about food preparation for the Shabbat. In these films, the specific ethnic, religious and cultural aspects of the ritual meals are stressed.

Salt water, a traditional Jewish foodstuff symbolising the tears shed by the Hebrew slaves in Egypt and hence eaten during the Seder meal, serves as a means to anchor Jews who are concealing their identities by mimicking gentility. In *The Governess* Rosina celebrates Passover alone in the privacy of her bedroom, and the required salt water proves to be a literal solution as a fixative for non-permanent photographic images when she spills some of it onto a photograph. This ritual element, therefore, develops into an important part of the plot, which revolves around the invention of photography as well as issues of concealment. The practice of eating an egg in salt water is also a key means by which Solly's ever-changing identity is rooted in *Hitlerjunge Salomon/Europa Europa*. He remembers the Seder ceremony in which salt water is consumed, and dreams of his family eating eggs dipped in it.

In *Avalon* (dir. Barry Levinson, 1990), the Jewish family meal is a critique of the divesting of ethnic traits in pursuit of assimilation. The Russian-Jewish Krichinsky family is never shown performing Jewish, but only American, rituals. One Thanksgiving meal climaxes in a dispute that cleaves the extended Jewish family. The meal serves as the pivotal point at which the Krichinsky family disintegrates into the atomised, separated, nuclear family structure of the dominant culture (*goyim naches*). The family traditionally does not begin eating until everyone arrives. However, older brother Gabriel (Lou Jacobi), who lives in the city and thus has farther to drive, is chronically late. The schism occurs when Sam (Armin Mueller-Stahl) agrees to break tradition and slices the turkey prematurely before Gabriel arrives, breaching the proper 'respect' and tradition. Gabriel exclaims, 'You started without me? You cut the turkey without me? Come on; we're going... They start without us, we leave... Your own flesh and blood, and you couldn't wait? You cut the turkey?' While the slicing of the turkey (potentially kosher but most likely not) obliquely invokes circumcision, it also marks the demise of the traditional family-centred focus of *Yiddishkeit*. As Eric A. Goldman points out 'Circumcision represents the induction into the Jewish family. But on this Thanksgiving, tradition is broken by the slice of a knife' (2003: 116). Assimilation into the mainstream culture of *goyim naches* is achieved at the expense of traditional *Yiddishkeit* and *menschlikayt*.

Food and survival

In *Munich*, food and Jewish survival are intimately linked. The film was designed as both an allegorical response to George Bush's 'war on terror' as well as Israel's targeted assassination policy. It interrogates the efficacy, appropriateness and ethics of state-sanctioned violence, revenge and counter-terrorist techniques at a time when these are much in evidence, to ask whether they are successful or ultimately futile and counter-productive. The theme of the connection between food and Jewish survival is evident elsewhere, but is most dramatically illustrated in Holocaust films. Like Avner, Mrs Silberschmidt (Marianne Saegebrecht) in the Belgian film *Left Luggage* ignores the past by compulsive cooking and baking, obsessively trying 'to bury the past under a pile of cakes'.

Schindler's List most strikingly details the theme of food and survival. Schindler's original factory manufactures crockery and kitchenware, but the Jews who work there barely eat at all. Furthermore, the film contains many sequences comparing the Nazis' diet of fine foods, including champagne, caviar, sardines and chocolate, with those of starving Jews eating meagre and undistinguishable items. 'Spielberg crosscuts scenes of food and death': Schindler welcomes his Jewish workers with 'hot soup and bread' while their wives are on an Auschwitz-bound train and a plump camp commandment reclines on his balcony while skeletal Jews undergo a medical selection (Barr 1996: 136). The Sonderkommando in *The Grey Zone* are shown feasting on food and alcohol denied to other Jews as a reward for their cooperation in the extermination. *The Pianist* develops several sequences in which food and survival are connected, coding the various stages of Nazi oppression. They begin with a special dinner held by the Szpilman family, but normality ends when a sign banning Jews is posted on the door of Wladyslaw's favourite restaurant. A young boy is beaten to death for attempting to smuggle food into the ghetto, while a man grabs a can of soup from a woman, and when it spills he voraciously licks it up off the ground. As the family awaits deportation by train at the Umschlagplatz, their father divides a caramel into six small pieces for each member of the family. A tin of pickles that Wladyslaw fails to open reveals his existence to a Wehrmacht captain, who saves his life by providing him with bread and jam.

Revenge: a dish best served cold?

Key scenes in contemporary cinema are situated at the Jewish dinner table, a worthy location for the delivery of Socratic dialogue. Using the extended discussion of morality in Allen's *Crimes and Misdemeanors* as a model, filmmakers clearly intend to show that important matters are discussed with the entire family present, and the entire family must be present for the evening and/or ritual meal. In *A Price Above Rubies*, for example, an extended family discusses morality, among other issues, over a Shabbat meal. In a departure from the book on which the film was based – George Jonas's *Vengeance* (2006) – key scenes and dialogue in *Munich* in which the morality, ethics, philosophy and consequences of counter-terrorism are discussed take place in sites of food preparation and consumption, as Spielberg literally delivers up food for thought. John Wrathall points out that the agents in the film spend a surprising amount of screen-time eating (2006: 68). The term 'food', for example, is used 16 times in the screenplay, primarily to describe the *mise-en-scène*. *Munich* therefore uses metaphors of food, family and home to make politically intricate or complex material more straightforward or simple, perhaps more relevant to audiences more accustomed to these concepts than they are to those associated with counter-terrorism. It is as if the film is debating, both literally and figuratively, the notion that 'revenge is a dish best served cold'.

Several of the film's major discussions occur amid ample, communal and homemade meals that Avner prepares and places on laden tables for his not-always-hungry colleagues. Avner 'keeps busy chopping and dicing for feasts that no one will consume, since they are too tortured about their mission' (Brown 2006). The first time he prepares a feast for his team, Avner is shown throughout the sequence wearing an apron. Not only does it reinforce his ordinariness and status as an 'everyman' – some of the primary reasons why he was chosen for the mission – but also his culinary skills cement his status as the leader of the group. Hans remarks, 'A team leader who cooks! What a luxury!' Avner replies, 'Years in the kibbutz kitchen.' Steve then asks Avner, 'You've done this before?' 'Done what?' he asks back. The lack of specificity in Steve's question creates an ambiguity as to what exactly he is asking Avner, whether he has cooked or killed before. This ambiguity, which again conflates cooking and killing, reinforces the killing/cooking metaphor at the heart of the film. As the film progresses, it is clear that Avner has cooked but not necessarily killed before.

Avner's apron also, and somewhat stereotypically, codes him as the team's maternal figure. Avner ensures his team has enough to eat; like the *baleboosteh* he replaces, he prepares more than they can possibly consume. At the same time, he plays the role of the stereotypical *Yiddische mama* by taking care of their emotional needs and welfare. Furthermore, since

Munich dining sequence.

Avner is the youngest member of the team he does not represent the father figure. Indeed, the idea of absent fathers is prevalent throughout the film. We never meet Avner's father, although he is referred to many times, yet we meet his mother. Avner himself becomes an absent father to his wife and child as a result of the dictates of his mission. The team becomes Avner's family, replacing the one he is forced to abandon for his work. The sequences of the team eating and discussing around the table reinforce this notion of the team as more than just a group of individuals assembled for a particular set of tasks, a tight unit resembling the family, which is at the heart of Jewish life both religious and secular. The directions in the screenplay convey this notion:

> Ephraim, still in his coat, is standing amidst the team, which is busy, everyone working like clockwork preparing dinner. Avner is in the kitchen, assisted by Hans, simmering a gravy, making spaetzle over a boiling pot, chopping dill. Steve and Robert are setting the table, while Carl selects and pours wine like a sommelier. They're, now a family, domesticated, concentrated [...]

The camerawork during this sequence further serves to reinforce this idea. Everyone sits and Avner starts serving. As they introduce themselves, the camera pans, almost lovingly, around the table, keeping the food and the table carefully foregrounded during the duration of the sequence. It is the last time that we see the whole team so happy.

Jews in conflict

The dining table also becomes the arena for articulating competing versions of Jewishness, in particular, inter-generational conflict. For Jews, the conflicts with their religious, ethnic and sexual selves are staged most pointedly at meals. Again, Allen set the benchmark. In his *Radio Days*, it is Yom Kippur, and the Jewish family is upset because their communist Jewish neighbours are playing the radio loudly and ignoring the fast. Abe (Josh Mostel) goes next door to complain, but does not return for an hour. When he does come back, he has rejected religion and is spouting the communist line, having broken the fast by eating pork chops, clams, French fries and chocolate pudding. When a relative tells him that God will punish him, Abe begins to have chest pains, but it turns out to be indigestion. This is also dramatised in the Swedish film *Freud flyttar hemifrån/Freud Leaving*

Home, in which Ruben and Rosha Cohen (Ghita Nørby) find it difficult to accept their son's homosexuality. Rochelle Wright explains: 'Divergent attitudes toward religious observance come into sharper focus that evening as the family prepares for Shabbat' (1998: 374). Deborah embraces the security of Orthodoxy, while her gay brother, David, 'rejects not only religious observance, but the self evident if relatively secular Jewishness of his parents, their traditions and their old-world values and aesthetics' (Wright 1998: 379). Deborah is annoyed that she must defend Jewish tradition in her parents' home, while David argues that the *haredim* are destroying the State of Israel. Meanwhile their father adheres to traditional practice, wearing a *yarmulke*, saying *kiddush* and blessing the *challah*, but generally trying to avoid tension.

In *Kissing Jessica Stein*, the Jewish family dining scenes become an arena where Jessica strives to assert her lesbian sexuality against the obvious wishes of her parents, who use these same mealtimes to try to match her with more suitable partners. Yet it is precisely at such a meal that Jessica has a change of heart, and realises that an old college friend, a single heterosexual Jew, offers a real opportunity for a romantic and long-lasting relationship. Similar issues are dealt with in *When Do We Eat?* in which a father seeks to reconcile with his lesbian daughter, who brings her Latina girlfriend along to the meal. Likewise, in *What's Cooking?* Rachel Seelig (Kyra Sedgwick) brings her lesbian life-partner, Carla (Julianna Margulies), home for Thanksgiving. Her parents, Herb (Maury Chaykin) and Ruth (Lainie Kazan), are unwilling to discuss openly their grown lesbian daughter's relationship with her lover around the dinner table. In these three scenes, food preparation and consumption illustrate the inter-generational clash in

The Seder meal in *When Do We Eat?*

which daughters bring home doubly unsuitable partners, both ethnically and sexually, and sons do not follow the wishes of their parents. They also show the decreasing level of observance among the younger generation, who accept homosexuality but reject traditional Jewish practice.

Ordeal, or meal, of civility

It is not just the foods that Jews eat, but how they behave while eating them, that are key signifiers of their difference from the Gentile world. John Murray Cuddihy explains what he calls this 'ordeal of civility':

> Jewish Emancipation involved Jews in collisions with the differentiations of Western society. The differentiations most foreign to the *shtetl* subculture of *Yiddishkeit* were those of public from private behavior and of manners from morals. Jews were being asked, in effect, to become bourgeois, and to become bourgeois quickly. The problem of behavior, then, became strategic to the whole problematic of 'assimilation.' The modernisation process, the civilisational process, and the assimilation process were experienced as one – as the 'price of admission' to the bourgeois civil society of the West [1978: 12–13].

Gentile etiquette, Stratton elaborates further, are 'those expressive and situational norms ubiquitously if informally institutionalised in the social interaction ritual of our modern Western societies', or 'the conventionalised system in which civility is practised' (2000: 285, 308). One of the markers of such civility is dining. Eating involves table manners, namely how to behave in a civilised manner, including knowing how to use the correct cutlery, not to eat noisily and not to speak with a full mouth (Bell and Valentine 1997: 64).

However, the 'association of Jewishness with vulgarity and lack of cultivation' is a fairly widespread belief, 'and not least among Jews' (Podhoretz 1967: 161). And nowhere is this more prominent than when eating (as well as excreting, as I will argue in the following chapter). The dinner table, therefore, is a test of Jewish civility.

> At the social dinner tasting is policed by a taste of a higher kind. The party becomes an aesthetic procession, a performance through which the individual's relation to and consumption of the other is regulated according to aesthetic norms of sociality and table etiquette. The individual learns to

present itself tastefully to the other by practising the protocols of 'civilised' conduct [Melville 2004: 209].

Eating is a performance of Jewish civility. By performing well at the dining table, the Jew/ess demonstrates good taste, as well as consciousness of the aesthetic that defines social class and status. Similarly, performing badly or tastelessly at the dining table is a clear indication of general ignorance about how to behave in a civilised society (Owen 2009: 31).

However, cinematic Jews rarely pass this test. They interrupt each other continually and argue heatedly, often with food in their mouths. Even ordinary conversations are conducted in loud voices, and their body language does not convey the expected reserve. *Annie Hall's* 'Grammy Ann' sequence, especially when compared in split screen with the Jewish family meal, sets the trend that is often replicated in contemporary cinema. In *Quiz Show*, for example, Dick Goodwin reveals his lack of breeding by speaking with his mouth full, licking his fingers and getting mustard on his chin. In *A Serious Man*, Judith Gopnik (Sari Lennick) and her daughter (Jessica McManus) are shown slurping soup in a disgusting manner (leading some Jews to label the film 'antisemitic'!).

The notion is extended in the dining sequences of *Meet the Parents* (dir. Jay Roach, 2000) and *Meet the Fockers*. When Greg accompanies his fiancée to visit her WASP parents on the north shore of Long Island, in scenes reminiscent of *Quiz Show*, everything there conspires to remind him that he is a Jew of low status. Jack places Greg under constant scrutiny and surveillance (he even rigs a series of hidden cameras to spy on the unwitting Greg) and thus the seemingly simplest situations, such as eating or using the toilet (discussed further in the following chapter), conceal hidden traps. The family meal is particularly important for establishing the cultural distance between the Jewish Focker and the WASP Byrnes families. Jack asks Greg to say grace at dinner. 'Greg is Jewish,' Jack is told. 'I'm sure Jews bless their food,' Jack smiles, and Greg launches into a tortured prayer that segues, to his own horror, into lyrics from *Godspell* (dir. David Greene, 1973) Mealtimes continue to be fraught with social danger. At breakfast, Greg is the last to arrive; still wearing his pyjamas, he is the only person shown eating a bagel – here used as a clear signifier of Jewish difference – further emphasising the wide social gap. In the first sequel, as we have seen, the meal is still replete with humiliation for Greg when it is revealed that he lost his virginity to the Latina housemaid and that his parents preserved his foreskin in a scrapbook following his botched circumcision. The meals, therefore, serve to highlight the distance between the 'uncivilised' Jews and the genteel Gentiles.

However, this checking-out-the-Jew-at-the-Gentile-family-table formula is often reversed in contemporary cinema. Films featuring exogamous relationships such as *Kissing Jessica Stein, Meet the Fockers* and *Suzie Gold* (dir. Ric Cantor, 2004), to name just a few examples, frequently include such sequences. In such dining scenes, it is usual for the Gentile to be subject to parental interrogation, assessing whether s/he is fit/kosher enough to marry into the family. Kosher is also slang for 'AOK', literally 'fitting and proper' in Hebrew (during the 1970s advertisements for the Israeli national carrier El Al would promise, 'We don't take off until everything is Kosher'). A slight reversal of this recipe is provided by the Spanish romantic comedy *Seres Queridos/Only Human*, in which a middle-class professional Jewess brings home her Palestinian fiancé while letting her family think that he is Jewish (because he has an Israeli passport and is circumcised).

Antisemite and Jew

Several films specifically deploy the dining table as a means to articulate the clash between the Jew and the antisemite. In the black comedy *The Last Supper* (dir. Stacy Title, 1995) a group of graduate students, one of whom is Jewish, use the dinner table to articulate and convert non-believers to their belief systems. They invite a variety of politically inappropriate – sexist, racist, fundamentalist, politically conservative, and so on – individuals to supper to try to persuade them to change their ideas, and poison them and bury them in the back yard if they remain unmoved. Significantly, Jewish student Marc (Jonathan Penner) kills the first guest, a vicious Holocaust-denying antisemite, thereby also reversing the stereotype of queer diaspora Jewish physical weakness.

This paradigm is reversed in *American History X* (dir. Tony Kaye, 1998). Neo-Nazi Derek Vinyard (Edward Norton) articulates his racist belief system at the dinner table, thereby clashing with his mother's Jewish boyfriend Murray (Elliot Gould). Although being 'sat at the table' carries connotations of negotiation, Derek is clearly unhappy about the new element in the household, sat at the dinner table, a sign that Murray has access to the intimacy of the family. The family discusses the politics of race, but when Derek fails to establish his position as patriarch, he loses his temper and resorts to a physical demonstration of his masculinity, manhandling his sister and mother. Older and physically weaker than Derek, Murray stands by motionless, passive and unable to intervene. Derek confronts Murray, ripping off his shirt, emphasising his musculature in contrast to Murray's shirt, jacket and tie. In an expletive-ridden, anti-Jewish diatribe, invoking many antisemitic stereotypes ('kike', 'Shylock', 'Kabbalah-reading motherfucker'), Derek tells him in no uncertain terms to 'Get the fuck out of my house.' As Murray leaves, Derek pulls down his vest to reveal a swastika tattoo over his heart. 'See this?' he asks Murray. 'That means: not welcome.' Murray has no choice but to submit and leave. He is the queer, weak, victimised Jew, and his status is revealed and compounded during a lengthy (ten-minute) dining sequence.

The Believer blends the two to produce a Jew who is simultaneously queer and tough. At the beginning of the film (before we know that he himself is Jewish), Danny beats up a *yeshiva bocher* type whom he accuses of, and despises for, being a Jewish weakling. His unmasking as a Jew also occurs in a pivotal scene in a diner, in which Danny rants against the Jews, but threatens to commit suicide if the reporter interviewing him prints that he is Jewish. Later, Danny and five fellow neo-Nazis deliberately target a kosher diner in order to provoke a disturbance. They sit down and provocatively order such *treyf* dishes as 'ham and cheese' and 'roast beef and Swiss' in the full knowledge that such combinations are forbidden by *kashrut*. Although mimicking a tough neo-Nazi, Danny is Jewish, and rather than resort to violence he uses his intellectual capacities to outwit the Jewish manager, asking him why chickens and milk cannot be mixed when the Bible forbids the cooking of a kid in its mother's milk. At the same time, such intimate knowledge of *kashrut* distances him from his fellow neo-Nazis, who are clearly much more ignorant.

Conclusion: just desserts

Food is a means in contemporary cinema to explore Jewish identity visually, whether the food itself is 'Jewish', kosher or *treyf*. In this chapter, I have brought together a variety of films and topics as a step towards beefing up the study of visual victuals, giving some illustrative (and hopefully tasty) examples of the rich selection of films to be productively researched further from a variety of perspectives: social, cultural, religious, class, gender and even sexual. Clearly, there is plenty of material for further exploration, and I hope that, in the future, the links between film, food and Jewish social dynamics will be confronted.

CHAPTER 8

Bathrooms

Lifting the lid

Much has been written on the cultural and semiotic connotations of the bathroom, particularly the public one. It is a place of structural oppositions: clean/dirty; public/private; hygienic/unhygienic; technical/organic. It is the boundary between the acceptable and unacceptable; a place in which submission to or defiance of authority is negotiated. The bathroom is also 'a place where masks are assumed and dropped' to show us how and what people really are. As Philip Kuberski (2004) explains:

> It is the first place that one enters in the morning and the last place one leaves at night. It is a room for bathing, washing, cosmetics, and self-preparation, but it is also a room for urination, defecation, masturbation and regurgitation. Like the kitchen, it is usually tiled, curtained, and plumbed, with mirrors as well as toilets, tubs, and sinks. It is a room dedicated to the flowing water and shining surfaces, chrome, glitter, reflection. It is luxurious and clinical, superficial and profound. It supplements faces and eliminates feces. There is an unavoidable doubleness about the bathroom. It is a palace of luxurious hardware and a slum of fetid waste: urine, feces, semen, blood, mucous, dirt, sweat.

The men's public bathroom, in particular, as Loshitzky points out, is 'an all-male public (yet semi-private/secret) space invested with associations of prostitution, AIDS, casual homosexual (including anal) sex' (2005:

139). 'The bathroom, whether public or private, has been used for various purposes, such as drug use or sex,' Irus Braverman adds. It is for these reasons, he argues, that 'the public washroom is the most regulated of all public spaces, at least in the United States', being the 'focus of hyper-juridical attention' (Braverman 2009: 53, 45).

These ideas have been extended to the public/private bathroom in film (Fuller 1993, Willis 1997, Gleason 2004, Kuberski 2004, Pheasant-Kelly 2009, Monaco 2009). Moving beyond these various readings (see also Barcan 2005, Gershonsen and Penner 2009), I wish to prod these studies into a new direction by introducing a specifically ethnic and religious Jewish dimension to the cinematic bathroom (I shall use this term hereafter to refer to any space, indoors or outdoors, in which washing, bathing and toileting occurs). I have observed elsewhere how the bathroom plays a central role in Jewish religion, literature, imagination, history, jokes and popular culture (Abrams 2009). Here, I will develop the argument with specific reference to film to demonstrate how the bathroom functions in terms of cinematic Jewishness to suggest that the toilet becomes a boundary marker between Jewish and *goyish*. It is semiotically coded as 'Jewish space', reinforcing the sense of Jewish Otherness and marginalisation. Yet, it is also functions as what Foucault (1967) called 'heterotopic' space: a 'counter-site' in which 'all the other real sites that can be found within the culture, are simultaneously represented, contested, and inverted.' It is the place in which the Jew/ess can achieve what s/he is denied elsewhere in the host society.

The Jew and the loo

'The laws regarding washrooms are quite intense in the Jewish tradition', especially when compared to Christianity, which, 'for some reason, seems more lax about the regulation of washroom conduct' (Braverman 2009: 59). Judaism places great importance on the act of going to the toilet and such related concerns as ritual purity and defilement that the toilet produces, as demonstrated in the Torah and later Talmudic literature. It even has its own dedicated blessing. Much emphasis is placed in the Bible on personal cleanliness as an essential requirement both for physical fitness and holiness, specifically ritual purity. Consequently, ancient latrines were situated beyond the confines of the military encampment in order to keep it clean, and each soldier was equipped with a spade (spike or trowel) so he could dig a hole to bury his excrement (Deut. 23: 13–15). Later, the rabbis also required that hands be washed after urination and/or defecation, and spent much time discussing whether a Jew could pray in or near a toilet and under what conditions, whether in the presence of urine and excrement. The concern here was that the toilet and/or its contents would defile such a holy act as prayer, and much thought and ink was deployed establishing a clear distinction between sacred and profane (that is toilet) space. Even today, in contemporary *haredi* culture, much attention is devoted to 'openings of the body, the flow of fluids in and out of it. Urinating, for example, has become a whole ceremony carried out under precise surveillance' (Aran 2006: 89).

Leaping ahead to the modern period, the toilet continues to be significant to the Jewish imagination beyond physical need. The toilet joke is important to the Jewish sense of humour, which tends towards the scatalogical. This is because, as Michael Wex explains, 'normal digestion is portrayed as a cosmic drama', hence every successful trip to the toilet 'is memorialised as a triumph over death' (2005: 60). Consequently, toilet jokes abound in Yiddish. The centrality of the toilet is perhaps also explained by the Yiddish mindset, in which the callow youth is described as a *pisher* (lit. 'pisser') and the old codger as an *alter kaka* (lit. 'old shit'). Thus, the life arc of the Jew is coded as evolving from urine to faeces.

The bathroom provides much grist for the mill elsewhere in Jewish popular culture. In Jewish literature at least one, usually male, member of the family suffers from a chronic dietary-related ailment, such as constipation and/or irritable bowel syndrome. No doubt this is due to an Ashkenazi cuisine rich in salt and fat, which the son is forced to eat in copious quantities by his overbearing *Yiddische mama*, both as mother and wife. Philip Roth's classic and controversial novel *Portnoy's Complaint* (1969) sets the tone. Roth extolled the *shvitz* (Yiddish: 'sweat bath') as the ideal world of Jewish masculinity, 'a place without goyim and women' (1969: 40), and its eponymous narrator spends a great deal of time in the bathroom, masturbating there, whether at home, in the cinema or at school.

Since a high number of key Jewish characters in television and film are placed in the bathroom, they become instantly recognisable as Jewish by a media-savvy audience able to detect and decode the signs. For example, the character of George Costanza (Jason Alexander) in the seminal sitcom *Seinfeld* – while not explicitly a Jewish character, but clearly playing a Jewish archetype modelled on the show's creator, Larry David – is constantly in the bathroom, usually at Jerry's apartment. He is often shown taking in something to read, too, thus elongating his stay and reinforcing the connection. David's own show, *Curb Your Enthusiasm* (HBO, 2000–), also makes much play of the toilet/bathroom.

The celluloid water closet as Jewish space

Similarly, the cinematic bathroom is often used as a visual means of establishing Jewish characters. In *Pi* and *La Haine* we first meet Max and get to know Vinz in the bathroom. David in *Seres Queridos/Only Human* expresses his new religiosity by pre-tearing sheets of toilet paper in preparation for the Shabbat, when ripping is expressly forbidden. During Friday-night supper, where his love interest is present, the Hebrew Hammer excuses himself from the dining table ('I have to go to the bathroom') and off-screen we hear the toilet door close, the sound of flushing, followed by repeated attempts to depress the handle, and Mordechai utter, 'What a mess.' Uncle Arthur (Richard Kind) in *A Serious Man* is constantly in the bathroom draining a sebaceous cyst. In *The Fantastic Four* (dir. Tim Story, 2005) Reed Richards (Ioan Gruffud) is caught short without toilet paper. Fortunately for him, however, and in an act of wish fulfilment, as a result of a genetic abnormality he is able to stretch his limbs, which he does, reaching under the door to grab some, thus avoiding any potential humiliation. This 'freakishness' is the first clue to his Jewishness, confirmed by the film's end, when he gives his girlfriend a star of David pendant.

In *Punch-Drunk Love* (dir. Paul Thomas Anderson, 2002), conceptually Jewish character Barry (Adam Sandler) owns a small novelty-toilet-accessory business. Barry sells toilet plungers from a warehouse. 'Even if he did make a lot of money, he wouldn't be able to brag about what he does as a sign of masculine pride' (Stanley 2006: 237). The film thus connects the sissy/queer Jew with the toilet. This link is elaborated upon later in the film. Asked out on a date by Lena (Emily Watson), it is cut short when she mentions a childhood story about Barry throwing a hammer through a window. Barry denies that it ever happened, and then excuses himself to go to the toilet. 'Upon entering the bathroom his chaotic rage bursts through his surface tranquillity as he tears the bathroom apart, kicking down doors, ripping fixtures off the walls' (Stanley 2006: 239–40). Calmer, he returns to Lena for dinner, but the manager requests to speak with him. The exchange ends with Barry and Lena leaving the restaurant. He later apologises: 'At that restaurant, I beat up the bathroom. I'm sorry.' The bathroom fulfils several functions here. It is the place where masks are dropped. It is the site of uncontrolled aggression, the cathartic expression of inner rage. It is a location of refuge for Barry, where he can exorcise his demons. Finally, it allows him to be violent, something denied to him in public space. His masculinity might be such that he is unable to attack another human being, but, in his telling words, he can 'beat up the bathroom', an inanimate set of objects. The bathroom also perhaps symbolises his failures, as it is precisely that to which he owes his living.

Multiple sequences place Barton Fink in or around bathrooms. Indeed, the script uses 'bathroom' or related terms some 11 times; for example, 'Barton stands at a urinal. He stares at the wall in front of him as he pees.' There he is introduced to fellow writer, and key character, W.P. (Bill) Mayhew (John Mahoney). Later, as Audrey Taylor (Judy Davis) seduces Barton, 'The camera wanders discreetly downwards to show shoes being slipped off, before tiptoeing into the bathroom, down the drain and through an endless shaft that leads to a wailing underworld' (Desalm 1999: 135). The camera pans away from their kiss, framing up on the door to the bathroom and tracking in towards the sink. The continuing track brings us up to and over the lid of the sink to frame up its drain, a perfect black circle in the porcelain white. Meanwhile, we hear the creak of bedsprings and Audrey and Barton's breath, becoming laboured, and we track up to the drain enveloped by the sounds of lovemaking as they mix into the groaning of pipes. At least one effect of these shots is to cement the link between the Jew and the loo.

Furthermore, Jews are often defined by gastrointestinal or similar problems. This mocks the above-mentioned and familiar trope of the Jew's dietary problems. In *Along Came Polly* (dir. John Hamburg, 2004), Reuben Feffer (Ben Stiller) has irritable bowel syndrome. Bernie Focker is introduced to us via his answering machine message, a recurring joke in which, unable to work the device, he unwittingly records an outgoing greeting in which he whines about wanting to eat chimichangas but cannot because they give him 'gas', much to his wife's displeasure. In *American Buffalo*, Teach explains, 'I never eat cantaloupe. It gives me the runs.' And, in *Harold & Kumar Go to White Castle/*

Get the Munchies, Goldstein complains that instead of buying 'soft toilet paper at the supermarket', Rosenberg has got 'sandpaper for my ass', and that as a result his 'piles are bleeding'. Rosenberg counters that 'It's fine on my ass', to which Goldstein responds, 'Well you must have an ass made of iron.'

The Jewess is also introduced to us in the bathroom. In *The Hebrew Hammer*, Mordechai's mother discusses her 'problems with the gas' ('after I started taking two charcoal pills before I ate, it cleared the whole problem right up'). We first meet Maggie Feller (Cameron Diaz) in *In Her Shoes* (dir. Curtis Hanson, 2005) in the bathroom, when, during her ten-year high-school reunion she drunkenly makes out with a fellow guest whose name she does not even know, before throwing up and passing out. We first meet Tania (María Botto) in *Seres Queridos/Only Human* as she shaves her underarm hair, while gossiping about her sister on the telephone. Five separate sequences in *Hey Hey It's Esther Blueburger* place Esther (Danielle Catanzariti) and her mother (Essie Davis) in the bathroom, where they use the toilet itself as a means to communicate with God. Certainly, as a result of the multiplicity of such scenes, the bathroom can be semiotically coded as 'Jewish space'.

Anxiety and danger

The bathroom represents a gendered threat in many situations where the Jew is compelled to hide his religion and ethnicity, to pass as white, either in order to survive or as a way to move up the socioeconomic ladder. The bathroom hence becomes a site for the potential unmasking of his invisibility by displaying the primary signifier of his Jewish masculinity: the circumcised penis. This is typically a feature in films dealing with the subject of antisemitism and/or the Holocaust, where the Jew attempts to mimic the Gentile. Here the public bathroom represents a clear and present danger, for the real identity of the Jew can be unmasked at any time and the naked Jew is at his most physically and emotionally vulnerable, revealing that he is 'almost the same, but not quite'.

Nowhere is this clearer than in *Hitlerjunge Salomon/Europa Europa*, a film that 'charts with black humour the danger of betrayal by one's penis' (Coates 2005: 172). Solly's story is intimately linked to his ability to hide his circumcision. Thus, the film opens with a fairly graphic depiction of the act, including the practice of *metzitzah* (the sucking of blood through a straw). 'I remember my circumcision,' Solly claims. While this may be doubtful, he is certainly given cause never to forget it as the film progresses, as it is the 'curse' he carries and tries to conceal in order to save his life during the Holocaust (Coates 2004: 280). In order to survive, Solly becomes a Zelig-like figure who disguises his Jewishness and mimics in turn a member of the Komsomol (Soviet youth movement), the Wehrmacht and the Hitler Youth. When captured by the Germans, but accepted into their ranks as one of their own because of his ability to speak fluent German, every toileting and bathing situation thereafter represents a source of possible danger. Solly thus must run deep into the forest to urinate while his fellow soldiers rest. Subsequently accepted into a prestigious Hitler Youth school in Germany, his fears intensify. 'It would be harder than at the front. I could be found at any moment.' This whole time 'nakedness means vulnerability', as it will mean discovery of his real identity.

Solly attempts to mask his circumcision by various means. His first act at the new school is to survey the bathrooms and toilets, and he notes with relief that another schoolmate showers with his underpants on. He later tries to thread the skin forward over the tip of his penis, but this fails and causes him too much pain. He even resorts to faking toothache, and allows a healthy tooth be extracted so he can forego the annual medical inspection that would reveal his Jewishness. Although he changes costume and persona with consummate ease, he is clearly aware that 'I couldn't flee my own body. I still had to hide.' Throughout these changes it is his circumcised penis that anchors him to his original identity and is his 'sole constant compass' (Coates 2005: 172, 170); 'it serves precisely the role for which it was intended by protecting his Jewish identity even when he is entirely willing to give it up' (Bartov 2005: 139). Only at the end of the film is Solly able to urinate freely, without restraint and fear of discovery, and he stands, silhouetted in the frame of a door, newly reunited with his brother, urinating in the open air in an act of liberation, release and celebration of his Jewish identity.

Rachel in *Zwartboek/Black Book* is also in constant fear of discovery, even if she lacks a signifier as obvious as a circumcised penis. It is in a toilet that she almost drops her mask when, recognising the Nazi who killed her family, she runs to vomit. At the same time, the bathroom allows her to assume the mask in the first place, as it is in front of the sink and mirror that we voyeuristically spy her dying her head and pubic hair blonde.

In *School Ties*, showering poses particular problems for David Greene, as it occurs in a non-private communal space. He is adept, however, at masking his Jewishness, for his identity is not revealed by his nudity (indeed, the film never reveals his circumcision, as he is always shot from the waist up). Instead, the bathroom sequences serve to highlight his mimicry as well as reveal the racism, bigotry and antisemitism of his fellow classmates at their elite private prep school.

The civilising process or the ordeal of civility

Brian Aldiss famously commented that 'Civilisation is the distance man has placed between himself and his excreta.' The cinematic bathroom thus functions as another space of anxiety for the Jew, serving to code the clash between Jewishness and civility/gentility, and the Jew's attempt to pass as white, as Gentile and genteel, or what Norbert Elias (1968) and Cuddihy (1978) call the 'civilising process' and 'the ordeal of civility' respectively. And because the 'public washroom is considered one of the marks of civilisation' (Braverman 2009: 53) it provides a clear marker as to whether the Jew is successful in passing this test. In any number of films, the Jew is confronted with toilet-related situations as a source of social danger and humour – what Kuberski calls 'the comic yet poignant intrusion of the body's ineluctable demands' (2004: 139) – in which he must overcome an obstacle in order to obtain the *shiksa* of his affection. The bathroom therefore represents a test to demonstrate that the Jew is worthy of being accepted into society, as genteel and Gentile. That he usually fails demonstrates that the 'washroom thus embodies and represents an unintentional cultural strategy for preserving existing social categories and for maintaining our most cherished classifications' (Braverman 2009: 49).

The bathroom then becomes a distancing device for establishing the cultural divide between Jews and Gentiles. In a number of his films, Ben Stiller's characters in particular are confronted with bathroom-related situations as a source of audience humour but which result in a trail of destruction, as they 'stumble from ignominy to ignominy in gentile society' (Stratton 2000: 6) when confronted with numerous toilet tests. In *Meet the Parents*, Greg is warned not to use the downstairs bathroom as it does not flush properly. One night he forgets, flooding the garden, in which his girlfriend's sister is set to get married, with faeces. When the Byrnes family visits Greg's parents in *Meet the Fockers*, the toilet continues to code the differences between Jewish and *goyish*. The Byrnes are given a tour of the Fockers' house in which there is only a single working bathroom. Bernie explains that 'if it's yellow let it mellow; if it's brown flush it down,' but notices that he has forgotten his own rule. Horrified, Jack suggests that his family use his mobile home, resulting in an incident whereby the Fockers' dog, Moses, is flushed down the chemical toilet. Later, as Jack is having a shower, Bernie unselfconsciously sits on the toilet reading his paper, much to Jack's obvious discomfort.

In *Along Came Polly*, the toilet becomes Reuben's worst nightmare. Ignoring his friend's advice ('You've got irritable bowel syndrome, dude. If she chose an ethnic restaurant, you're gonna be running to the bathroom every five seconds'), and attempting to impress the eponymous Polly (Jennifer Aniston), Reuben agrees to a date at a Moroccan restaurant against his better judgement. The subsequent meal is an excruciating experience for him as he slowly and painfully spoons the spicy food into his mouth, sweating profusely. He attempts to use the restaurant toilet, but it is occupied. After the meal, they return to Polly's tiny apartment. At this stage Reuben

Reuben Feffer in *Along Came Polly*.

is ready to explode, unable to contain his flatulence, which can clearly be heard beyond the confines of the bathroom. As he relieves himself, he attempts to mask the noise by running the bathtaps. But, as he finishes, he discovers that there is no toilet paper. He desperately searches for an alternative, eventually using for the closest item at hand – a towel hand-embroidered by Polly's grandmother – but which refuses to flush. In desperation, and like Esther Blueburger and her mother, Reuben beseeches God through the loo. However, the combination of steam emanating from the bathroom, the length of time Reuben is in there, and the seeping of water under the bathroom door leads Polly to burst in (in the rush he has forgotten to lock the door), literally catching Reuben with his pants down, clutching her very expensive loofer, as he attempts to plunge the offending item(s). His humiliation is complete. In these instances, the Jew fails the ordeal/test of civility.

Emasculation and feminisation

In many films the bathroom emphasises the queer status of the Jew, often emasculating and feminising him. Since the bathroom removes the Jew from the rest of the narrative for a brief moment, having to submit to the demands of nature, it highlights his powerlessness and lack of agency. It also reinforces his isolation from the group, as well as vulnerability – since he is literally alone and often caught with his trousers down. Furthermore, if modern urban society is emasculating, given that the Jew is overwhelmingly located in urban environments, the Jew is emasculated. He is too (sub)urbanised to function properly in the great outdoors. This is highlighted by an outdoor toileting sequence in *City Slickers II: The Legend of Curly's Gold* (dir. Paul Weiland, 1994) in which Phil Berquist (Daniel Stern) relieves himself behind a rock. He cries out in pain, believing a rattlesnake has bitten his buttock. Meanwhile, his friends Mitch (Billy Crystal) and Glen (Jon Lovitz) assume he is constipated ('He's having trouble. Relax, don't strain!' and 'too many tortilla chips'). Believing he is about to die, Phil panics ('Mitch, don't tell my kids I died taking a shit') and exhorts his friends to suck the poison out of his behind. As Mitch bends him over, Phil tells him to 'Suck already'. Thus, not only is the sequence emasculating, it is feminising, containing gay undertones.

In the end, it turns out that he has sat on a cactus, reinforcing his incompetent masculinity.

Far worse occurs to Ted (Stiller) in *There's Something About Mary*. As a shy high-school student, the hapless, awkward Ted arrives at his prom date's house, the eponymous Mary (Cameron Diaz). He goes to the toilet while she gets ready. The bathroom is visually constructed as a feminine space, with pink and blue flowery wallpaper and lace curtains. Thus the amplified sound of Ted urinating is especially incongruous and disgusting. As he stands at the toilet, Ted watches a pair of love birds sitting on a tree branch, directly in his line of vision to Mary's bedroom window. The birds fly away, providing a clear sight, and while Ted is urinating he spies Mary in her underwear. Mary's mother (Markie Post) looks down at him from the bedroom window and mistakenly assumes that he is masturbating. When Ted realises this, he hastily rushes to zip up his fly but manages to trap his penis and testicles in his zip in the process, depicted in an extreme close-up of his crotch. Mary's stepfather (Keith David) and mother enter to assist. A policeman (Steve Sweeney), alerted to the scene by a neighbour, climbs in the window. They are joined by a firefighter (Lenny Clarke). The policeman attempts to undo Ted's zip. Ted braces himself and we cut to the next scene, a paramedic shouting, 'We got a bleeder.' This prolonged scene then turns into one of very public humiliation, as not only is his date present, but so

Ted in *There's Something about Mary*.

are her parents, two fire trucks, four police cars, an ambulance and a crowd of neighbours. Thus 'the privacy of the bath[room] becomes a public meeting place' (Kuberski 2004). The assembled crowd and emergency crews (fire, police and ambulance) are heartily amused and, like Mary's mother, everyone assumes that he was masturbating. Needless to say, not only does the planned date never happen, but also the incident is so traumatic that Ted fails to consummate his relationship with Mary and bears deep psychological scars as a result.

While this scene is read for its psychoanalytic (penis/phallus, castration anxiety, Oedipal) qualities (Buchbinder 2008, Pheasant-Kelly 2009) its specifically Jewish properties are overlooked. While Ted is nowhere explicitly identified as Jewish, the viewer is given 'the possibility of reading him as a Jew – looks, behaviour, name – but no certainty.' For example, Ted's conduct resembles that of the 'classic Jewish *schlemiel*, a loser whose every effort at improvement works against him' (Stratton 2000: 5). Ted is juvenile, short and physically unattractive; several close-up shots emphasise his dental braces, highlighting his ugliness. The object of his affection is the beautiful blonde *shiksa* Mary. The sequence is thus loaded with Jewish meaning, suggesting a fear of double, albeit inadvertent, circumcision. As Stratton puts it, 'Ted's ambiguous Jewishness is played out in an anxious displacement of circumcision onto castration' (2000: 6). Ted is queered in this scene not only by his helpless passive vulnerability but also by the high-pitched scream he emits. The policeman comments, 'Neighbours said they heard a lady scream,' and a fireman calls him 'numb nuts'. 'The space of the toilet is again emasculating, as Ted is confined to a corner of the bathroom (and the frame), and is also object of the male characters' and the viewer's gaze' (Pheasant-Kelly 2009). Ted is infantilised and feminised, and his humiliation, suffering and passivity are made very public.

The event becomes the Jew's worst fear: uncovering of the primary identity of his Jewish masculinity, circumcision. Furthermore, the Jewish penis is exposed to the public gaze, when to do so is to invite invidious comparison of the Jewish penis to that of the Gentile. This is highlighted by the fact that the first person on the scene is Mary's African-American stepfather, who must put on his glasses to see Ted's penis, doubly playing on 'how American racial anxieties are played out in terms of penis size', particularly in Jewish terms (Stratton 2000: 6). The stepfather 'is simultaneously horrified and filled with laughter. Is this horror and amusement caused by his empathy with Ted's situation, or by the size of his penis (if Ted is Jewish and circumcised and therefore might already be thought to be castrated), or by a combination of both?' Stratton asks (2000: 6). The physical vulnerability of the Jewish penis is thus reinforced, contrasting with the notion of the Gentile penis as dominant, impervious and invincible. Furthermore, the presence of such *goyische* men as Mary's stepfather, the cop and the firefighter, as well as Mary's mother, all of whom stand as Ted's opposite, serve to highlight his inadequate and unmanly Jewish masculinity.

Furthermore, the bleeding genital wound clearly draws upon the erstwhile antisemitic canard of the Jew's menstruation. The idea that the Jew menstruated was a recurring theme in Europe, dating back to the thirteenth century. Antisemites considered haemorrhoids to be a classic Jewish disease, stemming from the Jew's scholarly lifestyle and its requisite hard benches. In turn, the bleeding anus was linked to male menstruation (Kassouf 1998). Such stereotypes are mocked, mimicked and reversed in other contemporary films in a form of *Jewissance*. In *Superbad*, menstrual blood is smeared on the front of Jonah's trousers when he dances very intimately with a drunken woman at a party. 'Why would I be bleeding?' he asks innocently. When the penny drops, he exclaims, 'Someone perioded [sic] on my fucking leg.' The sequence turns into one of public humiliation as other partygoers taunt his masculinity: 'That's a fucking man-gina man' and 'Do you need a tampon?' Elsewhere, when Reuben considers using a Tampax to wipe his behind in *Along Came Polly*, the idea of the menstruating Jew is again obliquely raised, as it is in *The Hebrew Hammer* when Mordechai asks his Mum 'Where do you keep the plunger?' and she replies 'It's under the sink next to my tampons!' Needless to say, the suggestion of menstruation emphasises the Jew's feminisation.

Ted is further queered by other public-toilet locations. As he recounts to his psychiatrist the above story, which is told in flashback, he says, 'I pulled into a rest area, parked the car, and just started shaking.' The psychiatrist scratches his chin and replies, 'You know ... rest areas are a homosexual hang-out? [...] Highway rest areas – they're the bathhouses of the nineties for some gay men.' Ted thinks about this, then glances back at the shrink and asks, 'What are you saying?' Missing the point, Ted later pulls into a rest area to urinate, inadvertently stumbling into a gay meeting place and is subsequently arrested, the police erroneously identifying him as propositioning a gay man in a public place. 'Here Ted's Jewishness, already associated with castration, is further, and conventionally, extended to his feminisation as he is situated, albeit mistakenly, as something less than a "proper" man. After this, he is mistaken for a murderer' (Stratton 2000: 6).

In the climax of his bathroom misadventures, Ted, as an adult in his thirties, nervous about his prospective date with Mary, masturbates in the bathroom of his hotel room toilet in order to calm his nerves. He is advised to 'clean the pipes' by his friend Dom Wooganowski (Chris Elliot), because otherwise 'it's like going out with a loaded gun… dangerous.' Dom's reasoning is that it will make for a better date. 'The most honest moment in a man's life is the five minutes after he's blown a load. That's a medical fact. And it's because you're no longer trying to get laid. You're actually thinking like a girl. They love that.' Ted obliges, brings himself to orgasm, but when he attempts to clean it up he cannot discover his ejaculate anywhere. He becomes increasingly desperate as he searches for it, checking his hands, trousers, shoes, the sink and even the ceiling, but to no avail. The use of cross-cutting, showing Mary's arrival at his hotel here reinforces the need for speed as Ted franticly tries to locate his semen, driving up the tension. Mary arrives first, and as Ted answers the door we see from her point-of-view that 'a HUGE LOAD is hanging off of Ted's earlobe like a drop earring'. Much to Ted's horror, since Mary has no clue as to what he has been just doing, she asks him if it is hair gel and then proceeds to remove it and apply it to her own hair. In the next scene, Mary sits with Ted in a bar, her fringe transformed into an erect blonde cockatoo crest, which only serves to increase Ted's discomfort as he stares continually at her stiff quiff.

The sequence is pregnant with Jewish meaning. Again, while various critics (Buchbinder 2008, Pheasant-Kelly 2009) discuss this scene, they ignore the specifically Jewish dimension of its setting. The hotel is the Cardozo – a name with many Jewish associations, such as Jewish Supreme Court Justice Benjamin Nathan Cardozo. Just as *American Pie* provides a link to *Portnoy's Complaint*, so this scene resembles an episode in the book where Portnoy is masturbating in the family bathroom and cannot locate his semen, only to find it sizzling from the light bulb. Although engaged in a highly masculine act, Ted is queered and feminised by a sequence that serves to undermine his masculinity in a number of ways. The bathroom is decorated in pink and blue. Unbeknownst to him, Ted is being manipulated by Dom in order to destroy his fledgling relationship with Mary. 'Dom's real intent, of course is to try to ensure the reduction of

Ted's libido while at the same time making him anxious about his ability to perform sexually' (Buchbinder 2008: 240). 'Ted's subordinate status in this scene is achieved and revealed, first, by his acquiescing in Dom's instructions, especially in relation to a sexual act like masturbation – there is something almost homoerotic about Dom's relish in informing Ted of this way of avoiding sexual humiliation' (Buchbinder 2008: 240). The very reason given for masturbating is so that he will think 'like a girl'.

The semen hanging from Ted's ear when he opens the door to Mary initially resembles a pendant earring, 'feminising – or, at any rate, demasculinising – Ted still further' (Buchbinder 2008: 240–41). At the same time, as mentioned earlier, earrings were the mark of the Jewess in place of circumcision. While the pendant or drop earring was later adopted by the Christian community in Renaissance Italy in order to distinguish itself from the *ear-ring* or loop that identified the Jewess,

> in decorating in 1508 the Spolverini chapel at Santa Eufemia in Verona with frescoes depicting the apocryphal Tobit, who piously maintained his Jewish faith in exile, Caroto rather exceptionally assigned the young Hebrew women not loops but rather the long pendant ear-rings that were beginning to be fitted into Christian ears [Hughes 1986: 44–45].

Thus, his semen, which is in its very essence male, is transformed into a feminine accessory and beauty product appropriated by a woman (Buchbinder 2008: 240–41).

Furthermore, Ted, who has not yet consummated his relationship with Mary, substitutes masturbation for 'real' sex here, suggesting the sexual deviance of the Jew. Yet, in the economy of antisemitic discourse, had Ted had sex it would have revealed his hyper-masculine sexual aggressiveness that corrupts the pure Gentile Christian woman. In such thinking, masturbation becomes evidence of the Jew's greater sexual appetite. It is also significant that Ted is left-handed. Finally, the act of bathroom masturbation infantilises him, recalling those teenage toileting practices as described so proficiently by the adolescent Portnoy! We do not know if Ted is a virgin or not, and although he ejaculates his sexual incompetence or inadequacy is magnified by his failure to locate his sperm – it is pointed out to him, and by a woman at that, one who appropriates his manly essence and uses it as a feminine hair product!

Shit and the Shoah

In films dealing with the Shoah the bathroom marks the boundary between life and death. Indeed, overall washing facilities coded death in the camps, as the gas chambers were concealed in mocked-up showers. The detailed mechanics of this are depicted in *The Grey Zone* and *The Boy in the Striped Pyjamas*. In *Schindler's List*, a group of women inmates is forced to strip and is herded into a large chamber labelled 'Bath and Inhalation Room'. Thinking they are about to die, they panic and shriek. The camera tilts up to focus on the showerheads. There is a delay as the women wait to see what emerges: water or gas, life or death. Like Alfred Hitchcock, Spielberg uses the shower to 'induce dread' (Baron 2010: 456). Elsewhere in the film, when a young Jewish concentration-camp inmate fails to clean the stains of the kommandant's bathtub by using soap instead of lye, Amon Goeth forgives the boy in his bathroom but later changes his mind and shoots him dead. Later, other children hide, literally, in the shit, to escape being rounded up and selected for the gas chambers. A very young boy looks for a place to hide. Finding that his chosen locations are already occupied, he jumps down through the hole of the wooden latrines into the sewage. Covered in faeces, we see that he is not alone, as a group of four other children tell him, 'Get out. This is our place. Get out.' The latrines in the camp thus become a place of refuge and safety. A similar scene occurs at the beginning of the film when Jews use the sewers to escape being forced out of the ghetto. At the same time, however, the sewers also lead to death, as other escapees are discovered and shot.

Significant with respect to the Shoah is the use of the toilet as a means of humiliation and degradation. The toilet was very public space, and given the sheer volume of numbers of Jews it was most likely coded as Jewish space. When the Jews were herded into cattle cars and transported to the death camps the trains did not contain any toilets, nor were there any toilet stops, for the Jews at least. Consequently, the acts of defecation and urination are remembered as very public and humiliating spectacles, designed by the Nazis to incrementally and excrementally dehumanise the Jews before killing them. Thus the disgusting physical state of the Jews facilitated the Nazis' murder machine, for it significantly distanced them from their humanity and therefore helped the perpetrators to believe that they were not killing humans but rather destroying 'Stücke' ('pieces')

– the Nazis' preferred term for the trainloads of Jews (Levi 2000: 22). An example of such is *The Grey Zone*, in which an elderly Jewess is shown using a bucket in the midst of a crowded train. The toilet is also used as a site of humiliation in *The Counterfeiters* when an SS guard urinates on Jewish concentration-camp prisoner Salomon Sorowitsch as he cleans the toilet. This act, and the space in which it occurs, serve to emphasise the unequal power relationship between captor and captive, using the bathroom 'as the locus for confrontations, both physical and verbal, of who's in charge' (Fuller 1993: 226).

In a much discussed and perplexing sequence in his *La Haine*, Kassovitz deliberately chose the public toilet as the location into which he introduces a Holocaust survivor (Tadek Lokcinski), cementing the association between victimisation, humiliation, toilets and the Shoah, or between 'God, shit and deportation' (Rose 2007: 487). It is further significant that it is the bathroom of a Parisian café. The character is clearly coded as Eastern European, specifically Polish, by his diminutive stature and Yiddish-accented French. The old Jew tells the three nonplussed youths a story about his shy friend Grunwalski, who, after going to the woods to relieve himself, failed to re-board his train en route to a Siberian gulag because, as the train was leaving, he reaches out his hands to board the train but his trousers fell down. Embarrassed at exposing himself, he pulled his trousers up, thus missing the train and freezing to death. Although the train was en route to a Russian labour camp, catching it could have saved Grunwalski's life since, like his friend, the majority of Polish Jews who survived the Holocaust were those who escaped to the Soviet Union after the German invasion of Poland.

Like the Coens' '*Goy*'s teeth' and *dybbuk* tales, the moral here is unclear. Is the old man telling the youths that they need to focus on the correct priorities, unlike his friend Grunwalksi; or is he using his *Yiddische kopf* to get himself out of a potentially threatening situation by bamboozling the three youths, who clearly do not get the point of his story? Loshitzky comments, 'This thought-provoking narrative digression confronts the spectator with Jewish weakness associated with the Holocaust, of the predicament of being literally "caught with their pants down"' (Loshitzky 2005: 139). And where this episode 'introduces the Holocaust through the back door', it also fits into a line of films that have done the same, at least in terms of Jewishness, an identity so wrapped up in the Shoah. *The Unborn* similarly uses the bathroom to introduce the Holocaust when a *dybbuk*, created as a result of Mengele's medical experimentation at Auschwitz, haunts the film's protagonist in toilet-related situations. Finally, a conversation takes place in the toilet in *Seres Queridos/Only Human* when a Palestinian and Jew argue over the Middle East conflict. Leni defends Israel's nuclear policy by referring to the Shoah: 'Since we left the concentration camps we've had to defend ourselves.'

Fantasy and escapism

The cinematic toilet is not only a marginalised Jewish space, but also a site for fantasy and wish-fulfilment unavailable to the Jew in the wider society of which he is a part. In *La Haine*, Vinz is able to be who he wants to be in the toilet, to exercise fantasies that he cannot enjoy in the external, 'real' world. He 'constantly seeks (in mirrors, on television and movie screens, in private fantasies) images that confirm his toughness and "authenticity"' (Rose 2007: 480). When we first meet Vinz at the beginning of the film, he is gazing into his bathroom mirror, mimicking (albeit in French) Travis Bickle (Robert de Niro) from *Taxi Driver*. He aims an imaginary gun at his reflection in the mirror, uncannily hinting at his own death later in the film, but ironically (although at this point unbeknownst to the viewer) reinforcing his inability to use an actual gun in the real world. Having practised in the bathroom, Vinz tries to perform this persona in the world beyond the toilet. In a Parisian apartment, however, his adversary Astérix not only steals his lines but also utters them much more convincingly than Vinz. When Vinz again performs in the café toilet, Hubert declares this performance to be unrealistic: 'Forget it Vinz. You're out of your depth.' Doughty and Griffiths further argue that 'Vinz's identity is further undermined by the space in which it is staged (another toilet) and by the emphatic and ironic toilet flushes with which it is punctuated' (2006: 118). Yet, the toilet confirms rather than undermines Vinz's identity as a Jew. Given his blonde, blue-eyed looks, it is the space of the toilet rather than phenotype or the other traditional markers of ethnicity that locate him. Furthermore, it allows him to assume an identity denied him in the outside, non-toilet, world.

Yet, not all Jews are shown as vulnerable in the toilet. Verna in *Miller's Crossing* punches Tom in the toilet. Detective Richie Roberts in *American Gangster* beats up a criminal in the bathroom and Judith in *Saving*

Silverman uses the toilet to assert her tough (conceptually Jewish) status by repeatedly holding the head of J.D. (Jack Black) under the water.

Unmasking

As I mentioned at the outset of this chapter, the bathroom is the place where masks are dropped. In *Hitlerjunge Salomon/Europa Europa*, the Jewishness of Solly Perel, who is masquerading as a German orphan whose parents were killed by the Bolsheviks, is exposed when a fellow Wehrmacht soldier surprises him while he is taking a bath. Fortunately for Solly, the soldier is gay and thus, as Bartov points out, 'by definition anti-Nazi' (2005: 341 n.33). He befriends Solly, helping him to conceal his Jewish identity. Solly is thus doubly unmasked: he is discovered to be Jewish and in doing so he discloses his own homosexuality. Therefore, in the bathroom, a clear connection is constructed between the 'queer'/queer Jew and the gay German, a connection that ultimately saves Solly's life.

Jewess Rachel in *Zwartboek/Black Book* transforms herself into Gentile Ellen by dying her hair blonde in front of the mirror. She also chooses to reveal her mimicry in the bathroom at the Nazi HQ, when she tells another woman that she is a spy ('That's like Greta Garbo in *Mata Hari*' is her friend's incredulous response). But Rachel's mimicry is too good, and she is incarcerated with other Dutch collaborators where, in a scene reminiscent of *Carrie* (dir. Brian De Palma, 1976), she is stripped to the waist and covered by the contents of a large bucket of faeces that is dropped on her (Condron 2008). And it is in the shower in *School Ties* that David Greene is revealed to be Jewish by his antisemitic schoolmate (Matt Damon), who calls him 'a lying, back-stabbing kike'.

Bree in *Transamerica* conceals both his male gender and his paternity from his/her son Toby, who not only does not know that s/he is a man, but also that s/he is his father. Going to the bathroom thus presents particular hazards for Bree: it is not so much the revelation of her/his Jewishness that is at issue here but her gender that s/he is trying to conceal. The problem is compounded by the fact that Bree constantly needs the 'ladies room' as her hormone pills are also diuretic. Consequently, multiple sequences place her in bathrooms or outdoors clutching a toilet roll. The mask is dropped, however, when Bree urinates behind their car and Toby spies her/him standing up in the rear-view mirror, her circumcised penis in plain sight. 'She's not even a real woman. She's got a penis,' Toby exclaims.

The real nature and Jewishness of the outwardly respectable Victor Ziegler in *Eyes Wide Shut* is revealed in the bathroom. We are first introduced to Ziegler when Bill (Tom Cruise) and Alice Harford (Nicole Kidman) attend an extravagant formal Christmas party he throws at his vast and opulent mid-town Manhattan mansion. Together with his wife, Ziegler presents the outward appearance of a decent New York socialite of high social prominence. But the party is 'a glittering display of artificiality, pretense, deceit – and enormous wealth' (Kuberski 2004), as some minutes later Bill is summoned to a bathroom, where that we learn that this pristine façade is a sham which, just like the bathroom, is hiding a proverbial underworld of sewage, shit and human waste. Ziegler's Jewishness is cemented in the bathroom, for it is there that his real but concealed nature is revealed. Of all the rooms in his vast mansion, of which there are presumably many, the bathroom is the place that Kubrick chose to situate Ziegler as his mask drops. It is here that he is 'exposed as the unclothed debauchee/pantaloon frightened by the prospect of a "hooker" dying in his own bathroom' (Nelson 2000: 293). It is also the location that Victor selects in order to engage in sexually depraved behaviour. In this bathroom, so many traits stereotypically attached to the Jew are depicted that it is difficult *not* to read

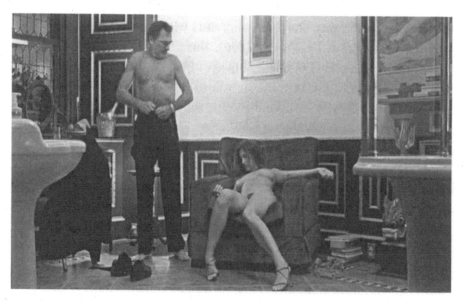

Victor Ziegler in *Eyes Wide Shut*.

Ziegler as Jewish. The bathroom is ornate and 'palatial' (Kuberski 2004). Luxurious and spacious, it is bigger and better furnished than most New York City apartments. It contains a bathtub, toilet, bidet, sink, armchair, fireplace with a mantle, and has paintings on the walls. An original artwork 'features an unflattering portrait of a naked woman, a portrait whose owner views women solely as sexual objects' (Rasmussen 2005: 337). Indeed, only a stereotypically tasteless Jew has a bathroom as lavishly and decadently decorated, what Thomas Allen Nelson calls 'Ziegler's American-rich version of a decadent Old World vulgarity' (2000: 275).

Upon entering the bathroom, we discover a half-naked, shirtless and shoeless Ziegler standing over a naked prostitute, slumped in a chair, semi-conscious from a drug overdose, clad only in a pair of high-heeled shoes and a necklace. Thus our first image of Ziegler, following the brief introductory scene with his wife, is an immediate post-coital one, involving a vulnerable woman. 'While downstairs Victor puts his opulently appointed wealth and power on display, clothed in a gracious but patronising civility, upstairs he hurriedly covers up his ugly naked vulnerability' (Nelson 2000: 275). Victor rapidly replaces his glasses and zips up his trousers. Several classic physical antisemitic images are accentuated here – hirsute (as a character quips in *Me Without You* [dir. Sandra Goldbacher, 2001], 'Jews are hairier'), big-nosed, bespectacled Jew. Indeed, Ziegler actually only puts on his shirt, and hides his hirsuteness, several minutes later towards the end of the bathroom scene after the prostitute is revived from her overdose. As the very first item that Ziegler chooses to put on while he is getting dressed is his glasses, attention is drawn to them, as well as his nose, thus dominating the viewers' image of Ziegler's face until Kubrick zooms in for close-ups. This is closely aligned with the suggested reference towards his Jewish penis by the action of zipping up, and hence stereotypical phenotype elements (glasses, nose, penis, and body hair) dominate the image for the majority of the scene.

The sequence is laden with antisemitic tropes. It recalls 'the hypersexual lascivious, sexually perverse and predatory Jew, mercilessly and callously exploiting a weak and powerless woman, through a combination of illegal drugs and sex; the Jew who corrupts and defiles beautiful young Gentile women (even if the presence of her shoes traditionally signifies a prostitute/courtesan)' (Kaplan 2010). As Kuberski (2004) puts it, 'the Zieglers' bathroom is a fully-furnished brothel and drug den.' Furthermore, Victor is misogynistic. Having bought the prostitute's services he patronises her ('That was one hell of a scare you gave us kiddo') and then attempts to remove her from his house as quickly as possible ('Is it OK if I get some clothes on her and get her out of here?'). He certainly shows no respect for her condition, refusing to cover up her nakedness, and only once she regains consciousness and presents no threat or embarrassment does he show any concern for her. When Bill revives the woman, Ziegler tells him, 'You saved my ass,' clearly indicating that her fate is irrelevant. Ziegler fetishises, objectifies and sexualises her in a manner little different to the painting on his wall. As Kuberski (2004) puts it, 'Bill has been summoned, like a plumber, to repair her.' Ziegler is the embodiment of a matrix of antisemitic discourses; Kubrick 'imbuing him with some of the most odious anti-Semitic stereotypes' (Kaplan 2010). He is powerful and wealthy, but a lying, hypocritical, hyper-sexual, misogynist, court Jew, covertly manipulative, and orchestrating and participating in the sexual corruption (and possible murder) of beautiful Gentile women (Rasmussen 2005, Kaplan 2010). Finally, the bathroom location suggests the dirty Jew doing his business in the conceptually filthiest of places, upstairs and out of sight of the genteel (and Gentile) guests downstairs.

The theme of unmasking in the bathroom also occurs in *Miller's Crossing*. As with Ziegler, although it is not the initial time that we meet Verna, it is the first time that we are given a revealing insight into her character. Tom intrudes into the 'ladies' room' while Verna is powdering her nose. The space is clearly defined as feminine not only by the presence of other women but also by its pastel colour scheme. Verna, however, engages in far from typically feminine behaviour: when Tom kisses her without permission she responds by punching him squarely in the face. It is the conversation that takes place there, though, that is most significant. As discussed in Chapter 3 Tom's boss Leo, with whom she is sleeping, thinks that she is the 'original Miss Jesus', suggesting that she has an air of innocence. Tom, on the other hand, calls her a 'tramp', indicating that he sees through her sexual wiles. Verna is sleeping with both Tom and Leo in order to protect her brother Bernie. Referring to the previous night, during which Verna seduced Tom, she asks, 'You think that last night was just more campaigning for my brother?' Tom responds, 'I can see the angles. You know if there was a market for little old ladies you'd have grandma Bernbaum first in line.' Thus, while clearly presented as a sexually alluring and physically attractive woman, the ladies' powder room sequence reveals Verna for what she really is: a coldly manipulative, hyper-sexual Jewess, but one who is simultaneously caring and family-minded, going to extraordinary lengths to take care of her brother in a display of *menschlikayt*.

Toilet erotics

James Monaco points out how sex plays less of a role in 'Hollywood bathtubs' than might be expected; often, there is the 'suggestion of nudity without the truth of it' (2009: 201). Even though the bathtub and Jewish sexuality have been intertwined since David spied Bathsheba bathing on her rooftop, rarely is the Jew/ess eroticised in the bathroom. Aaron Green (Jonah Hill) in *Get Him to the Greek* (dir. Nicholas Stoller, 2010), Eduardo and Mark in *The Social Network*, Rachel in *Zwartboek/Black Book* and David in *Carlito's Way* are rare exceptions to this rule. Even though Ziegler fornicates in his bathroom, he is not presented as an erotic figure. Indeed, this is fairly typical of the cinematic Jew/ess. Even in the film *In Her Shoes*, where we are introduced to the very attractive Maggie as she makes out with a former classmate at her ten-year high-school reunion, she drunkenly vomits into the toilet. Indeed, in Ziegler's case it is Eros's other that is in close proximity: the near-death experience of the overdosing prostitute. Similarly in *Barton Fink*, while many shots place him in and around bathrooms (in one sequence, a beautiful low-angle shot depicts Barton, seemingly alone, urinating at the end of a line of porcelain urinals), none of them serve to sexualise him. As I mentioned above, when Audrey seduces Barton, for example, the shot travels from their feet through the bedroom into the open door of the bathroom, establishing a causal link. As we hear the off-screen sounds of their lovemaking, the camera disappears down the plughole of the bathroom sink. Since the camerawork is a clear homage to the shower sequence in *Psycho* (dir. Alfred Hitchcock, 1960), it is an ominous foretelling of Audrey's fate: she is murdered. The next morning, having discovered that Audrey is dead, 'Barton stands in the bathroom, vulnerable and cold in his underwear' (Cheshire and Ashbrook 2000: 49). A further top-down objective shot of Barton slumped on the bathroom floor, traumatised by the discovery of Audrey's dead body and framed tightly between the corner of the white sink and green bathtub, emphasises his abject status and isolation, as if being punished for his sexual activity, and with a Gentile at that.

Conclusion: the final flush

Loshitzky might feel that 'the choice of the men's public toilet as the location for invoking the Holocaust is unusual' (2005: 139), but it connects to a wider Jewish discourse about Jewishness and the bathroom than perhaps she is aware. As Jewish space, it is represented as a site of potential danger, anxiety and unmasking, as well as a boundary marker between Jewish and Gentile, uncivilised and genteel, or the place of wish fulfilment and catharsis. As a heterotopic space, the bathroom is a key site for the production of Jewish resistance, critique and mockery of mainstream values by revealing what they really are. As a consequence, the bathroom no longer, in the words of Kuberski (2004), 'may seem to support a ritual of equalisation, in which men whatever their social status or financial position are forced, penis in hand, to acknowledge their same basic sameness before nature if not God'. However, it is an agent for Jewish normalisation, for what is more ordinary and quotidian than going to the toilet. Where Fuller sees 'support for the argument that men's rooms might truly be the last bastion for masculinity' (1993: 229), I would rewrite her assertion to state that the bathroom might truly be the last bastion for Jewishness.

Conclusion

'There is more than one way to be Jewish,' said Israeli novelist Sami Michael, opening a gay pride rally in Jerusalem in 2006. Contemporary cinema's depiction of the Jew/ess since 1990 convincingly demonstrates this, as 'Jews are comfortably "out" in a variety of senses' (Rosenberg 1996: 44). In addition to the stereotypes and self-images of the past, we have witnessed New Jews who are nasty, brutish, solitary, short, tough, fat, manly, unmanly, endogamous, exogamous, aggressive, passive-aggressive, traitors, losers, shysters, spaced-out, criminals, porn stars, assassins, killers, gangsters, cops, rebellious, in outer space, cowboys, skinheads, gay, lesbian, transsexual, superheroes, deviant, dysfunctional, liberated, working-class, Reform, Liberal, Conservative, *haredi*, Yiddish/Hebrew/Aramaic-speaking, immigrants, refugees, survivors, and so on. It is also in part a cinematic fulfilment of the dream of the first prime minister of Israel, David Ben Gurion, who said, 'We will know we have become a normal country when Jewish thieves and Jewish prostitutes conduct their business in Hebrew.' It represents Jewish normalisation, as if cinema was, in the words of Hannah Arendt, quoting Kafka, 'an instrument whereby' Jews 'might become "a people like other peoples"' (1944: 120).

These New Jews are located in contemporary narratives that are marked by a celebration, and a critique, of Jewish relations, by a sense that threats to Jewish continuity persist from within (assimilation/intermarriage) and without (antisemitism), as does resistance to both these threats. They are not marked by invisibility or the desire to become 'white', but rather celebrate New Jews in many guises. Such films are therefore quite overt and self-conscious about both the traditions of representation and their confident revisionist take on those representations as a source of ethnic pride. They display a 'relative freedom from classical film paradigms of Jewish experience' (Rosenberg 1996: 44). This shift towards more subtle, nuanced, playful and even outrageous representations signals that Jews feel more comfortable – *and not just in the United States* – that they have arrived; and for American Jews, even more so than they had done in the late 1960s and 1970s. Yet, at the same time, they are integrated to the extent that Jewishness has become accepted as normal or, as Brook put it, 'Jewish normalcy has become everyone's *normalcy*' (2003: 177). Consequently, the proliferation of post-1990s Jewish images is partly overcompensation for the sense of a recedingly distinctive Jewishness. The more Jews become accepted, the more their difference must be asserted. Jewish representation in the post-1990s period exists, therefore, in dialectical tension *between* assimilation and multiculturalism. It says much, then, that there are so many examples of this trend in contemporary cinema that not all of them could be listed or treated here.

Contemporary cinema manifests much Jewish assertiveness. What was once said about *The Producers* (dir. Mel Brooks, 1968), that it conveys 'considerable cultural confidence – loud and proud' and is 'a rebellion against invisibility' (Hoberman 2003: 229) is just as applicable today, but to a whole series of films in a range of countries. These New Jews a re not afraid of their 'surplus visibility' or 'burden of representation' – 'the feeling among minority members and others that whatever members of that group say or do, it is too much and moreover, they are being too conspicuous about it' – that is being considered 'too Jewish', (Zurawik 2003: 6). Indeed, it is often the non-Jew who is now the outsider. As Martin (Martin Starr) in *Knocked Up* states, 'Fuck you guys. I'm glad I'm not Jewish.' To which the response comes, 'So are we... You weren't chosen for a reason.' Contemporary cinema is, in the words of Eric L. Goldstein, 'unafraid to engage in "open cultural narcissism," undermining the assimilationist paradigm' (2006: 210). It reflects how Jewish filmmakers, actors, actresses, directors and screenwriters are increasingly representing themselves without the mediation or biases that either non-Jewish or older, more assimilatory directors may deploy in their films. In today's multicultural, postethnic and pluralist world these New Jews are less focused on Jewishness as a marker of an oppressed, diaspora-conscience minority.

To take just one measure discussed throughout this book: language. Where Yiddish (and Hebrew) was once perceived by a generation of Jews as an obstacle to acculturation, the language of mainstream contemporary cinema is more ethnically inflected, more 'Jewish'. A diverse range of films uses suggestive and un-translated phrases (as well as rhythms, cadences and even made-up words) in Hebrew, Aramaic and Yiddish, and other languages familiar to Jews, with no concern as to whether audiences understand them or not. And where once such utterances were confined to older characters and/or set in the past, today words in different languages and dialects are voiced by younger characters and often set in the present. And these characters sound normal; they speak like everyone else, not as if they had just got off the boat from Eastern or Central Europe. In doing so, contemporary cinema is more foul-mouthed and scatological than ever before. Walter's 'shomer fucking shabbes' is, of course, the classic example, but elsewhere Jewish gangster Mickey Cohen (Harvey Keitel) in *Bugsy* tells an Italian mobster to 'Kish mir in tuchis!' (Yiddish: 'Kiss my arse'). It says much that in 2010 the mainstream American remake of the French film *Le Diner de Cons* (dir. Francis Veber, 1998) can be titled *Dinner for Schmucks* (dir. Jay Roach, 2010).

Furthermore, the word 'Jew' is said much more often in film since 1990. It was never uttered in *The Life of Emile Zola* (dir. William Dieterle, 1937), for example, despite his famous diatribe against the Dreyfus case. Stanley Kubrick's films never used the word; his only overt Jewish references were the terms 'yahoodies' and 'kike' in his *A Clockwork Orange* (1971) and *Full Metal Jacket* (1987) respectively. Despite being set in the Catskills during its Jewish-holiday-resort heyday, it is never stated in *Dirty Dancing*. In *Avalon*, the words Jew or Jewish are never mentioned; indeed, the first-generation Jews speak in a Yiddish-inflected English accent, but do not actually use any Yiddish words (Furnish 2005: 65, 148). In fact, as was typical of the 1950s and early 1960s, the film removes any culturally specific references in a universalising, de-particularising, de-Judaising and de-Semitising strategy. At the grandmother's funeral, the only Jewish tinge is when the eulogist calls her 'a woman of valour'.

In the post-1990 period, in contrast, the avoidance of the word 'Jew' is reversed, and proliferates without any sense of such negativity or insult.[27] When, for example, Ben in *Knocked Up* is asked what product makes his hair so curly, he replies 'I use Jew' (perhaps he had been using some of *There's Something About Mary*'s Ted's hair gel?). The promotional poster for the British film *The Infidel* features the word 'Due' crossed out in the sentence 'Due out April 9' and replaced with the homophone 'Jew'. And in *The Believer*, Danny declares: 'J... E... W. Jew! You say it a million times, it's the only word that never loses its meaning. Jew. Jew. Jew. Jew. Jew. Jew. Jew. Jew. Jew. Jew. Jew.' *The Hebrew Hammer* even tries to recuperate the ethnic slurs 'kike' and 'Heeb'. If a film can be called '*Greenberg*' in 2010, it is not long before one appears simply entitled '*Jew*'. It is part of the 'process of de-hiding' (Rocha 2010: 39).

Furthermore, contemporary cinema offers a potentially shocking use of Jewish symbolism, demonstrating a consistent irreverence towards that which Judaism and Jews (literally at times) hold dear and holy. Not only does it walk a tightrope of political correctness, which could be perceived as crossing the line at times, but it also disrupts almost sacrosanct boundaries. Yet, judging by the lack of outrage such films have caused, it points to their acceptance in the contemporary period. Almost every millennia-old antisemitic canard is mimicked, mocked and reversed. Thus the mockumentary *Borat: Cultural Learnings of America for Make Benefit Glorious Nation of Kazakhstan* (dir. Larry Charles, 2006) can feature a British Jew mimicking a Jew-hating yet (in a clear form of double coding) paradoxically Hebrew-speaking Kazakh reporter in a film saturated with representations of antisemitism. After introducing the viewer through a tour of his home town, Borat (Sasha Baron-Cohen) announces, 'Although Kazakhstan glorious country, it have problem too: economic, social, and Jew.' Kazakhstan's 'Jewish problem' is mocked in a highly parodic moment, the 'running of the Jew'. In an obviously staged moment, a mimic of the Spanish tradition of bull-running is depicted, in which runners flee two enormous and crudely antisemitic puppets of a hooked nose and side-curled Jew and a meat-cleaver-wielding Jewess with a *challah*. A crowd of exuberant spectators, including Borat, who is reporting from the sidelines, jostle and jeer excitedly behind the barricades as horns play a loud fanfare. The event climaxes when the Jewess stops and lays a 'Jew egg'. Children are encouraged to rush and crush the egg before it hatches.

Elsewhere, when Borat visits the United States, his request for a gun to shoot Jews is met with equanimity and his antisemitic ditty ('Throw the Jew down the well/So my country can be free/You must grab him by his horns/Then we have a big party') is enthusiastically received in a Tucson bar. Neither of these scenes (shockingly), unlike the 'running of the Jew', was staged. Later in the film, Borat checks into a Jewish-owned bed and breakfast in rural Georgia. When cockroaches emerge from under the closed door of his room, he is convinced that they are the elderly Jewish proprietors, who have shifted shape and come to kill him. Throwing dollar bills on the floor in an attempt to distract them, and while suspenseful music plays in the background, he makes a quick escape.

A similar antisemitic stereotype is mocked in *Harold & Kumar Escape from Guantanamo Bay* when Federal Agent Ron Fox (Rob Corddry) tries to bribe information out of Rosenberg and Goldstein regarding the whereabouts of their friends by spilling a pile of pennies out on the table. They refuse to divulge, but once the frustrated agents leave the room and shut the door, they dive for the coins. *Four Lions* (dir. Christopher Morris, 2010) mocks the idea that Jews control global capitalism when slow-witted British Jihadist Barry (played by a Jewish actor Nigel Lindsay) declares, 'Spark plugs! Jews invented spark plugs to control global traffic.' And in *The Infidel*, Jews are described as the 'People of the chequebook'.

Indeed, no subject is beyond mockery or critique, including possibly the great Jewish taboo – the Holocaust. When asked in *Deconstructing Harry*, 'Do you care even about the Holocaust or do you think it never happened?' Harry responds, 'Not only do I know that we lost six million, but the scary thing is records are made to be broken.' When a woman explains JDate as a website for Jewish people in *Funny People*, 'So that way you can date whoever is listed.' George replies, 'That's interesting, I never thought Jews would like to be listed at all.' She looks at him blankly before he explains, 'Because of the whole Holocaust thing.' In *Adventureland*, Joel (Martin Starr) tries to prevent his friend from berating an antisemite by imploring that 'Worse things have happened to the Jews.' In *The Hangover* (dir. Todd Phillips, 2009) when one character complains that he lost his grandmother's Holocaust ring, another replies, 'I didn't know they gave rings out at the Holocaust,' ignorantly comparing the Shoah to the Superbowl. Finally, when in *Harold & Kumar Go to White Castle/Get the Munchies* Kumar asks, 'Oh dude, how were Katie Holmes's tits?' Goldstein replies, 'You know the Holocaust? Picture the exact opposite of that.'

While it could be argued that repetition of such discourses is at worst ignorant or disrespectful, and is thus a form of self-hatred, both Allen and Sandler use an underlying Jewishly inflected humour to make cogent and deeply serious points.[28] Where once such humorous creativity was once considered to be 'self-hatred', and such writers as Philip Roth were castigated as self-hating outcasts for producing similar fare, a sign of changed conditions is that the New Jews consider themselves, and are embraced by their Jewish communities, *qua* Jews. The New Jews, in the words of J.P. Steed, 'work to bring subversiveness, ironically and paradoxically, to the center. Largely through a new variation of Jewish humor [...] Jewish self-hatred is no longer anathema to the Jewish Self but rather a revolutionary force for remaking the Jewish Self' (2005: 61). Indeed, in films such as *The Believer*, *The Grey Zone* and *Homicide*, contemporary cinema even seriously tries to understand this phenomenon rather than simply dismiss it, as happened far too often in the past.

What these various examples point to is a clear demographic shift. 'For the current generation of Jews, the Holocaust is a historical event. It is real and horrible, but distant and communal. No one they actually knew died in Hitler's ovens' (Desser and Friedman 2004: 318). Likewise, many of the contemporary generation of directors, writers, actresses and actors have never experienced vicious, violent, physical, state-sponsored antisemitism first-hand. For them, such Judeophobia is as historical as the Holocaust. Indeed, at least one commentator suggested that

> We have entered a new qualitatively different epoch, which I choose to define as 'asemitic', i.e., one that is neither antisemitic nor philosemitic, but which treats 'the Jews' in a far calmer and more detached manner, as a group which definitely 'belongs' on the [European] continent and in each individual state, but which is to be treated on equal terms with everybody else [Pinto 2010].

This neutral context, 'which does not, either in positive or negative terms, attribute innate "differences", whether as special virtues or as unique "faults" (when not "crimes" as was often the case during Europe's millennial history) to the Jews *qua Jews*' (Pinto 2010), extends beyond the European continent to embrace most advanced pluralist democracies.[29] While Pinto perhaps overstates the case, this context, in which Jews, Jewishness and Judaism have become normalised, casual, 'matter of fact' and commonplace, has allowed Jewish cinema to flourish.

And it is in this context that this use of Jewish stereotypes and self-images in contemporary cinema is absolutely intentional. It reflects the post-assimilatory confidence of a younger generation of directors, actresses, actors and screenwriters who transform their forebears' anxieties and insecurities into feelings of assertiveness, unafraid to mock and reverse old caricatures. As I outlined in my introduction, stereotypes offer reassurance, as well as providing a surplus value, which itself produces pleasure or *Jewissance*: that joy derived from reading Jews, Jewishness and Judaism, stereotypical or otherwise, in film, where we least expect them, or *even* where their presence and Jewishness (whether ethnic, cultural or religious) is submerged, commonplace, doubly coded, superfluous and gratuitous, that is non-essential in plot, narrative or story terms. It gives a form of pleasure for its audiences, who can recognise the nod and the wink, perhaps where fellow audience members cannot. At the same time, these reverse stereotypes, through mimicry and mockery (and Baron-Cohen, like his British Jewish antecedent Peter Sellers, is the mimic *par excellence*) expose and undermine the continuation of anti-Jewish prejudices and fears.

Yet, as the above examples in particular clearly show, the contemporary use of these 'reverse stereotypes', or mimicry, is not simply diametrically opposed to the old stereotypes. As I noted at the outset, 'the stereotype is a complex, ambivalent, contradictory mode of representation' (Bhabha 1994: 100). 'After all, a reverse discourse, as Foucault describes it, does not simply produce a mirror reversal – a pure, one-to-one inversion of the existing discourses it reverses' (Halperin 1995: 60). Antisemitism does not function by means of a logical and rational set of propositions with an identifiable factual basis, rather it proceeds from a set of inconsistent concepts to be deployed and redeployed at will even if mutually contradictory. Thus, being immune to refutation by a strategy of rational argumentation, as its basic premises cannot be subjected to any rigorous, analytical examination, it is futile to attempt to disprove each premise (although many of the individual premises are easily invalidated), not least because as each is debunked it is replaced by a new set of propositions. Consequently, the mimicked, mocked and reversed stereotype or self-image may take almost exactly the same form as the original in its act of appropriation.

Another sign of change is that contemporary cinema is 'rife with very specific Jewish arcane, erudite knowledge that would only be familiar to a Jew steeped in Jewish lore' (Jackson and Moshin 2008: 205). Since many of these films include themes of classical Jewish tradition and folklore, as well as religious factors – namely Judaism – in their representations, they mine Jewish history for its specifically Jewish resonances and internal dialectics to break with the predominant paradigm in which Jews were largely treated as merely an ethnic group or cipher. In this way, by framing Jewishness as Judaism, only accessible through a presumed amount of knowledge, film since 1990 is de-universalising, re-Semitising, re-Judainising and re-particularising; emphasising that only certain audiences are truly meant to 'get' it. Contemporary cinema is thus coding the rebellion of the generation of New Jews against their mid-twentieth-century predecessors – those whose secularised Jewish identities were more ethnic than religious, whom Philip Roth described as 'Jews who needed no large terms of reference, no profession of faith or doctrinal creed, in order to be Jews, and they certainly needed no other language' (2004: 220).

Finally, prior to 1990, the Jew/ess in cinema suffered from the 'persistence of binaries', even in spite of 'their limited scope for representation' (Miguélez Carballeira 2010: 8). These included the queer or sissy/tough Jew, the Jewish Mother/JAP, hyper-sexual/hysteric, macho/feminised, *la belle juive*/ugly old kike, active/passive, victim/perpetrator, kosher/*treyf*, secular/*haredi*, Jewess/*shiksa* dualisms. If I have referred to them throughout this book, it is because so much of cinema, as well as the academic criticism of the place of 'the Jew' in it, relies on them. Yet, it is clear that while images of Jews, Jewishness and Judaism in contemporary cinema are still structured around these binaries, we cannot take their continued existence for granted as, in so many examples, they have been creatively blended to create new paradigms that are neither wholly one nor the other. Cinema has witnessed a move towards more unselfconscious, self-critical, deeper, subtle, nuanced, playful representations of Jews, Jewishness and Judaism that begin to populate the spectrum between these dichotomous poles. We have witnessed 'the willingness to suspend, though not discard, the conventional binaries' (Bial 2005: 141) to locate representations in 'the Gray Zone between Other and Not' (Bloom 2002). Jewish film is reflecting the cultural multiplicity of everyday Jewish life. Thus, in the final analysis, contemporary cinema is enacting – or, at least, attempting to provoke – a 'sea change in Jewish self-consciousness' by subverting the 'old fixed categories' of Jewish identity (Biale 1998: 31, 32).

Notes

1 However, it should be noted that Jewish actors John Garfield and Sam Jaffe played explicit Jews in *Gentleman's Agreement*.

2 I am, of course, invoking Laura Mulvey's notion, as found in her 'Visual pleasure and narrative cinema' (1975).

3 'Haredi' (plural: *haredim*) literally means 'one who trembles', deriving from Isaiah 66:5, in which the prophet admonishes his people to 'Hear the word of the Lord, you who tremble [*haredim*] at His word.' It is often confused with the much more common term, in American English at least, Hasidic. *Haredi* is translated as 'ultra-Orthodox', a definition that does not do justice to an extensive and nuanced term which covers a range of Jews who fall into this category but not all of whom are 'Orthodox' in the strictest definition of that term, and who can be further subdivided into Hasidic and Mitnagdic Jews. Hasidism, which is characterised by charismatic leadership, prayer and a mysticism-orientation is not 'Orthodox', but constitutes a large portion of *haredism*. So while all Hasidim are *haredim*, not all *haredim* are Hasidim. Mitnagdism, in contrast, has a study and ethics-centred orientation. Film has not assisted here in its tendency to elide all intra-Jewish differences and collapse *haredim* visually into the descriptive term 'black hat', used as an adjective but referring to the brimmed black hats that *haredi* men wear. This *haredi* is always male and Ashkenazi, ignoring the intricate visual differences that separate the groups within the *haredi* spectrum, as well as the national distinctions between the non-Ashkenazi *haredim* who are Sephardic and Mizrahic (Hebrew: 'Eastern'). This will be explored further in Chapter 6.

4 This is reinforced by the casting of Baldwin as Blake in *Glengarry Glen Ross*, a role specifically created for him for the film, in which he plays a non-Jew sales strategist brought in to motivate the other (Jewish) salesmen. Having said that, in *Along Came Polly* Baldwin played the Jewish character Stan Indursky.

5 Admittedly, Brandt's antisemitism occurs in a dream. As Larry Gopnik (Michael Stuhlbarg) dreams of the happy departure of his brother Arthur (Richard Kind) to Canada, the idyllic scene becomes horrific when he sees Arthur being shot in the head and falling into the lake. Brandt, who is seen lurking in the bushes, then shouts to Mitch, 'There's another Jew, son,' and he then proceeds to aim and shoot at Larry. At this point Larry wakes up screaming in terror about his nightmare. Brandt's name might also be an allusion to Karl Brandt, one of Hitler's leading medics in the early euthanasia programmes, as well as recalling that of Karl Mundt in *Barton Fink*.

6 Yiddish: a small town or village in the 'old country'.

7 Critics have pointed out, and Miller has confirmed, that Willy Loman is implicitly Jewish. George Ross (1951) makes the argument that the play is essentially Jewish in its treatment of business life, family relations and Yiddish cadences (see Popkin 1952: 46). Mamet himself commented, 'the greatest American play, arguably, is the story of a Jew told by a Jew and cast in "universal" terms. Willy Loman is a Jew in a Jewish Industry. But he is never identitied as such' (quoted in Kane 1999: 57).

8 Glasses and/or Jewish shortsightedness play into the much older anti-Jewish theological trope of Synagoga, the maiden whose blindfolded eyes are incapable of perceiving the true light of Christianity. At the same time, glasses also connote scholarliness. They are particularly prized by and are a matter of pride in contemporary *haredi* culture, where they are considered as much an identifying marker as the black hat, beard and *peyot* (side-locks), to the extent that there is peer pressure to wear them even when they are not required by the wearer (Aran 2006: 85–86). Félix's oversized glasses, then, can be read as both a reversal of anti-Jewish theology and an embracing of Jewish pride.

9 A small wooden oblong box containing rolled-up religious texts from Deuteronomy inscribed on parchment, and attached to the right-hand doorframe of Jewish households.

10 An obvious exception to the Jewish weakling syndrome, reflecting Jewish domination of the sport in the eighteenth and early twentieth centuries.

11 Lacking the obvious signifier of the Jew, hair has been an important stereotyping device for establishing the Jewess, in particular dark, curly or frizzy hair, otherwise known as a 'Jewfro' (Dowling 2009: 189–90).

12 Ironically, *The Jazz Singer* is playing, another reference to Karen's Jewishness.

13 Shoshanna is spelt both with and without the second 'h' in the film. I have retained the spelling with the 'h' as it is the correct spelling in general usage, as well as reflecting more accurately how the name is pronounced in the film.

14 The term 'mimic' here productively evokes Bhabha's useful analysis of the colonial subject as 'a subject of difference that is almost the same, but not quite', a fitting description for Shoshanna's (and Rachel's) blonde appearance for much of the film (1994: 123).

15 Ziegler is even left-handed, demonstrated when he flexes his serving arm, thus drawing upon age-old stereotypes of the Jew. In medieval art, Jews were always represented as being on the left-hand side of Christ at the Crucifixion, the Devil's side.

16 This is another marker of Jewish masculinity, in which the Jew's body was presumed to be apish and abnormally hairy, with 'more body hair than a yak' (Stetz 2010: 214).

17 This act echoes Daniel Boyarin's observation that 'Jewishness is like a concentrated dye' (1997: 263).

18 Bernie, who is gay, is himself in a relationship with Mink (John Buscemi), but, as with his sister, it is not for emotional needs, but rather a business arrangement. Together Bernie and Verna form 'a dysfunctional family riven by incest and overtones of homosexuality' (Cheshire et al. 2000: 37).

19 At the same time, Israeli fighter aircraft bearing the star of David stand alongside the US ones, invoking the US–Israeli strategic alliance. Brief shots of Israeli fighter pilots standing in front of the Israeli flag and aircraft also invoke the tough Zionist/*sabra* muscle-Jews.

20 Perhaps the unjustified killing is that of Yitzchok and his two bodyguards, who bear no responsibility for the death of Slevin's parents. 'Yitzchok' is Hebrew for Isaac, and given that he is Shlomo's only son, his 'name and fate evoke ha-akedah', the binding and sacrifice of Isaac, who some commentators say was actually killed by Abraham, a notion at the heart of *The Believer* (Wright 2009: 104).

21 *Inglourious Basterds* also reverses the earlier Second World War film *Saving Private Ryan* the defining sequence of which depicts the homoerotic death of Jewish GI Private Stanley Mellish (Adam Goldberg) at the hands (literally) of an anonymous SS Officer.

22 In both *The Grey Zone* and *Schindler's List*, for example, a young girl is used 'as a symbolic figure, standing in for the millions of nameless victims of the Holocaust' (Bangert 2008: 21). Where the girl in *Schindler's List* wears a red coat so as to demarcate her from the undifferentiated mass of Jewish victims, literally and figuratively presented as black and white, the little girl in *The Grey Zone* is clothed in a white dress. As young girls, both are 'an embodiment of innocence' invested with 'a considerable degree of sentimentality' (Bangert 2008: 21).

23 Redmon (2010) astutely observes how the graphic that alerts the audience that Emmanuelle is Shoshanna echoes that used to introduce Hugo Stiglitz (Til Schweiger), a German soldier with a penchant for brutally killing Gestapo officers, who is recruited by the Basterds. The insert, according to Redmon, quickly identifies the character, but 'draws attention to the otherwise latent similarities between Shosanna and Hugo Stiglitz. Both characters associate with people they are not – Shosanna, Gentiles in Paris; Stiglitz, the Jewish-American Basterds. Both characters don the guise of those against whom they seek restitution. For this costuming to work as it must if audiences are to deem their violence acceptable, these characters must slip into the disguises of their enemies without becoming them. Tarantino refuses to maintain the strict line between perpetrator and avenger, especially in the case of Shosanna.'

24 An educational establishment for male Jews where scripture and Talmud are studied.

25 Reuben was the eldest son of Jacob and Leah, from whom one of the 12 tribes of Israel took its name.

26 Terry Barr (1996) produces a counter-reading of this sequence, but one which is unsupported by its cinematography and narrative.

27 This is not to suggest that it did not happen at all prior to 1990. An exception to the rule is when Woody Allen drew particular attention to the word 'Jew' in his famous joke in *Annie Hall* where Alvy's antisemitic paranoia extends to his mis-hearing 'D'you eat?' as 'Jew eat?'

28 Unfortunately, elements of the Jewish community still drag out the term to decry films that are not as public-relations minded as they would wish. *The Hebrew Hammer* and *A Serious Man* were accused of just that.

29 While antisemitism has declined in the United States and among non-Muslims in Europe, tragically it has seemingly increased among many Muslims in Europe, and especially in the Middle East, where there has been a distinct revival of virulent antisemitism – generated and exacerbated by Israeli policy – which has become prevalent (indeed, this is what makes Borat's egg-crushing scene so chilling). As a sign of this, un-reversed antisemitic stereotypes continue to circulate in a number of films, such as *The Passion of the Christ* (dir. Mel Gibson, 2004) or the less obvious *Peter Pan* (dir. P.J. Hogan, 2003) (Stetz 2010: 134–35).

Bibliography

Aaron, Michele (2004) 'Cinema's queer Jews: masculinity and Yiddish cinema', in Phil Powrie, Ann Davies and Bruce Babington (eds), *The Trouble With Men: Masculinities in European and Hollywood cinema*. London and New York: Wallflower, pp. 90–99.

— (2010) 'The new queer Jew: Jewishness, masculinity, and contemporary film', in Harry Brod and Shawn Israel Zevit (eds), *Brother Keepers: New perspectives on Jewish masculinity*. Harriman, TN: Men's Studies Press, pp. 174–82.

Abramowitz, Rachel (n.d.) 'Tough Jews in cinema', *LA Times*, http://www.latimes.com/entertainment/news/la-et-tough-jews-pictures,0,1789514.photogallery. Last accessed May 2010.

Abrams, Nathan (2004) '"I'll have whatever she's having": Jewish food on film', in Anne Bowers (ed.), *Reel Food: Essays on food and film*. New York and London: Routledge, pp. 87–100.

— (2008) 'From Jeremy to Jesus: the Jewish male body on film, 1990 to the present', in Santiago Fouz-Hernández (ed.), *Mysterious Skin: Male bodies in global cinema*. London and New York: I.B.Tauris, pp. 13–26.

— (2009) 'The Jew on the loo: the toilet in Jewish popular culture, memory, and imagination', in Olga Gershenson and Barbara Penner (eds), *Ladies and Gents: Public toilets and gender*. Philadelphia, PA: Temple University Press, pp. 218–26.

— (2010) 'Hidden: Jewish film in the United Kingdom, past and present'. *Journal of European Popular Culture* 1(1), 53–68.

— (2011) '"My religion is American": a *midrash* on Judaism in American films, 1990 to the present', in Jeanne Cortiel, Kornelia Freitag, Christine Gerhardt and Michael Wala (eds), *Religion in the United States*. Heidelberg: Winter Verlag, pp. 209–25.

Abrams, Nathan, Ian Bell and Jan Udris (2010) *Studying Film*, 2nd edn. London: Bloomsbury Academic.

Aizen, Rebecca (2005) 'Like gefilte fish out of water: constructing Jewish femininity in Australia'. Unpublished PhD diss., University of Melbourne.

— (2009) '"The People of the Schtup?": Reflections on Jews, Sex and Pornography'. Unpublished manuscript in author's possession.

Alderman, Geoffrey (1994) 'British Jewry: religious community or ethnic minority?', in Jonathan Webber (ed.), *Jewish Identities in the New Europe*. Oxford: Littman, pp. 189–92.

Alfaro-Velcamp, Theresa (2006) '"Reelizing" Arab and Jewish ethnicity in Mexican film', *The Americas* 63(2), 261–80.

Almog, Oz (2000) *The Sabra: The creation of the New Jew*. Berkeley, CA: University of California Press.

Antler, Joyce (1998) 'Jewish women on television: too Jewish or not enough?', in Joyce Antler (ed.), *Talking Back: Images of Jewish women in American popular culture*. Hanover, NH and London: Brandeis University Press, pp. 242–52.

— (2008) *You Never Call! You Never Write! A History of the Jewish Mother*, New York and Oxford: Oxford University Press.

Aran, Gideon (2006) 'Denial does not make the haredi body go away: ethnography of a disappearing(?) Jewish phenomenon', *Contemporary Jewry* 26(1), 75–113.

Arendt, Hannah (1944) 'The Jew as pariah: a hidden tradition', *Jewish Social Studies* 6, 99–122.

Ascheid, Antje (2006) 'Safe rebellions: romantic emancipation in the "woman's heritage film"', *Scope* 4, http://www.scope.nottingham.ac.uk/article.php?issue=4&id=124. Last accessed in August 2011.

Ashcroft, Bill, Gareth Griffiths and Helen Tiffin (2000) *Post-colonial Studies: The key concepts*. London and New York: Routledge.

Avisar, Ilan (1988) *Screening the Holocaust: Cinema's images of the unimaginable*. Bloomington, IN: Indiana University Press.

Aviv, Caryn and David Shneer (2005) *New Jews: The end of the Jewish diaspora*. New York and London: New York University Press.

Bangert, Axel (2008) 'Changing narratives and images the Holocaust: Tim Black Nelson's film *The Grey Zone* (2001)', *New Cinemas* 6(1), 17–32.

Barcan, Ruth (2005) 'Dirty spaces: communication and contamination in men's public toilets', *Journal of International Women's Studies* 6(2) (online). Last accessed in August 2011.

Baron, Lawrence (2003) 'X-Men as J Men: the Jewish subtext of a comic book movie', *Shofar* 22(1), 44–52.

— (2005) *Projecting the Holocaust into the Present: The changing focus of contemporary Holocaust cinema*. Lanham, MD: Rowman & Littlefield.

— (2010) 'Film', in Peter Hayes and John K. Roth, *The Oxford Handbook of Holocaust Studies*. Oxford: Oxford University Press, pp. 444–60.

Barr, Terry (1996) 'Eating kosher, staying closer', *Journal of Popular Film and Television* 24(3), 134–44.

Barton, Bruce (2005) *Imagination in Transition: Mamet's move to film*. Brussels and New York: P.I.E./Peter Lang.

Bartov, Omer (2005) *The 'Jew' in American Cinema: From the Golem to Don't Touch My Holocaust*. Bloomington and Indianapolis, IN: Indiana University Press.

Baskind, Samantha (2007) 'The Fockerized Jew?: Questioning Jewishness as cool in American popular entertainment', *Shofar* 25(4), 3–17.

Baum, Charlotte, Paula Hyman and Sonia Michel (1977) *The Jewish Woman in America*. New York: New American Library.

Beinart, Peter (2010) 'The Failure of the American Jewish Establishment', *New York Review of Books* (10 June) (online version). Last accessed in August 2011.

Bell, David and Gill Valentine (1997) *Consuming Geographies: We are where we eat*. London and New York: Routledge.

Benshoff, Harry M. and Griffin, Sean (2009) *America on Film: Representing race, class, gender, and sexuality at the movies*. 2nd edn, Oxford: Wiley Blackwell.

Bergan, Ronald (2001) *The Coen Brothers*. London: Phoenix.

Berger, A.A. (2001) *Jewish Jesters: A study in American popular comedy*. Cresskill, NJ: Hampton Press.

Berger, Maurice (1996) 'The mouse that never roars: Jewish masculinity on American television', in Norman L. Kleeblatt (ed.), *Too Jewish? Challenging Traditional Identities*. New York and New Brunswick, NJ: Rutgers University Press, pp. 93–108.

Bhabha, Homi (1994) *The Location of Culture*. London: Routledge.

— (1998) 'Joking aside: the idea of a self-critical community', in Bryan Cheyette and Laura Marcus (eds), *Modernity, Culture and 'the Jew'*. Cambridge: Polity, pp. xv–xx.

Bial, Henry (2005) *Acting Jewish: Negotiating ethnicity on the American stage and screen*. Ann Arbor, MI: University of Michigan Press.

Biale, David (1997) *Eros and the Jews: From biblical Israel to contemporary America*. Berkeley, CA: University of California Press.

— (1998) 'The melting pot and beyond: Jews and the politics of American identity', in David Biale, Michael Galchinsky and Susan Heschel (eds), *Insider/Outsider: American Jews and multiculturalism*. Berkeley: University of California Press, pp. 17–33.

— (2000) 'Israeli secularists' revenge', *Tikkun* 15(4), 69.

Biberman, Matthew (2004) *Masculinity, Anti-semitism and Early Modern English Literature: From the satanic to the effeminate Jew*. Aldershot: Ashgate.

Blech, Benjamin (2009) 'If only the Coen brothers were serious', http://www.aish. com/ci/a/63956022.html. Last accessed April 2010.

Bloom, Davida (2002) 'White, but not quite: the Jewish character and anti-semitism negotiating a location in the gray zone between other and not', *Journal of Religion and Theatre* 1(1), http://www.rtjournal.org/vol_1/no_1/bloom.html. Last accessed March 2011.

Bloom, Lisa E. (2008) '"Barbie's Jewish roots": Jewish women's bodies and feminist art', in Nathan Abrams (ed.), *Jews and Sex*. Nottingham: Five Leaves, pp. 121–37.

Bombaci, Nancy (2002) '"Well of course, I used to be absolutely gorgeous Dear": the female interviewer as subject/object in Djuna Barnes's journalism', *Criticism* 44(2), 161–85.

Bonfil, Robert (1994) *Jewish Life in Renaissance Italy*, trans. Anthony Oldcorn. Berkeley, CA, Los Angeles and London: University of California Press.

Borden, Diane M. (2001) 'Man without a gun: Mamet, masculinity, and mystification', in Christopher C. Hudgins and Leslie Kane (eds), *Gender and Genre: Essays on David Mamet*. New York: Palgrave, pp. 235–54.

Boyarin, Daniel (1997) *Unheroic Conduct: The rise of heterosexuality and the invention of the Jewish man*. Berkeley, CA: University of California Press.

— (1998) 'Jewish Cricket', *PMLA* 113(1), 40–45.

— (2000) 'Freud, Sigmund (1856–1939)', in George E. Haggerty (ed.), *Gay Histories and Cultures: An encyclopedia*. New York: Garland, pp. 351–56.

Bradshaw, Peter (2011) '*Don't Look Now* and Roeg's red coat', http://www.guardian. co.uk/film/2011/jan/18/dont-look-now-red-coat. Last accessed October 2011.

Braverman, Irus (2009) 'Loo law: the public washroom as a hyper-regulated place', *Hastings Women's Law Journal* 20(1), 45–71.

Breines, Paul (1990) *Tough Jews: Political fantasies and the moral dilemma of American Jewry*. New York: Basic Books.

Brodkin, Karen (1998) *How Jews Became White Folks: And what that says about race in America*. New York: Rutgers University Press.

Brook, Stephen (1989) *The Club: The Jews of modern Britain*. London: Constable.

Brook, Vincent (2003) *Something Ain't Kosher Here: The rise of the 'Jewish' sitcom*. New Brunswick, NJ: Rutgers University Press.

— (2006) (ed.), *You Should See Yourself: Jewish Identity in Postmodern American Culture*. New Brunswick, NJ: Rutgers University Press.

Brown, Hannah (2006) '*Munich*: portentous and preachy', *Jerusalem Post*, 19 January (online). Last accessed in August 2011.

Buchbinder, David (2008) 'Enter the schlemiel: the emergence of inadequate or incompetent masculinities in recent film and television', *Canadian Review of American Studies/Revue canadienne d'études américaines* 38(2), 227–45.

Byers, Michele (2009) 'The pariah princess: agency, representation, and neoliberal Jewish girlhood', *Girlhood Studies* 2(2), 33–54.

Caplan, Nina (1999) '*A Price Above Rubies*', *Sight & Sound* (June), http://www.bfi. org.uk/sightandsound/review/133. Last accessed May 2007.

Chapman, Rowena (1996) 'The great pretender: variations on the New Man theme', in Rowena Chapman and Jonathan Rutherford (eds), *Male Order: Unwrapping masculinity*. London: Lawrence & Wishart, pp. 225–48.

Cheshire, Ellen and Ashbrook, John (2000), *The Coen Brothers*. Harpenden: Pocket Essentials.

Cheyette, Bryan (1993) *Constructions of 'the Jew' in English Literature and Society: Racial representations, 1875–1945*. Cambridge: Cambridge University Press.

Coates, Paul (2004) 'East-Central European cinema: beyond the Iron Curtain', in Elizabeth Ezra (ed.), *European Cinema*. Oxford and New York: Oxford University Press, pp. 265–82.

— (2005) *The Red and the White: The cinema of people's Poland*. London and New York: Wallflower.

Cohan, Steven and Ina Rae Hark (1993) *Screening the Male: Exploring masculinities in Hollywood cinema*. London: Routledge.

Cohen, Rich (1988) *Tough Jews*. New York: Simon & Schuster.

Cohen, Sarah Blacher (ed.) (1983) *From Hester Street to Hollywood: The Jewish-American stage and screen*. Bloomington, IN: Indiana University Press.

Cohen, Steven M. and Ari Kelman (2007) *Beyond Distancing: Young adult American Jews and their alienation from Israel*. New York: Andrea and Charles Bronfman Philanthropies.

Condron, Ann-Marie 'Of Heroines and Whores: The Changing Face of Female Resistance in Contemporary European Cinema.' Paper delivered at the European Cinema Research Forum Conference, Dublin Institute of Technology, June 2008.

Cuddihy, John Murray (1978) *The Ordeal of Civility: Freud, Marx, Lévi-Strauss, and the Jewish struggle with modernity*. Boston: Beacon Press.

Dargis, Manohla (2008) 'Innocence is lost in postwar Germany', *New York Times Review*, 10 December (online). Last accessed in August 2011.

Davidson, Alan (2002) *The Penguin Companion to Food*. London: Penguin.

Dencik, Lasse (2003) *Paideia Report: 'Jewishness' in postmodernity: The case of Sweden*. Sweden: The European Institute for Jewish Studies.

Desalm, Brigitte (1999) '*Barton Fink*', in Peter Körte and Georg Seesslen (eds), *Joel and Ethan Coen*. London: Titan Books, pp. 115–40.

Desser, David (2001) 'Jews in space: the "ordeal of masculinity" in contemporary American film and television', in Murray Pomerance (ed.), *Ladies and*

Gentlemen, Boys and Girls: Gender in film at the end of the twentieth century. Albany, NY: State University of New York Press, pp. 267–81.

Desser, David and Lester Friedman (2004) *American Jewish Filmmakers.* Chicago: University of Illinois Press.

Dines, Gail (2006) 'Invisible in Hollywood', *Boston Globe*, 16 January, http://www.boston.com/news/globe/editorial_opinion/oped/articles/2006/01/16/invisible_in_hollywood_jewish_women/. Last accessed May 2010.

Doneson, Judith E. (2002) *The Holocaust in American Film.* Philadelphia: Jewish Publication Society.

Doughty, Ruth and Kate Griffiths (2006) 'Racial reflection: *La Haine* and the art of borrowing', *Studies in European Cinema* 3(2), 117–27.

Dowling, Jennifer (2009) "'Oy Gevalt!'": a peek at the development of Jewish superheroines', in Angela Ndalianis (ed.), *The Contemporary Comic Book Superhero.* New York and London: Routledge, pp. 184–202.

Elber, Lynn (1997) 'Putting faith in film. Hollywood takes back-door approach to religion', http://www.southcoasttoday.com/apps/pbcs.dll/article?AID=/19970423/NEWS/304239936&emailAFriend=1. Last accessed August 2011.

Elias, Norbert (1968) *The Civilizing Process: The history of manners*, vol. 1, trans. Edmund Jephcott. New York: Urizen Books.

Epstein, Jan (2005) 'Jewish representation', in Brian McFarlane and Anthony Slide (eds), *The Encyclopedia of British Film*, London: BFI/Methuen, p. 366.

Erdman, Harley (1997) *Staging the Jew: The performance of an American ethnicity, 1860–1920.* New Brunswick, NJ: Rutgers University Press.

Erens, Patricia (1984) *The Jew in American Cinema.* Bloomington, IN: Indiana University Press.

— (2009) 'Film industry in the United States', in *Jewish Women: A comprehensive historical encyclopedia.* Jewish Women's Archive, http://jwa.org/encyclopedia/article/film-industry-in-united-states. Last accessed February 2011.

Evans, Nicola (1998) 'Games of hide and seek: race, gender and drag in *The Crying Game* and *The Birdcage*', *Text and Performance* quarterly 18(3), 199–216.

Fackenheim, Emil L. (1968) 'Jewish faith and the Holocaust', *Commentary* 46(2), 30–36.

Fiedler, Leslie A. (1984) *What Was Literature? Class culture and mass society.* New York: Simon & Schuster.

Finkelkraut, Alain (1994) *The Imaginary Jew*, trans. Kevin O'Neil and David Suchoff. Lincoln, NE and London: University of Nebraska Press.

Fishman, Sylvia Barack (1998) *I of the Beholder: Jews and gender in film and popular culture.* Hadassah Research Institute on Jewish Women Working Paper Series, no. 1.

Foreman, Jonathan (2009) '*Pulp Fiction* meets the Holocaust', *Jewish Chronicle*, 20 August (online). Last accessed in August 2011.

Foucault, Michel (1967) 'Des space autres (of other spaces)', http://foucault. info/documents/heteroTopia/foucault.heteroTopia.en.html. Last accessed February 2011.

— (1990) *The History of Sexuality*, vol. 1: *An Introduction*, trans. Robert Hurley. London: Penguin.

Fouz-Hernández, Santiago and Alfredo Martínez-Expósito (2007) *Live Flesh: The male body in contemporary Spanish cinema*. London and New York: I.B.Tauris.

Freedman, Jonathan (2005) 'Miller, Monroe and the remaking of Jewish masculinity', in Enoch Brater (ed.), *Arthur Miller's America: Theater and culture in a time of change*. Ann Arbor, MI: University of Michigan Press, 2005, pp. 135–52.

Freiberg, Freda (1994) 'Lost in Oz? Jews in the Australian cinema', *Continuum* 8(2) (online). Last accessed in August 2011.

Freud, Sigmund (1967) *Moses and Monotheism*. New York: Vintage.

— (1994) *Jokes and Their Relation to the Unconscious*. Harmondsworth: Penguin.

Friedman, Jonathan C. (2007) *Rainbow Jews: Jewish and gay identity in the performing arts*. Lanham, MD: Lexington Books.

Friedman, Lester D. (1982) *Hollywood's Image of the Jew*. New York: Ungar.

— (2006) *Citizen Spielberg*. Urbana, IL: University of Illinois Press.

Fuller, Linda K. (1993) 'Last bastion of masculinity: men's rooms in American popular film', in Paul Loukides and Linda K. Fuller (eds), *Beyond the Stars*, vol. 4: *Locales in American Popular Film*. Madison, WI: University of Wisconsin Press, 1993, pp. 223–29.

Furnish, Ben (2005) *Nostalgia in Jewish-American Theatre and Film, 1979–2004*. New York: Peter Lang.

Gabler, Neal (1988) *An Empire of Their Own: How the Jews invented Hollywood*. London: W.H. Allen.

Garb, Tamar (1995) 'Modernity, identity, textuality', in Linda Nochlin and Tamar Garb (eds), *The Jew in the Text: Modernity and the construction of identity*. London: Thames & Hudson, pp. 20–30.

Gershenson, Olga (2008) 'Ambivalence and identity in Russian-Jewish cinema', in Simon J. Bronner (ed.), *Jewish Cultural Studies*, vol. 1: *Jewishness: Expression, identity, and representation*. Oxford: Littman Library of Jewish Civilization, pp. 175–95.

Gershenson, Olga and Barbara Penner (2009) (eds) *Ladies and Gents: Public Toilets and Gender*. Philadelphia: Temple University Press.

Gertel, Elliot B. (2003) *Over the Top Judaism: Precedents and trends in the depiction of Jewish beliefs and observances in film and television.* Lanham, MD: University Press of America.

Gilman, Sander L. (1991) *The Jew's Body.* London and New York: Routledge.

— (1995) *Franz Kafka: Jewish patient.* London and New York: Routledge.

— (1996) *Smart Jews: The construction of the idea of Jewish superior intelligence at the other end of the bell curve.* Lincoln, NE: University of Nebraska Press.

— (2002) 'Jewish self-hatred and *The Believer*', in Henry Bean (ed.), *The Believer: Confronting Jewish self-hatred.* New York: Thunder's Mouth Press, pp. 221–42.

Girgus, Sam B. (2002) *The Films of Woody Allen.* Cambridge and New York: Cambridge University Press.

Gleason, Robin (2004) 'The unbearable lightness of being cool: appropriation and prospects of subversion in the works of Quentin Tarantino', *Bright Lights Film Journal* 45, http://www.brightlightsfilm.com/45/toilets.htm. Last accessed in August 2011.

Goldberg, Jeffrey (2009) 'Hollywood's Jewish Avenger', *The Atlantic* (September) (online). Last accessed in August 2011.

Goldman, Eric A. (2003) '*Avalon* and *Liberty Heights*: toward a better understanding of the American Jewish experience through cinema', *American Jewish History* 91(1), 109–27.

Goldstein, Eric L. (2006) *The Price of Whiteness: Jews, race, and American identity.* Princeton, NJ and Oxford: Princeton University Press.

Graham, David (2004) *European Jewish Identity at the Dawn of the 21st Century: A working paper.* Report for the American Jewish Joint Distribution Committee and Hanadiv Charitable Foundation presented to the European General Assembly of the European Council of Jewish Communities, Budapest, 20–23 May.

Grochowski, Thomas (2004) 'Neurotic in New York: the Woody Allen touches in *Sex in the City*', in K. Akass and J. McCabe (eds), *Reading Sex in the City.* London and New York: I.B.Tauris, pp. 149–60.

Grodstein, Laurie (2006) 'Jewess Studies: Don't call me Monica', *Jewcy.com*, 15 November 2006, http://www.jewcy.com/first_person/11-15/jewess_studies. Last accessed in August 2011.

Halperin, David M. (1995) *Saint Foucault: Towards a gay hagiography.* New York and Oxford: Oxford University Press.

Heeb magazine (2009) 'The 100 Greatest Jewish Movie Moments' http://www.heebmagazine.com/03-05/2777.htm?url=/blog/view/2777. Last accessed April 2010.

Heinze, Andrew R. (1990) *Adapting to Abundance: Jewish immigrants, mass consumption and the search for American identity.* New York: Columbia University Press.

Higbee, Will (2005) 'The return of the political, or designer visions of exclusion? The case for Mathieu Kassovitz's *"fracture sociale"* trilogy', *Studies in French Cinema* 5(2), 123–35.

— (2006) *Mathieu Kassovitz*. Manchester: Manchester University Press.

Hiller, Jordan (2009) '25 essential Jewish films: *A Serious Man*', http://www.bangitout.com/articles/viewarticle.php?a=2901. Last accessed November 2009.

Hills, Elizabeth (1999) 'From "figurative males" to action heroines: further thoughts on active women in the cinema', *Screen* 40(1), 38–50.

Hirsch, J.F. (2004) *Afterimage: Film, trauma, and the Holocaust*. Philadelphia: Temple University Press.

Hoberman, J. (2003) 'Flaunting it: the rise and fall of Hollywood's "nice" Jewish (bad) boys', in J. Hoberman and Jeffrey Shandler (eds), *Entertaining America: Jews, movies, and broadcasting*. Princeton, NJ and Oxford: Princeton University Press, pp. 220–43.

Hoberman, J. and J. Shandler (2003) *Entertaining America: Jews, movies, and broadcasting*. Princeton, NJ and Oxford: Princeton University Press.

Horkheimer, Max and Theodor Adorno (1973) *Dialectic of Enlightenment*, trans. John Cumming. London: Allen Lane.

Horst, Sabine (1999) '*Miller's Crossing*', in Peter Körte and Georg Seesslen (eds), *Joel and Ethan Coen*. London: Titan Books, pp. 87–114.

Hughes, Diane Owen (1986) 'Distinguishing signs: ear-rings, Jews, and Franciscan rhetoric in the Italian Renaissance city', *Past and Present* 112(8), 3–59.

Hyman, Paula (1995) *Gender and Assimilation in Modern Jewish History: The roles and representation of women*. Seattle: University of Washington Press.

Inness, Sherrie A. (2004) *Action Chicks: New images of tough women in popular culture*. Basingstoke: Palgrave Macmillan.

Insdorf, Annette (2003) *Indelible Shadows: Film and the Holocaust*. Cambridge and New York: Cambridge University Press.

Itzkovitz, Daniel (2006) 'They are all Jews', in Vincent Brook (ed.), *You Should See Yourself: Jewish identity in postmodern American culture*. New Brunswick, NJ and London: Rutgers University Press, pp. 230–51.

Jackson, Ronald L. II and Jamie Moshin (2008) 'Scripting Jewishness within the satire *The Hebrew Hammer*', in Kathleen Glenister-Roberts and Ronald Arnette (eds), *Communication Ethics: Cosmopolitanism and provinciality*. New York: Peter Lang, pp. 187–212.

Jewish Women's Archive (2006) 'Jewesses: Jappy, bizarre, or cool?', *Jewesses with Attitude*, 28 March, http://jwablog.jwa.org/jewesses. Last accessed May 2010.

Johnston, Ruth D. (2006) 'Joke-work: the construction of Jewish postmodern identity in contemporary theory and American film', in Vincent Brook (ed.),

You Should See Yourself: Jewish identity in postmodern American culture. New Brunswick, NJ: Rutgers University Press, pp. 207–29.

Jonas, George (2006) *Vengeance*. London: Harper Perennial.

Kane, Leslie (1999) *Weasels and Wisemen: Ethics and ethnicity in the work of David Mamet*. Basingstoke and London: Macmillan.

Kaplan, Bruce (2010) 'Open and shut: Stanley Kubrick's Victor Ziegler as anti-semitic stereotype'. Paper presented at Film and History Annual Conference, Milwaukee, WI.

Kassouf, Susan (1998) 'The shared pain of the golden vein: the discursive proximity of Jewish and scholarly diseases in the late eighteenth century', *Eighteenth-Century Studies* 32(1), 101–10.

Katz, Jackson (2010) 'Not-so-nice Jewish boys: notes on violence and the construction of Jewish-American masculinity in the late 20th and early 21st centuries', in Harry Brod and Shawn Israel Zevit (eds), *Brother Keepers: New perspectives on Jewish masculinity*. Harriman, TN: Men's Studies Press, pp. 57–74.

Kelman, Ari Y. and Eliana Schonberg (2008) *Legwork, Framework, Artwork: Engaging the next generation of Jews*. Denver, CO: Rose Community Foundation.

Kempner, Aviva (1999) 'Finally: Jewish women have sex on the screen', *Lilith* (31 March), 38–39.

Kirkham, Pat (1995) 'Loving me: Frank Borzage, Charles Farrell and the reconstruction of masculinity in 1920s Hollywood cinema', in Pat Kirkham and Janet Thumim (eds), *Me Jane: Masculinity, movies and women*. London: Lawrence & Wishart, pp. 94–112.

Koepnick, Lutz (2002) 'Reframing the past: heritage cinema and Holocaust in the 1990s', *New German Critique* 87, Special Issue on Postwall Cinema, 47–82.

Körte, Peter (1999) 'The Big Lebowski', in Peter Körte and Georg Seesslen (eds), *Joel and Ethan Coen*. London: Titan Books, pp. 191–208.

Kotsko, Adam (2010) *Awkwardness: An essay*. Alresford: Zero Books.

Krieger, Rosalin (2003) '"Does he actually say the word Jewish?" – Jewish representations in *Seinfeld*', *Journal for Cultural Research* 7(4), 387–404.

Kronish, Amy (2009) 'Filmmakers, Israeli', *Jewish Women: A comprehensive historical encyclopedia*. Jewish Women's Archive, http://jwa.org/encyclopedia/article/filmmakers-israeli. Last accessed February 2011.

Kuberski, Philip (2004) 'Plumbing the abyss: Stanley Kubrick's bathrooms', *The Arizona Quarterly* 60(4) (online). Last accessed in August 2011.

Kuhn, Annette and Susannah Radstone (1994) *The Woman's Companion to International Film*. Berkeley, CA: University of California Press.

Kun, Josh (2002) 'The sacrifice of Daniel, on *The Believer*', *Social Identities* 8(2), 369–73.

Lehman, Peter (2004) '"They look so uncomplicated once they're dissected": the act of seeing the dead penis with one's own eyes', in Phil Powrie, Ann Davies and Bruce Babington (eds), *The Trouble with Men: Masculinities in European and Hollywood cinema*. London and New York: Wallflower, pp. 196–206.

Lehman, Peter and Susan Hunt (2008) 'The naked and the dead: the Jewish male body and masculinity in *Sunshine* and *Enemy at the Gates*', in Daniel Bernardi (ed.), *The Persistence of Whiteness: Race and contemporary Hollywood cinema*. London and New York: Routledge, pp. 157–64.

Lenzner, Steven J. (2001) 'A cinematic call for self-knowledge: an interpretation of *Miller's Crossing*', *Perspectives on Political Science* 30(2) (online). Last accessed in August 2011.

Levi, Primo (2000) *If This is a Man*. London: Abacus.

Levine, Amy-Jill (1997) "A Jewess, more and/or less," in Miriam Peskowitz and Laura Levitt (eds), *Judaism Since Gender*. New York: Routledge, pp. 149–57.

Levine, Daniel J. (2006) '*Munich*: warp-speed storytelling and the war on terror', *Theory and Event* 9(3) (online). Last accessed in August 2011.

Lewin, Judith (2008a) 'Semen, semolina and salt water: the erotic Jewess in Sandra Goldbacher's *The Governess*', in Nathan Abrams (ed.), *Jews and Sex*. Nottingham: Five Leaves, pp. 88–100.

— (2008b) 'The sublimity of the Jewish type: Balzac's *belle juive* as virgin magdalene aux camelias', in Simon J. Bronner (ed.), *Jewish Cultural Studies: Expression, identity, and representation*. Oxford: Littman Library of Jewish Civilization, pp. 239–71.

Linville, Susan E. (1995) 'Agnieszka Holland's *Europa, Europa*: deconstructive humor in a Holocaust film', *Film Criticism* 19(3), 44–53.

Loshitzky, Yosefa (2005) 'The post-Holocaust Jew in the age of postcolonialism: *La Haine* revisited', *Studies in French Cinema* 5(2), 137–47.

Lubiano, Wahneema (1997) 'Don't talk with your eyes closed: caught in the Hollywood gun sights', in Martin B. Duberman (ed.), *Queer Representations: Reading lives, reading cultures*. New York: NYU Press, pp. 139–45.

Lungstrum, Janet (1998) 'Foreskin fetishism: Jewish male difference in *Europa Europa*', *Screen* 39, 53–66.

Lustig, Sandra and Ian Leveson (2006) 'Introduction', in Sandra Lustig and Ian Leveson (eds), *Turning the Kaleidoscope: Perspectives on European Jewry*. New York and Oxford: Berghahn Books, pp. 1–23.

Martin-Jones, David (2006) 'No literal connection: images of mass commodification, US militarism, and the oil industry', in *The Big Lebowski*, *Sociological Review* 54(1), 131–49.

Mather, Nigel (2005) *Tears of Laughter: Comedy-drama in 1990s British cinema.* Manchester: Manchester University Press.

Mazierska, Ewa (2007) *Roman Polanski: The cinema of a cultural traveller.* London and New York: I.B.Tauris.

McDonald, Tamar Jeffers (2007) *Romantic Comedy: Boy meets girl meets genre.* London and New York: Wallflower.

Medved, Harry (1998) 'A Jewish new wave', *Jewish Journal of Greater Los Angeles* (13 February).

Melville, Peter (2004) 'A "friendship of taste": the aesthetics of eating well in Kant's anthropology from a pragmatic point of view', in Timothy Morton (ed.), *Cultures of Taste/Theories of Appetite: Eating romanticism.* Palgrave Macmillan: New York, pp.203–16.

Meyers, Helene (2008) 'Educating for a Jewish gaze: the close doubling of antisemitism and philosemitism in Sandra Goldbacher's *The Governess*', in Phyllis Lassner and Lara Trubowitz (eds), *Antisemitism and Philosemitism in the Twentieth and Twenty-first Centuries: Representing Jews, Jewishness, and modern culture.* Newark, DE: University of Delaware Press, pp.103–18.

Miguélez-Carballeira, Helena (2007) 'Perpetuating asymmetries: the interdisciplinary encounter between translation studies and Hispanic studies', *Hispanic Research Journal* 8(4), 359–74.

— (2010) '"I am not from here": a translation for María do Cebreiro', in Maria do Cebreiro, *I am Not from Here*, trans. Helena Miguélez-Carballeira. Exeter: Shearsman Books, pp.8–14.

Miles, Margaret R. (1996) *Seeing and Believing: Religion and values in the movies.* Boston: Beacon Press.

Mizejewski, Linda (2008) 'Movies and the off-white gangster', in Chris Holmlund (ed.), *American Cinema of the 1990s: Themes and variations.* New Brunswick, NJ: Rutgers University Press, pp.24–44.

Monaco, James (2009) *How to Read a Film: Movies, media, and beyond*, 4th edn. Oxford University Press: New York and Oxford.

Mosse, George (1964) *The Crisis of German Ideology: Intellectual origins of the Third Reich.* New York: Grosset & Dunlap.

Mulder, Stacy S. (2002) '"*Tikkun* and *Teshuvah*": continuity in the novels of Henry Roth'. Unpublished diss., Ball State University, IN.

Mulvey, Laura (1975) 'Visual pleasure and narrative cinema', *Screen* 16(3), 6–18.

Nathan, Joan (1995) *Jewish Cooking in America.* New York: Alfred A. Knopf.

Naremore, James (2007) *On Kubrick.* London: BFI.

Nelson, Thomas Allen (2000) *Kubrick: Inside a film artist's maze.* Bloomington, IN: Indiana University Press.

Neofotistos, Vasiliki P. (2008) 'The Muslim, the Jew and the African American: America and the production of alterity in *Borat*', *Anthropology Today* 24(4), 13–17.

Nordau, Max (1898) Speech delivered at the Second Zionist Congress (Basel, 28–31 August), in *Stenographisches Protokoll der Verhandlungen des II. Zionisten-Congresses*. Vienna: Verlag des Vereines 'Erez Israel', pp. 14–27.

Novak, William and Moshe Waldoks (eds) (1981) *The Big Book of Jewish Humor*. New York: Harper & Row.

Novick, Peter (1999) *The Holocaust in American Life*. Boston and New York: Houghton Mifflin.

Owen, Gerwyn (2009) *Taste of Film: Food and drink in the films of Max Ophuls*. Unpublished MA diss., Bangor University.

Pawel, Ernst (1997) *Franz Kafka: A nightmare of reason*. New York: Farrar, Straus and Giroux.

Pearl, Jonathan and Judith Pearl (1999) *The Chosen Image: Television's portrayal of Jewish themes and characters*. Jefferson, NC: McFarland.

Pellegrini, Ann (1997) 'Whiteface performances: "race," gender, and Jewish dodies', in Jonathan Boyarin and Daniel Boyarin (eds), *Jews and Other Differences: The new Jewish cultural studies*. Minneapolis, MN: University of Minnesota Press, pp. 108–49.

Pheasant-Kelly, Frances (2009) 'In the men's room: death and derision in cinematic toilets', in Olga Gershenson and Barbara Penner (eds), *Ladies and Gents: Public toilets and gender*. Philadelphia: Temple University Press, 2009, pp. 195–207.

Phillips, Gene D. and Rodney Hill (2002) *The Encyclopedia of Stanley Kubrick*. New York: Facts on File.

Piette, Alain (2004) 'The 1980s', in Christopher Bigsby (ed.), *The Cambridge Companion to David Mamet*. Cambridge: Cambridge University Press, pp. 74–88.

Pinczuk, Michele (2007) 'American gangster: "Can ya dig it?"' December, http://www.jvibe.com/Pop_culture/American_Gangster.php. Last accessed September 2009.

Pinto, Diana (2010) 'Asemitism, or a society without antisemitism or philosemitism: dream or nightmare?' European Conference of the European Union for Progressive Judaism, Paris, March 3–7.

Pizzello, Chris (2003) 'DVD Playback', *American Cinematographer* 84(8) (14, 16, 18 August) (online). Last accessed in August 2011.

Plotkin, Janis (2009) 'Filmmakers, independent European', *Jewish Women: A comprehensive historical encyclopedia*. Jewish Women's Archive, http://jwa.org/encyclopedia/article/filmmakers-independent-european. Last accessed February 2011.

Podhoretz, Norman (1967) *Making It*. New York: Random House.

Popkin, Henry (1952) 'The vanishing Jew of our popular culture', *Commentary* 14, 46–55.

Portuges, Catherine (2005) 'Traumatic memory, Jewish identity: remapping the past in Hungarian cinema', in Anikó Imre (ed.), *East European Cinemas*. New York and London: Routledge, pp. 121–33.

Powrie, Phil, Ann Davies and Bruce Babington (2004) 'Introduction: turning the male inside out', in Phil Powrie, Ann Davies and Bruce Babington (eds), *The Trouble With Men: Masculinities in European and Hollywood cinema*. London and New York: Wallflower, pp. 1–15.

Pozefsky, Peter (2008) 'Russian gangster films as popular history: genre, ideology and memory in Pavel Lungin's *Tycoon*', *Studies in Russian and Soviet Cinema* 2(3), 299–325.

Prell, Riv-Ellen (1996) 'Why Jewish princesses don't sweat: desire and consumption in postwar American Jewish culture', in N.L. Kleeblatt (ed.), *Too Jewish? Challenging traditional identities*. New York and New Brunswick, NJ: Rutgers University Press, pp. 74–93.

— (1999) *Fighting to Become Americans: Assimilation and the trouble between Jewish women and Jewish men*. Boston, MA: Beacon Press.

— (2009) 'Stereotypes in the United States', *Jewish Women: A comprehensive historical encyclopedia*. Jewish Women's Archive, http://jwa.org/encyclopedia/article/stereotypes-in-united-states. Last accessed February 2011.

Rasmussen, Randy (2005) *Stanley Kubrick: Seven films analyzed*. Jefferson, NC: McFarland.

Ravits, Martha A. (2000) 'The Jewish mother: comedy and controversy in American popular culture', *Melus* 25(1), 3–31.

Redmon, Allen H. (2010) 'The revelation to Tarantino as it is given in *Inglourious Basterds*', JG Cinema, http://www.jgcinema.com/single.php?sl=Violence-holocaust-jews-nazi-revenge-apocalypse. Last accessed in July 2010.

Reichl, Ruth (2004) *The Gourmet Cookbook*. New York: Houghton Mifflin.

Richter, David H. (2005) 'Your cheatin' art: double dealing in cinematic narrative', *Narrative* 13(1), 11–28.

Rivo, Sharon Pucker (1998), 'Projected images: portraits of Jewish women in early American film', in Joyce Antler (ed.), *Talking Back: Images of Jewish women in American popular culture*. Hanover, NH and London: Brandeis University Press, pp. 30–49.

Roberts, Sofie Angharad (2010) 'A serious matter? The Coen brothers and the representation of Judaism'. Unpublished MA essay, Bangor University.

Rocha, Carolina (2010) 'Jewish cinematic self-representations in contemporary Argentine and Brazilian films', *Journal of Modern Jewish Studies* 9(1), 37–48.

Rockler, Naomi R. (2006) '*Friends*, Judaism, and the holiday armadillo: mapping a rhetoric of postidentity politics', *Communication Theory* 16, 453–73.

Rogin, Michael (1996) *Blackface, White Noise: Jewish immigrants in the Hollywood melting pot*. Berkeley: University of California Press.

— (1998) *Independence Day*. London: BFI.

Root, Regina A. (2005) 'Fashioning Independence: Gender, Dress and Social Space in Postcolonial Argentina', in Regina A. Root (ed.), The Latin American Fashion Reader. Oxford: Berg, pp.31–44.

Rose, Sven-Erik (2007) 'Mathieu Kassovitz's *La Haine* and the ambivalence of French-Jewish identity', *French Studies* 61(4), 476–91.

Rosenbaum, Jonathan (2006) 'In dreams begin responsibilities', in Geoffrey Cocks, James Diedrick and Glenn Perusek (eds), *Depth of Field: Stanley Kubrick, film, and the uses of history*. Madison, WI: University of Wisconsin Press, pp.245–54.

Rosenberg, Joel (1996) 'Jewish experience on film – an American overview', *American Jewish Year Book*, 1996, 3–50.

Rosenberg, Warren (2006) 'Coming out of the ethnic closet: Jewishness in the films of Barry Levinson', *Shofar* 22(1), 29–43.

Rosenfeld, Isaac (1949) 'Adam and Eve on Delancey Street', *Commentary* 8(4), 385–87.

Rosenthal, Rachel (2006) 'What's in a Name? The future of post-denominational Judaism', *Kedma* 1, 20–32.

Rosten, Leo (1969) *The Joys of Yiddish*. London: Penguin.

Roth, Laurence (2004) *Inspecting Jews: American Jewish detective stories*. New Brunswick, NJ and London: Rutgers University Press.

Roth, Philip (1969) *Portnoy's Complaint*. New York: Random House.

— (2004) *The Plot Against America*. Boston: Houghton Mifflin.

Rowe, David L. (2004) 'Preachers and prophets: using film to teach American religious history', *Teaching Theology and Religion* 7(4), 230–37.

Rubel, Nora L. (2010) *Doubting the Devout: The ultra-Orthodox in the Jewish-American imagination*. New York: Columbia University Press.

Rubin, Rachel (2002) 'Gangster generation: crime, Jews and the problem of assimilation', *Shofar* 20(4), 1–17.

Rubin-Dorsky, Jeffrey (2003) 'Woody Allen after the fall: literary gold from amoral alchemy', *Shofar* 22(1), 5–28.

Russell, C.R. (2001) *The Films of Joel and Ethan Coen*. Jefferson, NC: McFarland & Co.

Russell, James (2007) *The Historical Epic and Contemporary Hollywood: From Dances with Wolves to Gladiator*. New York and London: Continuum.

Sammons, Jeffrey T. (1988) *Beyond the Ring: The role of boxing in American society*. Urbana, IL: University of Illinois Press.

Samuels, Stuart (1978) 'The Evolutionary Image of the Jew in American Film', in Randall M. Miller (ed.), *Ethnic Images in American Film and Television*. Philadelphia: The Balch Institute, pp.23–34.

Sartre, Jean-Paul (1965) *Anti-Semite and Jew*, trans. George J. Becker. New York: Schocken.

Saval, Malina Sarah (2003) 'Gangsta hassid', *Jerusalem Post*, 11 April, 16.

Schaffer, Gavin (2008) *Racial Science and British Society, 1930–62*. Basingstoke and New York: Palgrave Macmillan.

Schoenfeld, Gabriel (2006) 'Spielberg's *Munich*', *Commentary* (February) (online). Last accessed in August 2011.

Schrank, Bernice (2007) '"Cutting off your nose to spite your race": Jewish stereotypes, media images, cultural hybridity', *Shofar* 25(4), 18–42.

Schubart, Rikke 'Cunts, dicks, and postfeminist politics: torture-porn, the horror heroine, and *Hostel II*'. Article accepted for Constantine Verevis, Claire Perkins, Alexia Kannas (eds), *B for Bad Cinema*. Detroit: Wayne State University Press (forthcoming).

Shandler, Jeffrey (1994) 'Is there a Jewish way to watch television? Notes from a tuned-in ethnographer', *Jewish Folklore and Ethnology Review* 16(1), 19–22.

— (1999) *While America Watches: Televising the Holocaust*. New York and Oxford: Oxford University Press.

Shelton, Emily (2002) 'A star is porn: corpulence, comedy, and the homosocial cult of adult film star Ron Jeremy', *Camera Obscura* 17(3), 115–46.

Sherzer, Dina (1999) 'Comedy and interracial relationships: *Romuald et Juliette* (Serreau, 1987) and *Métisse* (Kassovitz, 1993)', in Phil Powrie (ed.), *French Cinema in the 1990s: Continuity and difference*. Oxford: Oxford University Press, pp. 148–59.

Shohat, Ella (1991) 'Ethnicities-in-relation: toward a multicultural reading of American cinema', in Lester D. Friedman (ed.), *Unspeakable Images: Ethnicity and the American cinema*. Urbana and Chicago, IL: University of Illinois Press, pp. 215–50.

— (2010) *Israeli Cinema: East/West and the politics of representation*, 2nd edn. London and New York: I.B.Tauris.

Silverman, Eric Kline (2006) *From Abraham to America: A history of Jewish circumcision*. Lanham, MD: Rowman & Littlefield.

Smith, Allison (2009) 'Judaism and Jewishness in film', in William L. Blizek (ed.), *The Continuum Companion to Religion and Film*. London and New York: Continuum, pp. 167–76.

Soler, Jean (1979) 'The dietary prohibitions of the Hebrews', *New York Review of Books* (14 June) (online). Last accessed in August 2011.

Stanley, Timothy (2006) 'Punch-drunk masculinity', *Journal of Men's Studies* 14(2), 235–42.

Steed, J.P. (2005) 'The subversion of the Jews: post-World War II anxiety, humor, and identity in Woody Allen and Philip Roth', *Philip Roth Studies* 1(2), 45–62.

Stein, Howard F. and Robert F. Hill (1977) *The Ethnic Imperative: Examining the new white ethnic movement*. University Park, PA: Pennsylvania State University Press.

Stetz, Margaret D. (2010) '*Esther Kahn*: Antisemitism and Philosemitism at the Turns of Two Centuries', in Phyllis Lassner and Lara Trubowitz (eds), *Antisemitism and philosemitism in the twentieth and twenty-first centuries: representing Jews, Jewishness, and modern*. Newark: University of Delaware Press, pp. 119–37.

Stone, Jay (2009) 'It's a kind of Dirty Dozen with vengeful Jewish undertones', *Vancouver Province* (21 August), B3.

Stratton, Jon (2000) *Coming Out Jewish: Constructing ambivalent identities*. London: Routledge.

— (2008) *Jewish Identity in Western Pop Culture: The Holocaust and trauma through modernity*. Basingstoke and New York: Palgrave Macmillan.

Tal, Rami (ed.) (2007) *Jewish People Policy Planning Institute Annual Assessment 2007*. Jerusalem: Gefen Publishing House.

Tannen, Deborah (1989) *Talking Voices: Repetition, dialogue, and imagery in conversational discourse*. Cambridge: Cambridge University Press.

Tasker, Yvonne (1993) *Spectacular Bodies: Gender, genre and the action cinema*. London and New York: Routledge.

Taub, Michael (2005) *Films About Jewish Life and Culture*. Lewiston, NY, Queenston and Lampeter: Edward Mellen.

Taylor, Charles (2010) 'Violence as the best revenge: fantasies of dead Nazis', *Dissent* 57(1), 103–6.

Trachtenberg, Joshua (1984) *The Devil and the Jews: The medieval conception of the Jew and its relation to modern anti-semitism*. Philadelphia, PA: Jewish Publication Society of America.

Tyree, J.M. and Ben Walters (2007) *The Big Lebowski*. London: BFI.

Valman, Nadia (2007) *The Jewess in Nineteenth-Century British Literary Culture*. Cambridge: Cambridge University Press.

Wasserstein, Bernard (1996) *Vanishing Diaspora: The Jews in Europe since 1945*. Cambridge, MA: Harvard University Press.

Webber, Jonathan (1994) 'Modern Jewish identities', in Jonathan Webber (ed.), *Jewish Identities in the New Europe*. Oxford: Littman Library of Jewish Civilization, pp. 74–85.

Weinfeld, 'The Heartbreak Yid: Intermarriage Discourse and the JAP in the 1960s and 1970s', in Nathan Abrams (ed.), *Jews & Sex* (Nottingham: Five Leaves, 2008), pp. 189-200

Weitzman, Lenore J. (1998) 'Living on the Aryan side in Poland: gender, passing, and the nature of resistance', in Dalia Ofer and Lenore J. Weitzman (eds), *Women in the Holocaust*. New Haven, CT and London: Yale University Press, pp. 187–222.

Wex, Michael (2005) *Born to Kvetch: Yiddish language and culture in all of its moods*. New York: Harper Perennial.

White-Stanley, Debra and Flinn, Caryl (2008) 'Movies and homeland insecurity', in Chris Holmlund (ed.) American cinema of the 1990s: themes and variations. New Brunswick, NJ: Rutgers University Press, pp.157–79.

Whitfield, Stephen J. (1986) 'Our American Jewish heritage: the Hollywood version', *American Jewish History* 75, 322–40.

— (1999) *In Search of American Jewish Culture*. Hanover, NH and London: University Press of New England.

Wiegman, Robyn (1998) 'Race, ethnicity, and film', in John Hill and Pamela Church Gibson (eds), *The Oxford Guide to Film Studies*. Oxford and New York: Oxford University Press, pp. 158–68.

Williams, Linda Ruth (2007) 'Sleeping with the enemy', *Sight & Sound* 17 (2) (online). Last accessed in August 2011.

Willis, Sharon (1997) 'Borrowed style: Quentin Tarantino's figures of masculinity', *High Contrast: Race and gender in contemporary Hollywood film*. Durham, NC: Duke University Press, pp. 189–258.

Wood, Mary P. (2007) *Contemporary European Cinema*. London: Hodder Arnold.

Wrathall, John (2006) '*Munich*', *Sight & Sound* 16 (3), 68.

Wright, Melanie J. (2006) *Religion and Film: An introduction*. London: I.B.Tauris.

— (2009) 'Judaism', in John Lyden (ed.), *The Routledge Companion to Religion and Film*. London and New York: Routledge, pp. 91–108.

Wright, Rochelle (1998) *The Visible Wall: Jews and other ethnic outsiders in Swedish film*. Carbondale, IL and Edwardsville, IL: Southern Illinois University Press.

Yaquinto, Marilyn (2004) 'Tough love: Mamas, molls, and mob wives', in Sherrie A. Inness (ed.), *Action Chicks: New images of tough women in popular culture*. Basingstoke: Palgrave Macmillan, pp. 207–30.

Yosef, Raz (2004) *Beyond Flesh: Queer masculinities and nationalism in Israeli cinema*. New Brunswick, NJ and London: Rutgers University Press.

Zimerman, Moshe (2002) 'Jewish and Israeli film studies', in Martin Goodman (ed.), *The Oxford Handbook of Jewish Studies*. Oxford: Oxford University Press, pp. 911–42.

Zizek, Slavoj (1989) *The Sublime Object of Ideology*. London: Verso.

Zurawik, David (2003) *The Jews of Primetime*. Hanover, NH: Brandeis University Press/University Press of New England.

Filmography

27 Dresses (dir. Anne Fletcher, 2008)
The 40-Year-Old Virgin (dir. Judd Apatow, 2005)
Adventureland (dir. Greg Mottola, 2009)
Aimée & Jaguar (dir. Max Färberböck, 1999)
Airplane! (dirs Jim Abrahams and David Zucker, 1980)
Alles auf Zucker!/Go for Zucker! (dir. Dani Levy, 2004).
Along Came Polly (dir. John Hamburg, 2004)
American Buffalo (dir. Michael Corrente, 1996)
American Gangster (dir. Ridley Scott, 2007)
American History X (dir. Tony Kaye, 1998)
American Pie (dir. Paul Weitz, 1999)
American Pie 2 (dir. James B. Rogers, 2001)
American Pie: The Wedding (dir. Jesse Dylan, 2003)
Amy's O (dir. Julie Davis, 2001)
An American Werewolf in London (dir. John Landis, 1981)
Analyze That (dir. Harold Ramis, 2002)
Analyze This (dir. Harold Ramis, 1999)
Annie Hall (dir. Woody Allen, 1977)
O Ano em Que Meus Pais Saíram de Férias/The Year My Parents Went on Vacation
    (dir. Cao Hamburger, 2006)
The Antique Vase (dir. H.O. Martinek, 1913)
Assassin(s) (dir. Mathieu Kassovitz, 1997)
Avalon (dir. Barry Levinson, 1990)
A Bad Day for Levinsky (dir. T.J. Gobbett, 1909)
Barton Fink (dir. Joel Coen, 1991)
Basic Instinct (dir. Paul Verhoeven, 1992)
Beaufort (dir. Joseph Cedar, 2007)
Bee Season (dirs Scott McGehee and David Siegel, 2005)

Being Ron Jeremy (dir. Brian Berke, 2003)

The Believer (dir. Henry Bean, 2001)

Ben-Hur (dir. William Wyler, 1959)

Bent (dir. Sean Mathias, 1997)

The Big Lebowski (dir. Joel Coen, 1998)

The Birdcage (dir. Mike Nichols, 1996)

Black Hawk Down (dir. Ridley Scott, 2001)

Blade Runner (dir. Ridley Scott, 1982)

Body and Soul (dir. Robert Rossen, 1947)

Boogie Nights (dir. Paul Thomas Anderson, 1997)

Borat: Cultural Learnings of America for Make Benefit Glorious Nation of Kazakhstan (dir. Larry Charles, 2006)

The Boy in the Striped Pyjamas (dir. Mark Herman, 2008)

Bringing Down the House (dir. Adam Shankman, 2003)

The Bubble (dir. Eytan Fox, 2006)

Bugsy (dir. Barry Levinson, 1991)

Bulletproof (dir. Ernest R. Dickerson, 1996)

Bullets over Broadway (dir. Woody Allen, 1994)

Capturing the Friedmans (dir. Andrew Jarecki, 2003)

Carlito's Way (dir. Brian De Palma, 1993)

Carrie (dir. Brian De Palma, 1976)

Casino (dir. Martin Scorsese, 1995)

Cast A Giant Shadow (dir. Melville Shavelson, 1966)

Chariots of Fire (dir. Hugh Hudson, 1981)

A Child of the Ghetto (dir. D.W. Griffith, 1910)

Chopper (dir. Andrew Dominik, 2000)

The Chosen (dir. Jeremy Kagan, 1981)

Cinderella Man (dir. Ron Howard, 2005)

City Slickers II: The Legend of Curly's Gold (dir. Paul Weiland, 1994)

A Clockwork Orange (dir. Stanley Kubrick, 1971)

Clueless (dir. Amy Heckerling, 1995)

Cohen's Advertising Scheme (dir. Anon, 1904)

Cohen's Fire Sale (dir. Edwin S. Porter, 1907)

Cohen's Luck (dir. John H. Collins, 1915)

The Cotton Club (dir. Francis Ford Coppola, 1984)

The Counterfeiters (dir. Stefan Ruzowitzky, 2007)

Crimes and Misdemeanors (dir. Woody Allen, 1989)

Criminal (dir. Gregory Jacobs, 2004)

Crossfire (dir. Edward Dmytryk, 1947)

Crossing Delancey (dir. Joan Micklin Silver, 1988)
Curb Your Enthusiasm (HBO, 2000–)
The Debt (dir. John Madden, 2010)
Deconstructing Harry (dir. Woody Allen, 1997)
Deep Cover (dir. Bill Duke, 1992)
Defiance (dir. Edward Zwick, 2008)
The Diary of Anne Frank (dir. George Stevens, 1959)
Le Dîner de Cons (dir. Francis Veber, 1998)
Dinner for Schmucks (dir. Jay Roach, 2010)
Dirty Dancing (dir. Emile Ardolino, 1987)
Down in the Valley (dir. David Jacobson, 2005)
Dracula: Dead and Loving It (dir. Mel Brooks, 1995)
Driving Miss Daisy (dir. Bruce Beresford, 1989)
Dr. Strangelove (dir. Stanley Kubrick, 1964)
The Edge (dir. Lee Tamahori, 1997)
Edward Scissorhands (dir. Tim Burton, 1990)
Eight Crazy Nights (dir. Seth Kearsley, 2002)
Enemy at the Gates (dir. Jean-Jacques Annaud, 2001)
Esther Kahn (dir. Arnaud Desplechin, 2000)
Exodus (dir. Otto Preminger, 1960)
Eyes Wide Open (dir. Haim Tabakman, 2009)
Eyes Wide Shut (dir. Stanley Kubrick, 1999)
Eyewitness (dir. Peter Yates, 1981)
A Family Affair (dir. Helen Lesnick, 2001)
The Fantastic Four (dir. Tim Story, 2005)
Fiddler on the Roof (dir. Norman Jewison, 1971)
La fille du RER/The Girl on the Train (dir. André Téchiné, 2009)
Focus (dir. Neal Slavin, 2001)
For Your Consideration (dir. Christopher Guest, 2006)
Four Lions (dir. Christopher Morris, 2010)
Freud flyttar hemifrån/Freud Leaving Home (dir. Susanne Bier, 1991)
Full Metal Jacket (dir. Stanley Kubrick, 1987)
Funny Girl (dir. William Wyler, 1968)
Funny People (dir. Judd Apatow, 2009)
Gentleman's Agreement (dir. Elia Kazan, 1947)
A Gesture Fight in Hester Street (dir. Anon, 1900)
Get Him to the Greek (dir. Nicholas Stoller, 2010)
The Girlfriend Experience (dir. Steven Soderbergh, 2009)
Glengarry Glen Ross (dir. James Foley, 1992)

The Godfather (dir. Francis Ford Coppola, 1972)

The Godfather: Part II (dir. Francis Ford Coppola, 1974)

The Godfather: Part III (dir. Francis Ford Coppola, 1990)

Goodbye Columbus (dir. Larry Peerce, 1969)

Goodfellas (dir. Martin Scorsese, 1990)

The Governess (dir. Sandra Goldbacher, 1998)

The Graduate (dir. Mike Nichols, 1967)

Le Grand Pardon II/Day of Atonement (dir. Alexandre Arcady, 1992)

Greenberg (dir. Noah Baumbach, 2010)

The Grey Zone (dir. Tim Blake Nelson, 2001)

Ha-Hov (dir. Assaf Bernstein, 2007)

La Haine (dir. Mathieu Kassovitz, 1995)

The Hangover (dir. Todd Phillips, 2009)

Harold & Kumar Escape from Guantanamo Bay (dirs Jon Hurwitz and Hayden Schlossberg, 2008)

Harold & Kumar Go to White Castle/Harold & Kumar Get the Munchies (dir. Danny Leiner, 2004)

Harold and Maude (dir. Hal Ashby, 1971)

The Heartbreak Kid (dir. Elaine May, 1972)

The Hebrew Hammer (dir. Jonathan Kesselman, 2003)

Heist (dir. David Mamet, 2001)

Hester Street (dir. Joan Micklin Silver, 1975)

Hey Hey It's Esther Blueburger (dir. Cathy Randall, 2008)

His People (dir. Edward Sloman, 1925)

The History Boys (dir. Nicholas Hytner, 2006)

History of the World, Part 1 (dir. Mel Brooks, 1981)

Hitlerjunge Salomon/Europa Europa (dir. Agnieszka Holland, 1990)

The Holiday (dir. Nancy Meyers, 2006)

Holy Rollers (dir. Kevin Asch, 2010)

Homicide (dir. David Mamet, 1991)

L'homme est une femme comme les autres/Man is a Woman (dir. Jean-Jacques Zilbermann, 1998)

Hostel (dir. Eli Roth, 2005)

Hostel II (dir. Eli Roth, 2007)

Howl (dirs Rob Epstein and Jeffrey Friedman, 2010)

Hulk (dir. Ang Lee, 2003)

Husbands and Wives (dir. Woody Allen, 1992)

Independence Day (dir. Roland Emmerich, 1996)

The Infidel (dir. Josh Appignanesi, 2010)

In Her Shoes (dir. Curtis Hanson, 2005)

Inglourious Basterds (dir. Quentin Tarantino, 2009)

I Now Pronounce You Chuck and Larry (dir. Dennis Dugan, 2007)

Inside Man (dir. Spike Lee, 2006)

The Invaders (dir. Percy Stow, 1909)

It's My Turn (dir. Claudia Weill, 1980)

Jakob the Liar (dir. Peter Kassovitz, 1999)

The Jazz Singer (dir. Alan Crosland, 1927)

The Jazz Singer (dir. Michael Curtiz, 1952)

The Jazz Singer (dir. Richard Fleischer, 1980)

Judíos en el espacio/Jews in Space (dir. Gabriel Lichtmann, 2005)

Jew Süss (Lothar Mendes, 1934)

Judith of Bethulia (dir. D.W. Griffith, 1914)

Jud Süss (dir. Veit Harlan, 1940)

Kådisbellan/The Slingshot (dir. Åke Sandgren, 1993)

Kadosh/Sacred (dir. Amos Gitai, 1999)

Keeping the Faith (dir. Edward Norton, 2000)

Keeping up with the Steins (dir. Scott Marshall, 2006)

The Killers (dir. Robert Siodmak, 1946)

Kissing Jessica Stein (dir. Charles Herman-Wurmfeld, 2001)

Knocked Up (dir. Judd Apatow, 2007)

La cage aux folles (dir. Edouard Molinaro, 1978)

La vita è bella/Life is Beautiful (dir. Roberto Benigni, 1997)

Last Action Hero (dir. John McTiernan, 1993)

The Last Supper (dir. Stacy Title, 1995)

Lebanon (dir. Samuel Maoz, 2009)

Left Luggage (dir. Jeroen Krabbé, 1998)

Leon the Pig Farmer (dirs Vadim Jean and Gary Sinyor, 1992)

Lepke (dir. Menahem Golan, 1975)

Levi and Cohen: The Irish Comedians (dir. G.W. Bitzer, 1903)

Levitsky's Insurance Policy, or When Thief Meets Thief (dir. Anon, 1908)

Liberty Heights (dir. Barry Levinson, 1999)

The Life of Emile Zola (dir. William Dieterle, 1937)

The Little Drummer Girl (dir. George Roy Hill, 1984)

Little Fockers (dir. Paul Weitz, 2010)

The Little Jewess (dir. Anon, 1914)

The Long Goodbye (dir. Robert Altman, 1973)

Lord of War (dir. Andrew Niccol, 2005)

Love and Death (dir. Woody Allen, 1975)

Lucky Number Slevin (dir. Paul McGuigan, 2006)

Lyubov/Love (dir. Valery Todorovsky, 1991)

The Man Who Cried (dir. Sally Potter, 2000)

Manhattan (dir. Woody Allen, 1979)

Marci X (dir. Richard Benjamin, 2003)

Marjorie Morningstar (dir. Irving Rapper, 1958)

Meet the Fockers (dir. Jay Roach, 2004)

Meet the Parents (dir. Jay Roach, 2000)

Mendy (dir. Adam Vardy, 2003)

Métisse (dir. Mathieu Kassovitz, 1993)

Me Without You (dir. Sandra Goldbacher, 2001)

A Mighty Wind (dir. Christopher Guest, 2003)

Milk (dir. Gus Van Sant, 2008)

Miller's Crossing (dir. Joel Coen, 1990)

Mr & Mrs Smith (dir. Doug Liman, 2005)

Mr Saturday Night (dir. Billy Crystal, 1992)

The Mummy (dir. Stephen Sommers, 1999)

Munich (dir. Steven Spielberg, 2005)

Musíme si pomáhat/Divided We Fall (dir. Jan Hrebejk, 2000)

My Big Fat Greek Wedding (dir. Joel Zwick, 2002)

New York Stories (dirs Woody Allen, Frances Ford Coppola, Martin Scorsese, 1989)

Next Stop, Greenwich Village (dir. Paul Mazursky, 1976)

Nice Jewish Girls (dir. Matthew Blade, 2009)

Nick and Norah's Infinite Playlist (dir. Peter Sollett, 2008)

North by Northwest (dir. Alfred Hitchcock, 1959)

Novia que te vea/Like a Bride (dir. Guita Schyfter, 1994)

Nueve reinas/Nine Queens (dir. Fabián Bielinsky, 2000)

Ocean's Eleven (dir. Steven Soderbergh, 2001)

Ocean's Thirteen (dir. Steven Soderbergh, 2007)

Ocean's Twelve (dir. Steven Soderbergh, 2004)

Old Isaacs, the Pawnbroker (dir. D.W. Griffith, 1908)

Oligarkh/Tycoon (dir. Pavel Lungin, 2002)

Oliver Twist (dir. Roman Polanski, 2005)

Once Upon a Time in America (dir. Sergio Leone, 1984)

One-Eyed Monster (dir. Adam Fields, 2008)

Orgazmo (dir. Trey Parker, 1997)

Paradise Now (dir. Hany Abu-Assad, 2005)

The Passion of the Christ (dir. Mel Gibson, 2004)

A Passover Miracle (dir. Anon, 1914)

Peter Pan (dir. P.J. Hogan, 2003)

Pi (dir. Darren Aronofsky, 1998)

The Pianist (dir. Roman Polanski, 2002)

Pineapple Express (dir. David Gordon Green, 2008)

Pornstar: The Legend of Ron Jeremy (dir. Scott J. Gill, 2001)

Portnoy's Complaint (dir. Ernest Lehman, 1972)

Predators (dir. Nimród Antal, 2010)

A Price Above Rubies (dir. Boaz Yakin, 1998)

Prime (dir. Ben Younger, 2005)

The Prince of Egypt (dirs Brenda Chapman, Steve Hickner and Simon Wells, 1998)

Private Benjamin (dir. Howard Zieff, 1980)

The Producers (dir. Mel Brooks, 1968)

Psycho (dir. Alfred Hitchcock, 1960)

Punch-Drunk Love (dir. Paul Thomas Anderson, 2002)

The Quarrel (dir. Eli Cohen, 1991)

Quiz Show (dir. Robert Redford, 1994)

Radio Days (dir. Woody Allen, 1987)

The Reader (dir. Stephen Daldry, 2008)

Requiem for a Dream (dir. Darren Aronofsky, 2000)

Revolver (dir. Guy Ritchie, 2005)

Rewers/The Reverse (dir. Borys Lankosz, 2009)

The Robbers and the Jew (dir. Jack Smith, 1908)

Robin Hood: Men in Tights (dir. Mel Brooks, 1993)

Romance of a Jewess (dir. D.W. Griffith, 1908)

Samson and Delilah (dir. Cecil B. DeMille, 1949)

Saving Private Ryan (dir. Steven Spielberg, 1998)

Saving Silverman (dir. Dennis Dugan, 2001)

Schindler's List (dir. Steven Spielberg, 1993)

School Ties (dir. Robert Mandel, 1992)

Seinfeld (television series, NBC, 1990–98)

Serenity (dir. Joss Whedon, 2005)

Seres Queridos/Only Human (dirs Dominic Harari and Teresa de Pelegrí, 2004)

A Serious Man (dirs Joel and Ethan Coen, 2009)

Sex and the City (dir. Michael Patrick King, 2008)

Shoah (dir. Claude Lanzmann, 1985)

Showgirls (dir. Paul Verhoeven, 1995)

Sixty Six (dir. Paul Weiland, 2006)

Sleeper (dir. Woody Allen, 1973)

Snatch (dir. Guy Ritchie, 2000)

The Social Network (dir. David Fincher, 2010)
Solomon and Gaenor (dir. Paul Morrison, 1999)
Solomon and Sheba (dir. King Vidor, 1959)
Some Like It Hot (dir. Billy Wilder, 1959)
Song of Songs (dir. Josh Appignanesi, 2005)
Spaceballs (dir. Mel Brooks, 1987)
Star Trek (dir. J.J. Abrams, 2009)
Star Trek: The Motion Picture (dir. Robert Wise, 1979)
Star Trek II: The Wrath of Khan (dir. Nicholas Meyer, 1982)
Star Trek III: The Search for Spock (dir. Leonard Nimoy, 1984)
Star Trek IV: The Voyage Home (dir. Leonard Nimoy, 1986)
Star Trek V: The Final Frontier (dir. William Shatner, 1989)
Star Trek VI: The Undiscovered Country (dir. Nicholas Meyer, 1991)
Star Trek: First Contact (dir. Jonathan Frakes, 1996)
Star Trek: Generations (dir. David Carson, 1994)
Star Trek: Insurrection (dir. Jonathan Frakes, 1998)
Star Trek: Nemesis (dir. Stuart Baird, 2002)
Star Wars (dir. George Lucas, 1977)
Star Wars: Episode I – The Phantom Menace (dir. George Lucas, 1999)
The Stepford Wives (dir. Frank Oz, 2004)
A Stranger Among Us (dir. Sidney Lumet, 1992)
The Sum of All Fears (dir. Phil Alden Robinson, 2002)
Sunday Bloody Sunday (dir. John Schlesinger, 1971)
Sunshine (dir. István Szabó, 1999)
Superbad (dir. Greg Mottola, 2007)
Suzie Gold (dir. Ric Cantor, 2004)
Taking Woodstock (dir. Ang Lee, 2009)
Taxi Driver (dir. Martin Scorsese, 1976)
The Ten Commandments (dir. Cecil B. DeMille, 1956)
Tevye (dir. Maurice Schwartz, 1939)
Then She Found Me (dir. Helen Hunt, 2007)
There's Something About Mary (dirs Bobby Farrelly and Peter Farrelly, 1998)
Threads of Destiny (dir. Joseph W. Smiley, 1914)
Train of Life (dir. Radu Mihaileanu, 1998)
Transamerica (dir. Duncan Tucker, 2005)
Trembling Before G-d (dir. Sandi Simcha Dubowski, 2001)
Treyf (dirs Alisa Lebow and Cynthia Madansky, 1998)
The Trotsky (dir. Jacob Tierney, 2009)
Twenty-One (TV game show, 1956–58)

Two Lovers (dir. James Gray, 2008)

The Unborn (dir. David S. Goyer, 2009)

Ushpizin/Guests (dir. Giddi Dar, 2004)

Viehjud Levi/Jew-Boy Levi (dir. Didi Danquart, 1999)

Walk Hard: The Dewey Cox Story (dir. Jake Kasdan, 2007)

A Walk on the Moon (dir. Tony Goldwyn, 1999)

Walk on Water (dir. Eytan Fox, 2004)

Waltz with Bashir (dir. Ari Folman, 2008)

The Way We Were (dir. Sydney Pollack, 1973)

Wedding Daze (dir. Michael Ian Black, 2006)

Welcome to Collinwood (dirs Anthony Russo and Joe Russo, 2002)

We Own the Night (dir. James Gray, 2007)

What's Cooking? (dir. Gurinder Chadha, 2000)

When Do We Eat? (dir. Salvador Litvak, 2005)

When Harry Met Sally (dir. Rob Reiner, 1989)

Witness (dir. Peter Weir, 1985)

Wondrous Oblivion (dir. Paul Morrison, 2003)

X-Men (dir. Bryan Singer, 2000)

X-Men 2 (dir. Bryan Singer, 2003)

X-Men: First Class (dir. Matthew Vaughn, 2011)

X-Men: The Last Stand (dir. Brett Ratner, 2006)

Yentl (dir. Barbra Streisand, 1983)

Yossi & Jagger (dir. Eytan Fox, 2002)

You Don't Mess with the Zohan (dir. Dennis Dugan, 2008)

Zebra Head/The Colour of Love (dir. Anthony Drazan, 1992)

Zelig (dir. Woody Allen, 1983)

Zwartboek/Black Book (dir. Paul Verhoeven, 2006)

Index